Lecture Notes in Artificial Intelli

Edited by J. G. Carbonell and J. Siekmann

Subseries of Lecture Notes in Computer Science

Bettina Berendt   Andreas Hotho
Dunja Mladenic   Maarten van Someren
Myra Spiliopoulou   Gerd Stumme (Eds.)

Web Mining: From Web to Semantic Web

First European Web Mining Forum, EWMF 2003
Cavtat-Dubrovnik, Croatia, September 22, 2003
Invited and Selected Revised Papers

 Springer

Series Editors

Jaime G. Carbonell, Carnegie Mellon University, Pittsburgh, PA, USA
Jörg Siekmann, University of Saarland, Saarbrücken, Germany

Volume Editors

Bettina Berendt
Humboldt University Berlin, Institute of Information Systems
E-mail: berendt@wiwi.hu-berlin.de

Andreas Hotho
University of Kassel, Department of Mathematics and Informatics
E-mail: hotho@cs.uni-kassel.de

Dunja Mladenic
J. Stefan Institute, Ljubljana, Slovenia
and Carnegie Mellon University, Pittsburgh, USA
E-mail: Dunja.Mladenic@ijs.si

Maarten van Someren
University of Amsterdam, Department of Social Science Informatics
E-mail: maarten@swi.psy.uva.nl

Myra Spiliopoulou
Otto-von-Guericke-University of Magdeburg, ITI/FIN
E-mail: myra@iti.cs.uni-magdeburg.de

Gerd Stumme
University of Kassel, Department of Mathematics and Computer Science
E-mail: stumme@cs.uni-kassel.de

Library of Congress Control Number: 2004112647

CR Subject Classification (1998): I.2, H.2.8, H.3, H.4, H.5.2-4, K.4

ISSN 0302-9743
ISBN 3-540-23258-3 Springer Berlin Heidelberg New York

Springer is a part of Springer Science+Business Media

springeronline.com

© Springer-Verlag Berlin Heidelberg 2004
Printed in Germany

Typesetting: Camera-ready by author, data conversion by PTP-Berlin, Protago-TeX-Production GmbH
Printed on acid-free paper   SPIN: 11321798   06/3142   5 4 3 2 1 0

Preface

In the last years, research on Web mining has reached maturity and has broadened in scope. Two different but interrelated research threads have emerged, based on the dual nature of the Web:

- The Web is a practically infinite collection of documents: The acquisition and exploitation of information from these documents asks for intelligent techniques for information categorization, extraction and search, as well as for adaptivity to the interests and background of the organization or person that looks for information.
- The Web is a venue for doing business electronically: It is a venue for interaction, information acquisition and service exploitation used by public authorities, non-governmental organizations, communities of interest and private persons. When observed as a venue for the achievement of business goals, a Web presence should be aligned to the objectives of its owner and the requirements of its users. This raises the demand for understanding Web usage, combining it with other sources of knowledge inside an organization, and deriving lines of action.

The birth of the Semantic Web at the beginning of the decade led to a coercion of the two threads in two aspects: (i) the extraction of semantics from the Web to build the Semantic Web; and (ii) the exploitation of these semantics to better support information acquisition and to enhance the interaction for business and non-business purposes. Semantic Web mining encompasses both aspects from the viewpoint of knowledge discovery.

The *Web Mining Forum* initiative is motivated by the insight that knowledge discovery on the Web from the viewpoint of hyperarchive analysis and from the viewpoint of interaction among persons and institutions are complementary, both for the familiar, conventional Web and for the Semantic Web. The Web Mining Forum was launched in September 2002 as an initiative of the KDNet Network of Excellence [1]. It encompasses an information portal and discussion forum for researchers who specialize in data mining on data *from* and on data *about* the Web/Semantic Web and its usage. In its function as an information portal, it focusses on the announcement of events associated with knowledge discovery and the Web, on the collection of datasets for the evaluation of Web mining algorithms and on the specification of a common terminology. In its function as a discussion forum, it initiated the "European Web Mining Forum" Workshop (EWMF 2003) during the ECML/PKDD conference in Cavtat, Croatia.

EWMF 2003 was the follow-up workshop of the Semantic Web Mining workshop that took place during ECML/PKDD 2002, and also built upon the tradition of the WEBKDD workshop series that has taken place during the ACM SIGKDD conference since 1999.

The EWMF 2003 workshop hosted eight regular papers and two invited talks, by Sarabjot Sing Anand (University of Ulster) and by Rayid Ghani (Accenture). The presentations were organized into four sessions followed by a plenary discussion. Following the well-accepted tradition of the WEBKDD series, a postworkshop proceedings volume was prepared. It consists of extended versions of six of the papers and is further extended

---

[1] Funded by the EU 5th Framework Programme under grant IST-2001-33086

by four invited papers and a roadmap describing our vision of the future of Semantic Web mining.

The role of semantic information in improving personalized recommendations is discussed by Mobasher et al. in [7]: They elaborate on collaborative filtering and stress the importance of item-based recommendations in dealing with scalability and sparsity problems. Semantic information on the items, extracted with the help of domain-specific ontologies, is combined with user-item mappings and serves as basis for the formulation of recommendations, thus increasing prediction accuracy and demonstrating robustness over sparse data. Approaches for the extraction of semantic information appear in [4, 6,9]. Rayiv Ghani elaborates on the extraction of semantics features from product descriptions with text mining techniques, with the goal of enriching the (Web) transaction data [4]. The method has been implemented in a system for personalized product recommendations but is also appropriate for further applications like store profiling and demand forecasting. Mladenic and Grobelnik discuss the automated mapping of Web pages onto an ontology with the help of document classification techniques [6]. They focus on skewed distributions and propose a solution on the basis of multiple independent classifiers that predict the probability with which a document belongs to each class. Sigletos et al. study the extraction of information from multiple Web sites and the disambiguation of extracted facts [9] by combining the induction of wrappers and the discovery of named entities.

Personalization through recommendation mechanisms is the subject of several contributions. While the emphasis of [7] is on individual users, [8] elaborates on user communities. In the paper of Pierrakos et al., community models are built on the basis of usage data and of a concept hierarchy derived through content-based clustering of the documents in the collection [8]. The induction of user models is also studied by Esposito et al. in [3]: The emphasis of their work is on the evaluation of two user profiling methods in terms of classification accuracy and performance. Evaluation is also addressed by van Someren et al., who concentrate on recommendation strategies [10]: They observe that current systems optimize the quality of single recommendations and argue that this strategy is suboptimal with respect to the ultimate goal of finding the desired information in a minimal number of steps.

Evaluation from the viewpoint of deploying Web mining results is studied by Anand et al. in [1]. They elaborate on modelling and measuring the effectiveness of the interaction between business venues and the visitors of their Web sites and propose the development of scenaria, on the basis of which effectiveness should be evaluated. Architectures for the knowledge discovery, evaluation *and* deployment are described in [1] and [5]. While Anand et al. focus on scenario-based deployment [1], Menasalvas et al. stress the existence of multiple viewpoints and goals of deployment and propose a method for assessing the value of a session for each viewpoint [5]. Finally, the paper of Baron and Spiliopoulou elaborates on one of the effects of deployment, the change in the patterns derived during knowledge discovery [2]: The authors model patterns as temporal objects and propose a method for the detection of changes in the statistics of association rules over a Web-server log.

Acknowledgments

This volume owes much to the engagement of many scientists. The editors are indebted to the PC members of the EWMF 2003 workshop

Ed Chi (Xerox Parc, Palo Alto, USA)
Ronen Feldman (Bar-Ilan University, Ramat Gan, Israel)
Marko Grobelnik (J. Stefan Institute, Ljubljana, Slovenia)
Oliver Günther (Humboldt University Berlin, Germany)
Stefan Haustein (Universität Dortmund, Germany)
Jörg-Uwe Kietz (kdlabs AG, Zuerich, Switzerland)
Ee-Peng Lim (Nanyang Technological University, Singapore)
Alexander Maedche (Robert Bosch GmbH, Stuttgart, Germany)
Brij Masand (Data Miners, Boston, USA)
Yannis Manolopoulos (Aristotle University, Greece)
Ryszard S. Michalski (George Mason University, USA)
Bamshad Mobasher (DePaul University, Chicago, USA)
Claire Nedellec (Université Paris Sud, France)
George Paliouras (National Centre for Scientific Research "Demokritos", Athens, Greece)
Jian Pei (Simon Fraser University, Canada)
John R. Punin (Rensselaer Polytechnic Institute, Troy, NY, USA)
Jaideep Srivastava (University of Minnesota, Minneapolis, USA)
Rudi Studer (Universität Karlsruhe, Germany)
Stefan Wrobel (Fraunhofer Institute for Autonomous Intelligent Systems, Sankt Augustin, Germany)
Mohammed Zaki (Rensellaer Polytechnic Institute, USA)
Osmar Zaiane (University of Alberta, Edmonton, Canada)

and the reviewers of the papers in this volume

Philipp Cimiano (Universität Karlsruhe, Germany)
Marko Grobelnik (J. Stefan Institute, Ljubljana, Slovenia)
Dimitrios Katsaros (Aristotle University, Greece)
Jörg-Uwe Kietz (kdlabs AG, Zuerich, Switzerland)
Ee-Peng Lim (Nanyang Technological University, Singapore)
Zehua Liu (Nanyang Technological University, Singapore)
Brij Masand (Data Miners, Boston, USA)
Yannis Manolopoulos (Aristotle University, Greece)
Bamshad Mobasher (DePaul University, Chicago, USA)
Alexandros Nanopoulos (Aristotle University, Greece)
George Paliouras (National Centre for Scientific Research "Demokritos", Athens, Greece)
Ljiljana Stojanovic (FZI Forschungszentrum Informatik, Germany)
Rudi Studer (Universität Karlsruhe, Germany)
Stefan Wrobel (Fraunhofer AIS and Univ. of Bonn, Germany)
Mohammed Zaki (Rensselaer Polytechnic Institute, USA)
Osmar Zaiane (University of Alberta, Edmonton, Canada)

for the involvement and effort they contributed to guarantee a high scientific niveau for both the workshop and the follow-up proceedings.

We would like to thank the organizers of ECML/PKDD 2003 for their support in the organization of the EWMF 2003 workshop. Last but foremost, we are indebted to the KDNet network of excellence for the funding of the Web Mining Forum and for the financial support of the EWMF 2003 workshop, and especially to Ina Lauth from the Fraunhofer Institute for Autonomous Intelligent Systems (AIS), the KDNet project coordinator, for her intensive engagement and support in the establishment of the Web Mining Forum and in the organization of the EWMF 2003.

The EWMF workshop chairs

Bettina Berendt, Humboldt Universität zu Berlin (Germany)
Andreas Hotho, Universität Kassel (Germany)
Dunja Mladenic, J. Stefan Institute (Slovenia)
Maarten van Someren, University of Amsterdam (The Netherlands)
Myra Spiliopoulou, Otto-von-Guericke-Universität Magdeburg (Germany)
Gerd Stumme, Universität Kassel (Germany)

References

1. S.S. Anand, M. Mulvenna, and K. Chevalier. On the deployment of Web usage mining. (invited paper)
2. S. Baron and M. Spiliopoulou. Monitoring the evolution of Web usage patterns.
3. F. Esposito, G. Semeraro, S. Ferilli, M. Degemmis, N. Di Mauro, T. Basile, and P. Lops. Evaluation and validation of two approaches to user profiling.
4. R. Ghani. Mining the Web to add semantics to retail data mining. (invited paper)
5. E. Menasalvas, S. Millán, M. Pérez, E. Hochsztain, V. Robles, O. Marbán, A. Tasistro, and J. Peña. An approach to estimate user sessions value dealing with multiple viewpoints and goals.
6. D. Mladenić and M. Grobelnik. Mapping documents onto a Web page ontology. (invited paper)
7. B. Mobasher, X. Jin, and Y. Zhou. Semantically enhanced collaborative filtering on the Web. (invited paper)
8. D. Pierrakos, G. Paliouras, C. Papatheodorou, V. Karkaletsis, and M. Dikaiakos. Web community directories: A new approach to Web personalization.
9. G. Sigletos, G. Paliouras, C.D. Spyropoulos, and M. Hatzopoulos. Mining Web sites using wrapper induction, named-entities and post-processing.
10. M. van Someren, V. Hollink, and S. ten Hagen. Greedy recommending is not always optimal.

Table of Contents

A Roadmap for Web Mining: From Web to Semantic Web 1
Bettina Berendt, Andreas Hotho, Dunja Mladenic,
Maarten van Someren, Myra Spiliopoulou, Gerd Stumme

On the Deployment of Web Usage Mining 23
Sarabjot Singh Anand, Maurice Mulvenna, Karine Chevalier

Mining the Web to Add Semantics to Retail Data Mining 43
Rayid Ghani

Semantically Enhanced Collaborative Filtering on the Web 57
Bamshad Mobasher, Xin Jin, Yanzan Zhou

Mapping Documents onto Web Page Ontology 77
Dunja Mladenić, Marko Grobelnik

Mining Web Sites Using Wrapper Induction, Named Entities,
and Post-processing 97
Georgios Sigletos, Georgios Paliouras, Constantine D. Spyropoulos,
Michalis Hatzopoulos

Web Community Directories: A New Approach
to Web Personalization 113
Dimitrios Pierrakos, Georgios Paliouras, Christos Papatheodorou,
Vangelis Karkaletsis, Marios Dikaiakos

Evaluation and Validation of Two Approaches to User Profiling 130
F. Esposito, G. Semeraro, S. Ferilli, M. Degemmis, N. Di Mauro,
T.M.A. Basile, P. Lops

Greedy Recommending Is Not Always Optimal 148
Maarten van Someren, Vera Hollink, Stephan ten Hagen

An Approach to Estimate the Value of User Sessions Using Multiple
Viewpoints and Goals 164
E. Menasalvas, S. Millán, M.S. Pérez, E. Hochsztain, A. Tasistro

Monitoring the Evolution of Web Usage Patterns 181
Steffan Baron, Myra Spiliopoulou

Author Index 201

A Roadmap for Web Mining:
From Web to Semantic Web

Bettina Berendt[1], Andreas Hotho[2], Dunja Mladenic[3],
Maarten van Someren[4], Myra Spiliopoulou[5], and Gerd Stumme[2]

[1] Institute of Information Systems, Humboldt University Berlin, Germany.
berendt@wiwi.hu-berlin.de
[2] Chair of Knowledge & Data Engineering, University of Kassel, Germany,
{hotho,stumme}@cs.uni-kassel.de
[3] Jozef Stefan Institute, Ljubljana, Slovenia, Dunja.Mladenic@ijs.si
[4] Social Science Informatics, University of Amsterdam, The Netherlands,
maarten@swi.psy.uva.nl
[5] Institute of Technical and Business Information Systems, Otto–von–Guericke–University
Magdeburg, Germany, myra@iti.cs.uni-magdeburg.de

1 Introduction

The purpose of Web mining is to develop methods and systems for discovering models of objects and processes on the World Wide Web and for web-based systems that show adaptive performance. Web Mining integrates three parent areas: Data Mining (we use this term here also for the closely related areas of Machine Learning and Knowledge Discovery), Internet technology and World Wide Web, and for the more recent Semantic Web. The World Wide Web has made an enormous amount of information electronically accessible. The use of email, news and markup languages like HTML allow users to publish and read documents at a world-wide scale and to communicate via chat connections, including information in the form of images and voice records. The HTTP protocol that enables access to documents over the network via Web browsers created an immense improvement in communication and access to information. For some years these possibilities were used mostly in the scientific world but recent years have seen an immense growth in popularity, supported by the wide availability of computers and broadband communication. The use of the internet for other tasks than finding information and direct communication is increasing, as can be seen from the interest in "e-activities" such as e-commerce, e-learning, e-government, e-science.

Independently of the development of the Internet, Data Mining expanded out of the academic world into industry. Methods and their potential became known outside the academic world and commercial toolkits became available that allowed applications at an industrial scale. Numerous industrial applications have shown that models can be constructed from data for a wide variety of industrial problems (e.g. [1,2]).

The World-Wide Web is an interesting area for Data Mining because huge amounts of information are available. Data Mining methods can be used to analyse the behaviour of individual users, access patterns of pages or sites, properties of collections of documents. Almost all standard data mining methods are designed for data that are organised as multiple "cases" that are comparable and can be viewed as instances of a single pattern,

B. Berendt et al. (Eds.): EWMF 2003, LNAI 3209, pp. 1–22, 2004.

for example patients described by a fixed set of symptoms and diseases, applicants for loans, customers of a shop. A "case" is typically described by a fixed set of features (or variables). Data on the Web have a different nature. They are not so easily comparable and have the form of free text, semi-structured text (lists, tables) often with images and hyperlinks, or server logs. The aim to learn models of documents has given rise to the interest in Text Mining [3]: methods for modelling documents in terms of properties of documents. Learning from the hyperlink structure has given rise to graph-based methods, and server logs are used to learn about user behavior.

The Semantic Web is a recent initiative, inspired by Tim Berners-Lee [4], to take the World-Wide Web much further and develop in into a distributed system for knowledge representation and computing. The aim of the Semantic Web is to not only support access to information "on the Web" by direct links or by search engines but also to support its *use*. Instead of searching for a document that matches keywords, it should be possible to combine information to answer questions. Instead of retrieving a plan for a trip to Hawaii, it should be possible to automatically construct a travel plan that satisfies certain goals and uses opportunities that arise dynamically. This gives rise to a wide range of challenges. Some of them concern the infrastructure, including the interoperability of systems and the languages for the exchange of information rather than data. Many challenges are in the are of knowledge representation, discovery and engineering. They include the extraction of knowledge from data and its representation in a form understandable by arbitrary parties, the intelligent questioning and the delivery of answers to problems as opposed to conventional queries and the exploitation of formerly extracted knowledge in this process. The ambition of representing content in a way that can be understood and consumed by an arbitrary reader leads to issues in which cognitive sciences and even philosophy are involved, such as the understanding of an asset's intended meaning.

The Semantic Web proposes several additional innovative ideas to achieve this:

Standardised format. The Semantic Web proposes standards for uniform metalevel description language for representation formats. Besides acting as a basis for exchange, this language supports representation of knowledge at multiple levels. For example, text can be *annotated* with a formal representation of it. The natural language sentence "Amsterdam is the capital of the Netherlands", for instance, can be annotated such that the annotation formalises knowledge that is implicit in the sentence, e.g. Amsterdam can be annotated as "city", Netherlands as "country" and the sentence with the structured "capital-of(Amsterdam, Netherlands)". Annotating textual documents (and also images and possibly audio and video) thus enables a combination of textual and formal representations of knowledge. A small step further is to store the annotated text items in a structured database or knowledge base.

Standardised vocabulary and knowledge. The Semantic Web encourages and facilitates the formulation of shared vocabularies and shared knowledge in the form of ontologies: if knowledge about university courses is to be represented and shared, it is useful to define and use a common vocabulary and common basic knowledge. The Semantic Web aims to collect this in the form of ontologies and make them available for modelling new domains and activities. This means that a large amount of knowledge will be structured, formalised and represented to enable automated access and use.

Shared services. To realise the full Semantic Web, beside static structures also "Web services" are foreseen. Services mediate between requests and applications and make it possible to automatically invoke applications that run on different systems.

In this chapter, we concentrate on one thread of challenges associated with the Semantic Web, those that can be addressed with knowledge discovery techniques, putting the emphasis on the transition from Web Mining to mining the Semantic Web and on the role of ontologies and information extraction for this transition. Section 2 summarises the more technical aspects of the Semantic Web, in particular the main representation languages, section 3 summarises basic concepts from Data Mining, section 4 reviews the main developments in the application of Data Mining to the World Wide Web, section 5 extends this to the combination of Data Mining and the Semantic Web and section 6 reviews developments that are expected in the near future and issues for research and development. Each section has the character of a summary and includes references to more detailed discussions and explanations. This chapter summarises and extends [5], [6] and [7].

2   Languages for the Semantic Web

The Semantic Web requires a language in which information can be represented. This language should support (a) knowledge representation and reasoning (including infor- mation retrieval but ultimately a wide variety of tasks), (b) the description of document content, (c) the exchange of the documents and the incorporated knowledge and (d) stan- dardisation. The first two aspects demand adequate expressiveness. The last two aspects emphasise that the Semantic Web, like the Web, should be a medium for the exchange of a wide variety of objects and thus allow for ease-of-use and for agreed-upon pro- tocols. Naturally enough, the starting point for describing the Semantic Web has been XML. However, XML has not been designed with the intention to express or exchange knowledge. In this section, we review three W3C initiatives, XML, RDF(S) and OWL and their potential for the Semantic Web.

2.1   XML

XML (Extensible mark-up language) was designed as a language for mark-up or annota- tion of documents. An XML object is a labeled tree and consists of objects with attributes and values that can themselves be XML objects. Beside annotation for formatting, XML allows the definition of any kind of annotation, thus opening the way to annotation with ontologies and to use as data model for arbitrary information. This makes it extensible, unlike its ancestors like HTML.

XML Schema allows the definition of grammars for valid XML documents, and the reference to "name spaces", sets of labels that can be accessed via the internet. XML can also be used as a scheme for structured databases. The value of an attribute can be text but it can also be an element of a limited set or a number. XML is only an abstract data format.

Furthermore, XML does not include any procedural component. Tools have been developed for search and retrieval in XML trees. Tools can create formatted output from formatting annotations but in general any type of operation is possible. When tools are integrated in the Web and can be called from outside they are called "services". This creates a very flexible representation format that can be used to represent information that is partially structured.

Details about XML can be found in many books, reports and Web pages. In the context of the Semantic Web, the most important role for XML is that it provides a simple standard abstract data model that can be used to access both (annotated) documents and structured data (for example tables) and that it can be used as a representation for ontologies. However, XML and XML schema were designed to describe the structure of text documents, like HTML, Word, StarOffice, or LaTeXdocuments. It is possible to define tags in XML to carry meta data but these tags may not have a well-defined meaning. XML helps organizing documents by providing a formal syntax for annotation. Erdmann [8] provides a detailed analysis of the capabilities of XML, the shortcomings of XML concerning semantics and possible solutions. For Web Mining the standardisation created by XML simplifies the development of generic systems that learn from data on the web.

2.2 RDF(S)

The *Resource Description Framework (RDF)* is, according to the W3C recommendation [9], "a foundation for processing metadata; it provides interoperability between applications that exchange machine-understandable information on the Web."

RDF documents consist of three types of entities: resources, properties, and statements. Resources may be Web pages, parts or collections of Web pages, or any (real-world) objects which are not directly part of the World-Wide Web. In RDF, resources are always addressed by URIs, Universal Resource Identifiers, a generalisation of URLs that includes services besides locations. Properties are specific attributes, characteristics, or relations describing resources. A resource together with a property having a value for that resource form an RDF statement. A value is either a literal, a resource, or another statement. Statements can thus be considered as object–attribute–value triples.

The data model underlying RDF is basically a directed labeled graph. RDF Schema defines a simple modeling language on top of RDF which includes classes, is-a relationships between classes and between properties, and domain/range restrictions for properties. XML provides the standard syntax for RDF and RDF Schema.

Summarising, RDF and RDF Schema provide base support for the specification of semantics *and* use the widespread XML as syntax. However, the expressiveness is limited, disallowing the specification of facts that one is bound to expect, given the long tradition of database schema theory. They include the notion of key, as in relational databases, as well as factual assertions, e.g. stating that each print of this book can be either hardcover or softcover but not both. The demand for supporting more expressive semantics and reasoning is addressed in languages like DAML, OIL and the W3C recommendation OWL described below. More information on RDF(S) can be found on the W3C website (www.w3.org) and many books. As with XML, the standardisation provided by RDF(S) simplifies development and application of Web Mining.

2.3 OWL

Like RDF and RDF Schema, OWL is a W3C recommendation, intended to support more elaborate semantics. OWL includes elements from description logics and provides many constructs for the specification of semantics, including conjunction and disjunction, existentially and universally quantified variables and property inversion. Using these constructs, a reasoning module can make logical inferences and derive knowledge that was previously only implicit in the data. Using OWL for the Semantic Web implies that an application could invoke such a reasoning module and acquire inferred knowledge rather than simply retrieve data.

However, the expressiveness of OWL comes at a high cost. First, OWL contains constructs that make it undecidable. Second, reasoning is not efficient. Third, the expressiveness is achieved by increased complexity, so that ease-of-use and intuitiveness are no more given. These observations lead to two variations of OWL, *OWL DL* (stands for OWL Description Logic) and *OWL Lite*, which disallow the constructs that make the original *OWL Full* undecidable and at the same time aim for more efficient reasoning and for higher ease-of-use. To this end, OWL DL is more expressive than OWL Lite, while OWL Lite is even more restricted but easier to understand and to implement.

In terms of standardisation, it should be recalled that RDF and RDF Schema use XML as their syntax. OWL Full is upward compatible with RDF. This desirable aspect does not hold for OWL DL and OWL Lite. A legal OWL DL document is also a legal RDF document but not vice versa. This implies that reasoning and the targeted knowledge extraction are limited to the set of documents supporting OWL DL (resp. OWL Lite), while other documents, even if RDF Schema, cannot be taken into account in the reasoning process. For the transition of the Web to the Semantic Web, this is a more serious caveat than for other environments (e.g. institutional information sources) which need ontological support. More information on OWL can be found on the W3C website and many books.

The development of OWL and its application is still in an early stage. If it leads to the availability of large knowledge bases via the internet, this will increase the relevance of knowledge-intensive Data Mining methods, that combine data with prior (OWL) knowledge.

2.4 Ontologies

Beside the formal languages to be used for the Semantic Web there is the ambition to develop ontologies for general use. There are in practice two types of ontologies. The first type uses a small number of relations between concepts, usually the subclass relation and sometimes the part-of relation. Popular and commonly used are ontologies of Web documents, such as DMoz or Yahoo!, where the documents are hierarchically organized based on the content. For each content topic, there is an ontology node, with more general topics placed higher in the hierarchy. For instance, one of the top level topics in DMoz is "Computers" that has as one of the subtopics "Data Formats. Under it, there is a subtopic

"Markup Languages" that has "XML" as one of its subtopics. There are several hundred documents assigned to the node on "XML" or some of its subnodes.[1] Each Web document is very briefly described and this description together with the hyperlink to the document is placed into one or more ontology nodes. For instance, one item in the "XML" node is a hyperlink to W3C page on XML, http://www.w3.org/XML/, with the associated brief description: "Extensible Markup Language (XML) - Main page for World Wide Web Consortium (W3C) XML activity and information". We can say that here each concept (topic in this case) in the ontology is described by a set of Web documents and their corresponding short descriptions with hyperlinks. The only kind of relations that appear in such ontologies are implicit relations between more specific topic, that is a "subtopic of" a more general topic while the more general topic is a "supertopic of" a more specific topic.

The other kind of ontologies are rich with relations but have a rather limited description of concepts consisting usually of a few words. A well known example of a general, manually constructed ontology is the semantic network WordNet [10] with 26 different relations (e.g., hypernym, synonym). For instance, concepts such as "bird" and "animal" are connected with the relation "is a kind of", concepts "bird" and "wing" are connected with the relation "has part".

3   Data Mining

Before considering what the Semantic Web means with respect to Data Mining, we briefly review the main tasks that are studied in Data Mining. Data Mining methods construct models of data. These models can be used for prediction or explanation of observations or for adaptive behaviour. Reviews of the main methods can be found in textbooks such as [11,12,13]. The main tasks are classification, rule discovery, event prediction and clustering.

3.1   Classification

Classification methods construct models that assign a class to a new object on the basis of its description. A wide range of models can be constructed. In this context an important property of classification methods is the form in which objects are given to the data miner and the form of the models. Most learning methods take as input object descriptions in the form of attribute-value pairs where the scales of the variables are nominal or numerical. One class of methods, relational learning or Inductive Logic Programming, see for example [14], takes input in the form of relational structures that describe multiple objects with relations between them creating general models over structures.

Classification methods vary in the type of model that they construct. Decision tree learners construct models basically in the form of rules. A condition in a rule is a constraint on the value of a variable. Usually constraints have the form of identity (e.g. colour = red) or an interval on a scale (age > 50). The consequent of a rule is a class. Decision trees have a variable at each node and a partitioning of the values of this

---

[1] See http://dmoz.org/Computers/Data_Formats/Markup_Languages/XML/

variable. Each part of the values is associated with a subtree and the leaves of the tree are classes. Details on decision tree learning can be found in [11]

Bayesian methods construct models that estimate "a posteriori" probablity distributions for possible classes of an object using a form of Bayes Law. Popular models and methods are Naïve Bayes (assuming conditional independence of features within classes) and Bayesian Belief Networks. More details can be found in e.g. [11].

A third popular type of method is support vector machines. This is a method for minimising prediction errors within a particular class of models (the "kernel"). The method maximises the classification "margin": the distance between the data points of different classes that are closest to the boundary between the classes. The data points that are on the "right side" of the boundary and that are closest to the boundary are called "support vectors". SVM does not literally construct the boundary line (or in more dimensions, the hyperplane) that separates the classes but this line can be reconstructed from the support vectors. Implementations and more information are available from the Web, for example at http://www.kernel-machines.org/.

3.2 Rule Discovery

The paradigm of association rules discovery was first established through the work of Rakesh Agrawal and his research group, starting with [15,16]. Association rules are based on the notion of "frequent itemset", i.e. a set of items occuring together in more data records than an externally specified frequency threshold. From a frequent itemset, association rules can be derived by positioning some of the items in the antecedent and the remaining ones in the consequent, thereby computing the confidence with which the former imply the latter. A popular algorithm is the Apriori algorithm [17].

One of the most popular applications for association rules discovery is market basket analysis, for which sets of products frequently purchased together are identified. In that context, the association rules indicate which products are likely to give rise to the purchase of other products, thus delivering the basis for cross-selling and up-selling activities. In the context of Web Mining, association rule discovery focusses on the identification of pages that are frequently accessed together but also on the discovery of frequent sets of application objects (such as products, tourist locations visited together, course materials etc).

3.3 Clustering

Clustering methods divide a set of objects into subsets, called *clusters*, such that the objects in any cluster are similar to those inside it and different from those outside it. Some methods are hierarchical and construct clusters of clusters. The objects are described with numerical or nominal variables. Clustering methods vary in the measure for similarity (within and between clusters), the use of thresholds in constructing clusters, whether they allow objects to belong to strictly to one cluster or can belong to more clusters in different degrees and the structure of the algorithm. The resulting cluster structure is used as a result in itself, for inspection by a user, or to support retrieval of objects.

3.4   Sequence Discovery, Sequence Classification, and Event Prediction

In many applications, the data records do not describe sets of items but sequences of events. This is the case both for the navigation through a Web site and for carrying and filling a market basket inside a store. There are several Data Mining tasks involved here.

Sequence mining (or sequence discovery) extends the paradigm of association rules discovery towards the discovery of frequent sequences of events. Unlike conventional association rules, events are ordered. Hence, a rule emanating from a frequent sequence expresses the likelihood with which the last event will occur after the sequence of events in the antecedent. Sequence mining adds several new aspects to the original paradigm, such as the adjacency of events, the distance between the frequent events being observed and the sequentialisation of events recorded with different clocks. Methods for sequence mining are derived from rule discovery methods or from probabilistic models (Hidden Markov Models). A survey of sequence mining research is incorporated in the literature overview of [18].

Rules derived from frequent sequences can be used to predict events from a given series of observations. Data Mining can be used to find classifiers for frequent sequences. For example, certain types of sequences correspond to manufacturing errors or network intrusions. A classifier can be learned to predict which event will occur (immediately) after the sequence, enabling predictions. An example is page pre-fetching in file servers or Web servers e.g. [19,20]. Just as discovered rules are not optimal for classification, rules derived from frequent sequences are not automatically appropriate for event prediction. For example, the frequent sequences "A-B-C-D" and "A-B-C-E" indicate that events D and E are likely to occur after A, B and C in that order and allow for a quantification of this likelihood. However, if the goal is to find events, whose appearance leads to E, the sequence "A-B-C" is not necessarily a good predictor, because this sequence may as well be followed by the event D. Nonetheless, solutions based on sequence mining have been devised to assist in prediction of given events as in the early works of [21,22].

4   Data Mining and the World Wide Web

In this section we review how the Data Mining methods summarised in section 3 are used to construct models of objects and events on the World Wide Web and adaptive Web-based systems. Web Mining can involve the structured data that are used in standard Data Mining but it derives its own character from the use of data that are available on the Web. It should be kept in mind that data may be privacy-sensitive and that purpose limitations may preclude an analysis, in particular one that combines data from different sources gathered for different purposes.

4.1   Data on the Web

Learning methods construct models from samples of structured data. Most methods are defined for samples of which each element, each case, is defined as values of a fixed set of features. If we take documents as cases then a feature-value representation of a document must be constructed. A standard approach is to take words as features and occurrence of a word in a document as value. This requires a tokenising step (in which the series of basic symbols is divided into tokens - words, numbers, delimiters). Many documents are annotated with formatting information (often in HTML) that can be kept or removed. Refinements are the use of word stems, dropping frequent but uninformative words, merging synonyms, including combinations of words (pairs, triples, or more). In addition, other features of documents can be used (for example, length, occurrence of numbers, number of images).

The hyperlinks induce a graph structure on the set of Web pages. This structure has been used to identify central pages. The Page Rank algorithm [23] (implemented in the Google search engine) ranks for instance all Web pages based on the number of links from other important pages. When Google is answering a query, then it presents basically the answers to the query according to this order. The Hub & Authorities approach [24] follows a similar scheme, but differentiates between two types of pages. An authority is a page which is pointed to from many important hubs, and hubs are pages pointing to many important authorities.

Which data are recorded in user logs is an issue that has no general answer. . At the lowest level clicks on menu items and keystrokes can be recorded. At a higher level, commands, queries, entered text, drawings can be logged. The level of granularity and selection that is useful depends on the application and the nature of the interaction. The same is true of the context in which the user action is observed. The context can be the entire screen, a menu or other. The context can include textual documents. The content and usage of the Web can be viewed as single units but also as structures. The content consists of pieces that are connected to other pieces in several ways: by hyperlinks (possibly with labels), addresses, textual references, shared topics or shared users. Similarly, users are related by hyperlinks, electronic or postal addresses, shared documents, pages or sites. These relational data can be subject of Web Mining, modelling structural patterns, in combination with data about the components.

Web usage mining is characterised by the need of an extensive data preparation. Web server data are often incomplete, in the sense that important information is missing, including a unique association between a user and her activities and a complete record of her activities, in which also the order of retrieving locally cached objects is contained. Techniques to this end are either proactive, i.e. embedding to the Web server functionalities that ensure the recording of all essential data, or reactive, i.e. trying to reconstruct the missing data a posteriori. An overview of techniques for Web data preparation can be found in [25]. An evaluation of their performance is reported in [26].

4.2   Document Classification

Classifying documents is one of the basic tasks in Web Mining. Given a collection of classified documents (or parts of documents), the task is to construct a classifier that can classify new documents. Methods that are used for this task include the methods described in section 3.1. These methods are adapted to data on the Web, in particular textual documents. Features that are used to represent textual data mainly capture occurrences of words (or word stems) and in some cases also occurrence of word sequences. In the basic approach, all the words that occur in a whole set of documents are included in the feature set (usually several thousands of words). The representation of a particular document contains many zeros, as most of the words from the collection do not occur in particular document. To handle this, special methods are used (support vector machines) or relevant features are selected. The set of features is sometimes extended with, for example, text length, and features defined in terms of HTML tags (e.g. title, author). Document classification techniques have been developed and applied on different datasets including descriptions of US patents [27], Web documents [27,28], and Reuters news articles [29]. An overview can be found in [30].

A related form is classification of structures of documents instead of single documents. Information on the Web is often distributed over several linked pages that need to be classified as a whole. Relational classification methods are appropriate for this.

Applications of document classification are adaptive spam filters where email messages are labelled as spam or not and the spam filter learns to recognise spam messages (e.g. [31]), adaptive automated email routing, where messages are labelled by the person or department that needs to deal with them to enable automated routing, identifying relevant Web pages or newspaper articles, and assigning documents to categories for indexing and retrieval.

4.3 Document Clustering

Document clustering [32] means that large numbers of documents are divided into groups that are similar in content. This is usually an intermediate process for optimising search or retrieval of documents. The clusters of documents are characterised by documents features (single keywords or word combinations) and these are exploited to speed up retrieval or to perform keyword based search. Document clustering is based on any general data clustering algorithm adopted for text data by representing each document by a set of features in the same way as for document classification. The similarity of two documents is commonly measured by the cosine-similarity between the word-vector representation of the documents. Document clustering is used for collections that are at a single physical location (for example, the US national library of medicine) but also for search engines that give access to open collections over the internet. Document clustering is combined with document classification to enable maintenance: new documents are added to clusters by classifying them as cluster members. An example of an application of document clustering is [33].

4.4 Data Mining for Information Extraction

Information extraction means recognition of information in documents. Usually information extraction is combined with document classification: a document is recognised as a document that contains certain information and we need to find out where it is. A pattern is matched with the text in the document. If the pattern matches a fragment it indicates where the target information is. Such patterns can be constructed manually or learned inductively from documents in which the information is labelled. The patterns can be strings of symbols but can also include features: linguistic features (e.g. part of speech, capital letters) or semantic features (e.g. person name, number greater than 1000).

Although this can be viewed as a form of classification (classify all word sequences of length up to N as being the sought information or not) the classification models above are not directly applicable. Documents lack the structure of objects for which learning methods were originally developed: they may vary in length and it is not obvious what should be the features of an instance. On the other hand, documents on the Web are often encoded in HTML which imposes some structure that flat texts do not have.

Standard Data Mining methods must be adapted to the less structured setting of information extraction and are combined with ideas from grammar induction. Wrapper induction is the inductive construction of a wrapper, a system that mediates between what we might call a client and a server. It translates requests from the client into calls to the server. If we are interested in information from a Web page, the wrapper translates an information request into the format of the Web page, extracts the information from the page and sends it to the client. The wrapper exploits the structure of the Web page. If the Web page is structured as HTML or XML the wrapper can exploit this, otherwise it has to use patterns in the language, or a combination of the two.

Wrappers and extraction patterns in general can be learned from examples in which the relevant information is marked. The learner compares patterns around relevant information with general structure in the text and inductively constructs the wrapper. Examples of systems that perform this task are RAPIER [34] and BWI [35].

An example of an application of information extraction is wrapper maintenance [36]. A wrapper types components of an object or procedure from an external perspective to interface it with other systems or users. Information extraction patterns can be viewed as wrappers for documents or Web pages. The layout of documents or certain pages changes regularly and then wrappers must be revised. This can be done by comparing pages with the old and the new layout, identifying the components in the new layout and using this to revise the wrappers.

The use of Data Mining methods for learning extraction patterns and wrappers is currently a very active area of research. For an overview see [37].

4.5 Usage Mining

Web usage mining is a Web Mining paradigm in which Data Mining techniques are applied to Web usage data. As for Data Mining in general, the goal can be to construct a model of users' behaviour or to directly construct an adaptive system. A potential advantage of an explicit user model is that it can be used for different purposes where an adaptive system has a specific function. For modelling user behaviour, usage mining is combined with other information about users. Many aspects of users can be modelled: their interaction with a system, their interests, their knowledge, their geographical behaviour and also of course combinations of these. Modelling preferences needs information about users preferences for individual objects. This is often problematic because users are not always prepared to evaluate objects and enter the evaluations. Therefore other data are used like downloading, buying or time data.

Adaptive systems have the purpose to improve some aspect of the behaviour of the system. Improvements can be *system-oriented*, *content-oriented* (e.g. presenting information or products that relevant for the user), or *business-oriented* (e.g. presenting advertisements that the user is likely to buy, or that the vendor prefers to sell). Another dimension is wether the model or adaptation concerns individual users *personalisation* or generic system behaviour. An intermediate form is to use usage information obtained during a session to adapt system behaviour. This can also be combined with personalisation.

System-oriented adaptation based on usage mining is aimed at performance optimisation, e.g. for Web servers. This is of paramount importance in large sites that incur a lot of traffic. One of the factors leading to performance degradation is access to slow peripherals like disks, from which pages are pre-fetched upon user demand. Hence, it is of interest to devise intelligent pre-fetching mechanisms that allow for efficient caching. The problem specification reduces to a next-event prediction, where the next event is a page fetch request, combined with an appropriate mechanism for refreshing the cash, e.g. least frequently used or most frequently used. As described in the subsection 3.4 on event prediction above, the methods of choice here are Hidden Markov Models and, occasionally, sequence mining.

Personalisation. Although the terminology is not always used consistently, "personalisation" usually denotes adaptation to individual users that can be identified by the system (via a login step). Most systems have simple tools that a user can apply to adapt the interface to his preferences. For example, a user can store his favourite links to web pages. These are then later easily available when the user logs on to the system. Personalisation takes this further in two ways: (1) it includes aspects of systems that are less easy to specify with a few features and (2) the system automatically infers the preferences of the user and makes adjustments. Personalisation can be system-oriented, business-oriented or content-oriented and it can include a variety of data about an individual user.

Personalisation can be used for a variety of user tasks. A well-known example is shopping. The buying record in an electronic shop is used to infer user preferences of a user and direct advertising. Other applications center around information search. Examples are personalised newspapers (that include only material that is considered of interest to the user), personalised Web sites, active information gathering from the web, highlighting potentially interesting hyperlinks on a requested Web pages [28], query-expansion (by adding user-specific keywords to a query for a search engine), selection of TV programmes. Personalisation and recommending can be based on usage data, on documents that are associated with an individual user or a combination of these two.

System adaptation. Systems can also be adapted to a user community, rather than a single user, optimising average instead of user specific peformance.

For example, Etzioni et al. propose a clustering algorithm for correlated but not linked Web pages, allowing for overlapping clusters [38]; Alvarez et al. extend association rules discovery to cope with the demands of online recommendations [39]; Mobasher et al propose two methods for modelling user sessions and corresponding distance functions, to cluster sessions and derive user and usage profiles [40]. Finally, dedicated Web usage mining algorithms are also proposed, focussing mainly on the discovery of Web usage patterns, as in [41,42,43].

An important subject in Web usage mining concerns the evaluation of adaptive systems based on Web Mining. Methods for the evaluation of Web sites with respect to user friendliness, interactivity and similar user-oriented aspects have been devised early, building upon the research on hypermedia and upon cognitive sciences [44]. The business-oriented perspective leads to other evaluation criteria derived from marketing.

4.6 Modelling Networks of Users

Users do not act in isolation - they are part of various social networks, often defined by common interests and by phenomena such as opinion leadership and, more generally, different degrees of influence on one another. An understanding of a user's surrounding social network(s) improves the understanding of that user and can therefore contribute to reaching various Web mining goals. For example, Domingos and Richardson [45] use a collaborative filtering database to understand the differential influence users have and propose to use this knowledge for "viral marketing": to preferentially target customers whose purchasing and recommendation behaviour are likely to have a strong influence on others. Other data sources include email logs [46] and publicly-available online information [47]. This research combines aspects of Web content mining and Web structure mining. The latter view closes a circle: link mining has its origins in social network analysis and is now being applied to analyze the social networks forming on the Web.

5 Data Mining for and with the Semantic Web

The standardized data format, the popularity of content-annotated documents and the ambition of large scale formalization of knowledge of the Semantic Web has two consequences for Web Mining. The first is that more structured information becomes available to which existing Data Mining methods can be applied with only minor modifications. The second is the possibility of using formalized knowledge (in the form of concept hierarchies in RDF but even more in the form of knowledge represented in OWL) in combination with Web data for Data Mining. The combination of these two gives a form of closed-loop learning in which knowledge is acquired by Web Mining and then used again for further learning. We briefly summarise the implications of this for the main Web Mining tasks.

5.1 Document Classification for and with the Semantic Web

Document classification methods for the Semantic Web are like those for the World-Wide Web. Besides general features of documents, annotations can be used, as additional features or to structure features. Knowledge in the form of ontologies can be used to infer additional information about documents, potentially providing a better basis for classification. This form of document classification uses classification learning with background knowledge and feature construction [48]. Document classes can be added to the annotation of documents. Classification be applied to predefined segments of documents.

Issues for current and future research are the use of non-textual data such as images. Images can be tagged more or less like textual documents (see [49]) giving rise to the same learning tasks and opening the opportunity for learning about combinations of text and images. Future issues are video, voice and sound. From the current state of the art it is likely that this will be possible in the next five years, enabling a wide range of new applications such as multimedia communication.

5.2   Document Clustering for and with the Semantic Web

Like document classification, clustering of annotated documents can exploit the annotations and it can infer extra information about documents from ontologies. An example is [50], where texts are preprocessed by adding semantic categories derived from Wordnet. Evaluation on Reuters newsfeeds shows an improvement of the results by using background knowledge.

Hierarchical document clusters and the descriptions of these clusters can be viewed as ontologies based on subconcept relations. In this sense hierachical clustering methods construct ontologies of documents and then maintain these ontologies [51,7,29] by classifying new documents in the hierachy. Characterising clusters supports the construction of ontologies because the description of a cluster reflects relations between concepts, see [52,53,54].

5.3   Data Mining for Information Extraction with the Semantic Web

Learning to extract information from documents can exploit annotations of document segments for learning extraction rules - assuming these have been assigned consistently - and it can benefit from knowledge in ontologies. The other way round, existing ontologies can support solving different problems including learning of other ontologies and assigning ontology concepts to text (text annotation). Ontology concepts are assigned either to whole documents, as in the case of already described ontologies of Web documents or to some smaller parts of text. In the letter case, researchers have been working on learning annotation rules from already annotated text. This can bee seen as a kind of information extraction, where the goal is not to fill in the database slots by extracted information (see Section 4.4) but to assign a label (slot name) to a part of text (see [55]). As it is non-trivial to obtain already annotated text, some researchers investigate other techniques, such as natural language processing or clustering to find text units (eg., groups of nouns, clusters of sentences) and map them upon concepts of the existing ontology [56].

5.4   Ontology Mapping

Because ontologies are often developed for a specific purpose it is inevitable that similar ontologies are constructed and unifying these ontologies needs to be done to enable the use of knowledge from one ontology in combination with knowledge in the other. This requires the construction of a mapping between the concepts, attributes, values and relations in the two ontologies, either as a solution or as a step towards a single unified ontology. Several approaches to this problems are explored by several researchers [57, 58,59,60,61,62]. One line of attack is to first take information about concepts from the ontologies and then extract additional information for example from Web pages recognised as relevant for each concept. This information can then be used to learn a classifier for instances of a class. Applying this classifier to instances of concepts in the other ontology makes it possible to see which other concept (or combination of concepts) has most in common with the original concept.

5.5   User Modelling, Recommending, Personalisation, and the Semantic Web

The Semantic Web opens up interesting opportunities for usage mining because ontologies and annotations can provide information about user actions and Web pages in a standardised form that enables discovery of richer and more informative patterns. Examples for recommending are the work by Mobasher and by Ghani (both this volume). The annotations of products that are visited (and bought) by users add information to customer segments and make it possible to discover the underlying general patterns. Such patterns can be used, for example, to predict reactions to new products from the description of the new product. This would not have been possible if only the name, image and price of the product had been available and mining can be done much more effectively using a uniform ontology than from documents that describe products.

Applications of usage mining such as usage-based recommending, personalisation and link analysis will benefit from the use of annotated documents and objects. Only a few technical problems need to be solved to extend existing methods this. Large scale applications need larger ontologies that can be maintained and applied semi-automatically. Designing or automatically generating ontologies for decribing user interests and user behaviour are more challenging problems that need to be addressed in this context.

5.6   Learning About Services

The construction and design of ontologies for functions of Web services is an area that is currently topic of active research. As for descriptive concepts, a Web Mining approach can be applied to this problem. Requests to a service and the reaction of the server can be collected and learning methods can be applied to, at least for simple cases, reconstruct the function of the service. An illustration of this approach is shown in [63]. Advances to practical applications of this approach that are complex enough to make this approach competitive to manual construction of the service description are still beyond the state of the art and have to wait for suitable ontologies that can be used as background knowledge by the learner.

5.7   Infrastructure

In the sections above we reviewed research on Data Mining methods for the Semantic Web. Techniques and representations developed for the Semantic Web are not only applied as methods for which systems are developed. Notions from the Semantic Web are introduced in operating systems for single and distributed systems. These developments would facilitate the use and development of Web Mining systems and the unification imposed by system level standards will make it easier to exploit distributed ontologies and services. In this section we focus on the innovations in the infrastructure for systems that are based on such methods.

Current applications of Semantic Web ideas suffer partially from a lack of speed. The bigger problem is the lack of a large number of ontologies and annotations. Although access to ontologies and data via the internet is possible, existing applications strongly rely on local computing. Ontologies, instances, logfiles are imported and kept locally to achieve enough speed. This will clearly meet its limits when the Semantic Web will be used at a large scale. Bringing Semantic Web ideas into the lower level of the internet may allow distributed computing with distributed ontologies, instances and knowledge. This brings together the Semantic Web and Grid Computing and is pursued under the name of Semantic Grid.

Another development that will have a great influence in the Semantic Web is that the successor to the Windows operating system, the Longhorn operating system uses a version of XML to integrate the datamodel and applications. This is likely to make the Semantic Web languages known outside the current communities and also it will provide widely available support for Semantic Web tools. This in turn will create enormous opportunities for Web Mining methods both at the level of information and knowledge and at the level of systems.

6   Prospects

The future of Web Mining will to a large extent depend on developments of the Semantic Web. The role of Web technology still increases in industry, government, education, entertainment. This means that the range of data to which Web Mining can be applied also increases. Even without technical advances, the role of Web Mining technology will become larger and more central. The main technical advances will be in increasing the types of data to which Web Mining can be applied. In particular Web Mining for text, images and video/audio streams will increase the scope of current methods. These are all active research topics in Data Mining and Machine Learning and the results of this can be exploited for Web Mining.

The second type of technical advance comes from the integration of Web Mining with other technologies in application contexts. Examples are information retrieval, e-commerce, business process modelling, instruction, and health care. The widespread use of web-based systems in these areas makes them amenable to Web Mining.

In this section we outline current generic practical problems that will be addressed, technology required for these solutions, and research issues that need to be addressed for technical progress.

Knowledge Management. Knowledge Management is generally viewed as a field of great industrial importance. Systematic management of the knowledge that is available in an organisation can increase the ability of the organisation to make optimal use of the knowledge that is available in the organisation and to react effectively to new developments, threats and opportunities. Web Mining technology creates the opportunity to integrate knowledge management more tightly with business processes. Standardisation efforts that use Semantic Web technology and the availability of ever more data about business processes on the internet creates opportunities for Web Mining technology.

More widespread use of Web Mining for Knowledge Management requires the availability of low-threshold Web Mining tools that can be used by non-experts and that can flexibly be integrated in a wide variety of tools and systems.

E-commerce. The increased use of XML/RDF to describe products, services and business processes increases the scope and power of Data Mining methods in e-commerce. Another direction is the use of text mining methods for modelling technical, social and commercial developments. This requires advances in text mining and information extraction.

E-learning. The Semantic Web provides a way of organising teaching material, and usage mining can be applied to suggest teaching materials to a learner. This opens opportunities for Web Mining. For example, a recommending approach (as in [64]) can be followed to find courses or teaching material for a learner. The material can then be organized with clustering techniques, and ultimately be shared on the web again, e. g., within a peer to peer network [65]. Web mining methods can be used to construct a profile of user skills, competence or knowledge and of the effect of instruction. Another possibility is to use web mining to analyse student interactions for teaching purposes. The internet supports students who collaborate during learning. Web mining methods can be used to monitor this process, without requiring the teacher to follow the interactions in detail. Current web mining technology already provides a good basis for this. Research and development must be directed toward important characteristics of interactions and to integration in the instructional process.

E-government. Many activities in governments involve large collections of documents. Think of regulations, letters, announcements, reports. Managing access and availability of this amount of textual information can be greatly facilitated by a combination of Semantic Web standardisation and text mining tools. Many internal processes in government involve documents, both textual and structured. Web mining creates the opportunity to analyse these governmental processes and to create models of the processes and the information involved. It seems likely that standard ontologies will be used in governmental organisations and the standardisation that this produces will make Web Mining more widely applicable and more powerful than it currently is. The issues involved are those of Knowledge Management. Also governmental activities that involve the general public include many opportunities for Web Mining. Like shops, governments that offer services via the internet can analyse their customers behaviour to improve their services. Information about social processes can be observed and monitored using Web Mining, in the style of marketing analyses. Examples of this are the analysis of research proposals for the European Commission and the development of tools for monitoring and structuring internet discussion fora on political issues (e.g. the E-presentation project at Fraunhofer Institute [66]). Enabling technologies for this are more advanced information extraction methods and tools.

Health care. Medicine is one of the Web's fastest-growing areas. It profits from Semantic Web technology in a number of ways: First, as a means of organizing medical knowledge - for example, the widely-used taxonomy International Classification of Diseases and its variants serve to organize telemedicine portal content (e.g., http://www.dermis.net) and interfaces (e.g., http://healthcybermap.semanticweb.org). The Unified Medical Language System (http://www.nlm.nih.gov/research/umls) integrates this classification and many others. Second, health care institutions can profit from interoperability between the different clinical information systems and semantic representations of member institutions' organization and services (cf. the Health Level 7 standard developed by the International Healthcare XML Standards Consortium: http://www.hl7.org). Usage analyses of medical sites can be employed for purposes such as Web site evaluation and the inference of design guidelines for international audiences [67,68], or the detection of epidemics [69]. In general, similar issues arise, and the same methods can be used for analysis and design as in other content classes of Web sites. Some of the facets of Semantic Web Mining that we have mentioned in this article form specific challenges, in particular: the privacy and security of patient data, the semantics of visual material (cf. the Digital Imaging and Communications in Medicine standard: http://medical.nema.org), and the cost-induced pressure towards national and international integration of Web resources.

E-science. In E-Science two main developments are visible. One is the use of text mining and Data Mining for information extraction to extract information from large collections of textual documents. Much information is "buried" in the huge scientific literature and can be extracted by combining knowledge about the domain and information extraction. Enabling technology for this is information extraction in combination with knowledge representation and ontologies. The other development is large scale data collection and data analysis. This also requires common concept and organisation of the information using ontologies. However, this form of collaboration also needs a common methodology and it needs to be extended with other means of communication, see [70] for examples and discussion.

Webmining for images and video and audio streams. So far, efforts in Semantic Web research have addressed mostly written documents. Recently this is broadened to include sound/voice and images. Images and parts of images are annotated with terms from ontologies.

Privacy and security. A factor that limits the application of Web Mining is the need to protect privacy of users. Web Mining uses data that are available on the web anyway but the use of Data Mining makes it possible to induce general patterns that can be applied to personal data to inductively infer data that should remain private. Recent research addresses this problem and searches for selective restrictions on access to data that do allow the induction of general patterns but at the same time preserves a preset uncertainty about individuals, thereby protecting privacy of individuals, e.g., [71,72].

Information extraction with formalised knowledge. In section 5.3 we briefly reviewed the use of concept hierarchies and thesauri for information extraction. If knowledge is represented in more general formal Semantic Web languages like OWL, in principle there are stronger possibilities to use this knowledge for information extraction.

In summary, the main foreseen developments are:

– *The extensive use of annotated documents facilitates the application of Data Mining techniques to documents.*

- *The use of a standardised format and a standardised vocabulary for information on the web will increase the effect and use of Web Mining.*
- *The Semantic Web goal of large-scale construction of ontologies will require the use of Data Mining methods, in particular to extract knowledge from text.*

At the moment of writing the main issues to address are:

- *Methods for images and sound: an increasing part of the information on the web is not in textual form and methods for classification, clustering, rule and sequence learning and information extraction are needed, and thus require a combination with methods for text and structured data.*
- *Knowledge-intensive learning methods for information extraction from texts. Building powerful information extraction knowledge is likely to be a necessary condition to enable the Semantic Web.*

References

1. Michalski, R., Bratko, I., (eds), M.K.: Machine Learning and Data Mining: methods and applications. John Wiley and Sons, Chichester (1998)
2. Paliouras, G., Karkaletsis, V., (eds), C.S.: Machine Learning and its Applications. Springer-Verlag, Heidelberg (2001)
3. Franke, J., Nakhaeizadeh, G., Renz, I., eds.: Text Mining, Theoretical Aspects and Applications. Physica-Verlag (2003)
4. Berners-Lee, T., Fischetti, M.: Weaving the Web. Harper, San Francisco (1999)
5. Berendt, B., Stumme, G., Hotho, A.: Usage mining for and on the semantic web. In: Data Mining: Next Generation Challenges and Future Directions. AAAI/MIT Press, Menlo Park, CA (2004) 467–486
6. Berendt, B., Hotho, A., Stumme, G.: Towards semantic web mining. In: [73]. (2002) 264–278
7. Mladenić, D., Grobelnik, M.: Feature selection on hierarchy of web documents. Journal of Decission support systems 35 (2003) 45–87
8. Erdmann, M.: Ontologien zur konzeptuellen Modellierung der Semantik von XML. Isbn: 3831126356, University of Karlsruhe (2001)
9. W3C: RDF/XML Syntax Specification (Revised). W3C recommendation, http://www.w3.org/TR/2004/REC-rdf-syntax-grammar-20040210/ (2004)
10. Fellbaum, C.: WordNet: An Electronic Lexical Database. MIT Press, Cambridge, MA (1998)
11. Mitchell, T.: Machine Learning. McGraw Hill (1997)
12. Hand, D., Mannila, H., Smyth, P.: Principles of Data Mining. MIT Press (2001)
13. Weiss, M., Indurkhya, N.: Pedictive Data-Mining: A Practical Guide. organ Kaufmann, San Francisco (1997)
14. Lavrac, N., Dzeroski, S.: Inductive Logic Programming: Techniques and Applications. Ellis Horwood, New York (1994)
15. Agrawal, R., Imielinski, T., Swami, A.: Mining association rules between sets of items in large databases. In: SIGMOD'93, Washington D.C., USA (1993) 207–216
16. Agrawal, R., Srikant, R.: Fast algorithms for mining association rules. In Bocca, J.B., Jarke, M., Zaniolo, C., eds.: Proc. 20th Int. Conf. Very Large Data Bases, VLDB, Morgan Kaufmann (1994) 487–499
17. Adamo, J.M.: Data Mining and Association Rules for Sequential Patterns: Sequential and Parallel Algorithms. Springer, New York (2001)

18. Roddick, J., Spiliopoulou, M.: A survey of temporal knowledge discovery paradigms and methods. IEEE Trans. of Knowledge and Data Engineering (2002)
19. Lan, B., Bressan, S., Ooi, B.: Making web servers pushier. In: Proceedings WEBKDD-99. Springer Verlag, Berlin (2000) 108–122
20. Scheffer, T., Wrobel, S.: A sequential sampling algorithm for a general class of utility criteria. In: Knowledge Discovery and Data Mining. (2000) 330–334
21. Zaki, M., Lesh, N., Ogihara, M.: Mining features for sequence classification. In: Proc. of 5th ACM SIGKDD Int. Conf. on Knowledge Discovery and Data Mining KDD'99, ACM (1999) 342–346
22. Weiss, G.M., Hirsh, H.: Learning to predict rare events in event sequences. In Agrawal, R., Stolorz, P., Piatesky-Shapiro, G., eds.: Proc. of 4th Int. Conf. KDD, New York, NY (1998) 359–363
23. Brin, S., Page, L.: The anatomy of a large-scale hypertextual web search engine source. In: Proceedings of the seventh international conference on World Wide Web, Elsevier Science Publishers (1998)
24. Kleinberg, J.M.: Authoritative sources in a hyperlinked environment. Journal of the ACM **46** (1999) 604–632
25. Cooley, R., Mobasher, B., Srivastava, J.: Data preparation for mining world wide web browsing patterns. Journal of Knowledge and Information Systems **1** (1999) 5–32
26. Spiliopoulou, M., Mobasher, B., Berendt, B., Nakagawa, M.: A framework for the evaluation of session reconstruction heuristics in web usage analysis. INFORMS Journal on Computing, Special Issue on "Mining Web-based Data for E-Business Applications" (eds. Rashid, Louiqa and Tuzhilin, Alex) (2003)
27. McCallum, A., Rosenfeld, R., Mitchell, T., Ng, A.: Improving text classification by shrinkage in a hierarchy of classes. In: Proceedings of the 15th International Conference on Machine Learning (ICML-98), Morgan Kaufmann, San Francisco, CA (1998)
28. Mladenic, D.: Web browsing using machine learning on text data. In Szczepaniak, P., ed.: Intelligent exploration of the web, 111,Physica-Verlag (2002) 288–303
29. Koller, D., Sahami, M.: Hierarchically classifying documents using very few words. In: Proceedings of the 14th International Conference on Machine Learning ICML97. (1997) 170–178
30. Sebastiani, F.: Machine learning in automated text categorization. ACM Computing Surveys **34** (2002) 1–47
31. Androutsopoulos, I., Koutsias, J., Chandrinos, K., Paliouras, G., Spyropoulos, C.: An evaluation of naive bayesian anti-spam filtering. In Potamias, G., Moustakis, V., van Someren, M., eds.: Proceedings of the workshop on Machine Learning in the New Information Age. (2000)
32. Steinbach, M., Karypis, G., Kumar, V.: A comparison of document clustering techniques. In Grobelnik, M., Mladenic, D., Milic-Frayling, N., eds.: Proceedings of the KDD Workshop on Text Mining. (2000)
33. Zamir, O., Etzioni, O.: Web document clustering: A feasibility demonstration. In: Research and Development in Information Retrieval. (1998) 46–54
34. Califf, M.E., Mooney, R.J.: Bottom-up relational learning of pattern matching rules for information extraction. Journal of Machine Learning Research **4** (2003) 177–210
35. Freitag, D., Kushmerick, N.: Boosted wrapper induction. In: Proceedings AAAI-00. (2000) 577–583
36. X. Meng, D. Hu, C.L.: Schema-guided wrapper maintenance for web-data extraction. In: ACM Fifth International Workshop on Web Information and Data Management (WIDM 2003). (2003)
37. Kushmerick, N., Thomas, B.: Adaptive information extraction: Core technologies for information agents. In: Intelligent Information Agents R&D in Europe: An AgentLink perspective. Springer, Berlin (2004) 79–103

38. Perkowitz, M., Etzioni, O.: Adaptive web sites: Automatically synthesizing web page. In: Proc. of AAAI/IAAI'98. (1998) 727–732
39. Lin, W., Alvarez, S., Ruiz, C.: Efficient adaptive-support association rule mining for recommender systems. Data Mining and Knowledge Discovery **6** (2002) 83–105
40. Mobasher, B., Dai, H., Luo, T., Nakagawa, M.: Discovery and evaluation of aggregate usage profiles for web personalization. Data Mining and Knowledge Discovery **6** (2002) 61–82
41. Baumgarten, M., Büchner, A.G., Anand, S.S., Mulvenna, M.D., Hughes, J.G.: Navigation pattern discovery from internet data. In: Proceedings volume [74]. (2000) 70–87
42. Borges, J.L., Levene, M.: Data mining of user navigation patterns. In Spiliopoulou, M., Masand, B., eds.: Advances in Web Usage Analysis and User Profiling. Springer, Berlin (2000) 92–111
43. Spiliopoulou, M.: The laborious way from data mining to web mining. Int. Journal of Comp. Sys., Sci. & Eng., Special Issue on "Semantics of the Web" **14** (1999) 113–126
44. Cutler, M.: E-metrics: Tomorrow's business metrics today. In: KDD'2000, Boston, MA, ACM (2000)
45. Domingos, P., Richardson, M.: Mining the network value of customers. In: Proceedings of the Seventh ACM SIGKDD International Conference on Knowledge Discovery and Data Mining, KDD-01, New York, ACM (2001) 57–66
46. Schwartz, M., Wood, D.: Discovering shared interests using graph analysis. Communications of the ACM **36** (1993) 78–89
47. Kautz, H., Selman, B., Shah, M.: Referralweb: Combining social networks and collaborative filtering. Communications of the ACM **40** (1997) 63–66
48. Bloehdorn, S., Hotho, A.: Boosting for text classification with semantic features. In: Proc. of the Mining for and from the Semantic Web Workshop at KDD 2004. (2004)
49. Zaiane, O., Simoff, S.: Mdm/kdd: Multimedia data mining for the second time. SIGKDD Explorations **3** (2003)
50. Hotho, A., Staab, S., Stumme, G.: Wordnet improves text document clustering. In: Procs. of the SIGIR 2003 Semantic Web Workshop, Toronto, Canada (2003)
51. McCallum, A., Rosenfeld, R., Mitchell, T., Ng, A.: Improving text classification by shrinkage in a hierarchy of classes. In: Proceedings of the 15th International Conference on Machine Learning ICML98, Morgan Kaufmann (1998)
52. Hotho, A., Staab, S., Stumme, G.: Explaining text clustering results using semantic structures. In: Proc. of the 7th European Conference on Principles and Practice of Knowledge Discovery in Databases, PKDD. (2003) 217–228
53. Maedche, A., Staab, S.: Ontology learning for the semantic web. IEEE Intelligent Systems **16** (2001) 72–79
54. Cimiano, P., Hotho, A., Staab, S.: Comparing conceptual, partitional and agglomerative clustering for learning taxonomies from text. In: Proceedings of the European Conference on Artificial Intelligence (ECAI'04). (2004)
55. Handschuh, S., Staab, S.: Authoring and annotation of web page in CREAM. In: Proc. Of WWW Conference 2002. (2002)
56. Hotho, A., Staab, S., Stumme, G.: Explaining text clustering results using semantic structures. In: Proceedings of ECML/PKDD, Springer Verlag (2003) 217–228
57. Hovy, E.: Combining and standardizing large-scale, practical ontologies for machine translation and other uses. In: Proc. 1st Intl. Conf. on Language Resources and Evaluation (LREC), Granada (1998)
58. Chalupsky, H.: Ontomorph: A translation system for symbolic knowledge. In: Principles of Knowledge Representation and Reasoning: Proceedings of the Seventh International Conference (KR2000). (2000) 471–482

59. McGuinness, D., Fikes, R., Rice, J., Wilder, S.: An environment for merging and testing large ontologies. In: In the Proceedings of the Seventh International Conference on Principles of Knowledge Representation and Reasoning (KR2000), Breckenridge, Colorado, USA (2000) 483–493

60. Noy, N., Musen, M.: Prompt: Algorithm and tool for automated ontology merging and alignment. In: Proceedings of the Seventeenth National Conference on Artificial Intelligence (AAAI-2000), Austin, Texas (2000) 450–455

61. Stumme, G., Maedche, A.: Fca-merge: Bottom-up merging of ontologies. In: Proceedings 17th International Conference on Artificial Intelligence (IJCAI-01). (2001) 225–230

62. Doan, A., Madhavan, J., Domingos, P., Halevy, A.: Ontology matching: A machine learning approach. In: Handbook on Ontologies. Springer, Berlin (2004) 385–404

63. Heß, A., Kushmerick, N.: Machine learning for annotating semantic web services. In: Proceedings of the First International Semantic Web Services Symposium. AAAI Spring Symposium Series 2. (2004)

64. Aguado, B., Merceron, A., Voisard, A.: Extracting information from structured exercises. In: Proceedings of the 4th International Conference on Information Technology Based Higher Education and Training ITHET03, Marrakech, Morocco. (2003)

65. Tane, J., Schmitz, C., Stumme, G.: Semantic resource management for the web: An elearning application. In: Proc. 13th International World Wide Web Conference (WWW 2004). (2004)

66. Althoff, K., Becker-Kornstaedt, U., Decker, B., Klotz, A., Leopold, E., Rech, J., Voss, A.: The indigo project: Enhancement of experience management and process learning with moderated discourses. In Perner, P., ed.: Data Mining in Marketing and Medicine. Springer, Berlin (2002)

67. Yihune, G.: Evaluation eines medizinischen Informationssystems im World Wide Web. Nutzungsanalyse am Beispiel www.dermis.net. PhD thesis, Ruprecht-Karls-Universität Heidelberg (2003)

68. Kralisch, A., Berendt, B.: Cultural determinants of search behaviour on websites. In: Proceedings of the IWIPS 2004 Conference on Culture, Trust, and Design Innovation. (2004)

69. Heino, J., Toivonen, H.: Automated detection of epidemics from the usage logs of a physicians' reference database. In: Proceedings of the 7th European Conference on Principles and Practice of Knowledge Discovery in Databases (PKDD'03), Berlin, Springer (2003) 180–191

70. Mladenic, D., Lavrac, N., Bohanec, M., Moyle, S., eds.: Data Mining and Decision Support: Integration and Collaboration. Kluwer Academic Publishers (2003)

71. Evfimievski, A., Srikant, R., Agrawal, R., Gehrke, J.: Privacy preserving mining of association rules. In: [75]. (2002) 217–228

72. Iyengar, V.: Transforming data to satisfy privacy constraints. In: [75]. (2002) 279–288

73. Horrocks, I., Hendler, J.A., eds.: The Semantic Web. In Horrocks, I., Hendler, J.A., eds.: Proceedings of the First International Semantic Web Conference, Springer (2002)

74. Masand, B., Spiliopoulou, M., eds.: Advances in Web Usage Mining and User Profiling: Proceedings of the WEBKDD'99 Workshop. LNAI 1836, Springer Verlag (2000)

75. Hand, D., Keim, D., Ng, R., eds.: KDD - 2002 – Proceedings of the Eighth ACM SIGKDD International Conference on Knowledge Discovery and Data Mining, New York, ACM (2002)

On the Deployment of Web Usage Mining

Sarabjot Singh Anand, Maurice Mulvenna, and Karine Chevalier*

School of Computing and Mathematics, University of Ulster at Jordanstown,
Newtownabbey, County Antrim, Northern Ireland BT37 0QB
{ss.anand, md.mulvenna}@ulster.ac.uk,
karine.chevalier@lip6.fr

Abstract. In this paper we look at the deployment of web usage mining results within two key application areas of web measurement and knowledge generation for personalisation. We take a fresh look at the model of interaction between business and visitors to their web sites and the sources of data generated during these interactions. We then look at previous attempts at measuring the effectiveness of the web as a channel to customers and describe our approach, based on scenario development and measurement to gain insights into customer behaviour. We then present Concerto, a platform for deploying knowledge on customer behaviour with the aim of providing a more personalized service. We also look at approaches to measuring the effectiveness of the personalization. Various standards that are emerging in the market that can ease the integration effort of personalization and similar knowledge deployment engines within the existing IT infrastructure of an organization are also presented. Finally, current challenges in the deployment of web usage mining are presented.

1 Introduction

A major issue with web usage mining to date is the inability of researchers and practitioners to put forward a convincing case for Return on Investment (ROI) in this technology. Web usage mining is complex if for no other reason, because of the sheer volume of data and the pre-processing requirements due to data quality [10]. Data generated by on-line businesses ranges from tens of Megabytes to several hundred Gigabytes per day. Complexity of the web infrastructure and the focus on scalability has led to numerous data quality issues related to page view identification, visitor identification and robot activity filtering. Prior to knowledge being discovered, this data must be cleaned, requiring large processing capabilities. The processed data must then be loaded into an optimised warehouse before even the simplest of statistics can be generated based on the data collected. This in turn means that businesses need to

---

*

Currently working as a Marie Curie Fellow at the PERSONET training site at the Northern Ireland Knowledge Engineering Laboratory. Her home university is Univertié Pierre et Marie Curie, Paris 6.

B. Berendt et al. (Eds.): EWMF 2003, LNAI 3209, pp. 23–42, 2004.
© Springer-Verlag Berlin Heidelberg 2004

make large investments in hardware and software before they can start gaining the benefits from analysing the data.

Analysing the data collected on-line on its own has not provided significant business benefits and more recently there is a trend towards integration of web data with non-web customer data prior to analysing it – the mythical 360 degree view of the customer. Such consolidation is evident from takeovers of web analytics companies such as Net Genesis by data mining/CRM companies such as SPSS.

In keeping with a number of data mining applications in industry, success of a web usage mining project depends on the development and application of a standard process. CRISP-DM[1] provides a generic basis for such a process that has been tried and tested in industry. It is also accepted by most practitioners that while pre-processing of the data is the most time-consuming phase of the process, planning for and executing on the deployment phase of the process is key to project success and delivery of ROI. We suggest that it is at this phase that web usage mining has failed to deliver.

In this paper we review past attempts, describe current research and develop future trends in the deployment of web usage mining results. In Section 2 we define web usage mining from a deployment perspective distinguishing between its two main applications: web measurement and knowledge generation. We elaborate on our model for customer interaction that forms the basis for data generated online, the input to analytical tools provided by web usage mining. Section 3 describes the web usage mining function of web measurement, probably the most common form of analytics associated with the web. We discuss the growth of the field of web metrics and describe a process based on business process monitoring called scenario measurement. The second key application of web usage mining is the generation of useful knowledge to be used for various business applications such as target marketing and personalisation and Section 4 describes the deployment of generated knowledge within the context of personalisation. In Section 5 we briefly describe Concerto, a scalable platform for flexible recommendation generation, highlighting the role of standards within the platform. Finally, Section 6 focuses on future trends within the development of deployment technologies for web usage mining.

2   Web Usage Mining

Web usage mining has been defined as the application of data mining techniques to large Web data repositories in order to extract usage patterns [5].

From a deployment perspective, there are two key applications of web usage mining. The first is Web Measurement, encompassing the use of web mining to understand the value that the web channel is generating for the business. This includes measuring the success of various marketing efforts and promotions, understanding conversion rates and identifying bottlenecks within the conversion process.

The second key application is the generation of knowledge about visitor behaviour. The aim here is to understand visitor behaviour with the aim of servicing them better

---

[1] www.crisp-dm.org

whether it is through the use of target marketing campaigns tailored to the individual needs of customers or more proactive personalisation of the interactions in real-time.

In either case, it is essential to understand the nature of the interaction of visitors with the business, the data that can be collected at each stage and the relationship between the various data items with each other. We now describe our model of online customer interactions that forms the basis for data collected for web usage mining.

2.1 A Model of Online Customer Interaction

From a web usage mining perspective, visitor interactions can be viewed as shown in Figure 1. A visitor visits the web site on a number of occasions (visits). During each visit, the visitor accesses a number of page impressions (also known as page views). Each page impression represents certain concepts from the business domain and each concept in turn is represented by a number of content objects (often called hits). Each content object is identified by a unique URI but also has a number of attributes that describe its content. This is especially useful for dynamic web sites where the URLs themselves do not explicitly present all content related information.

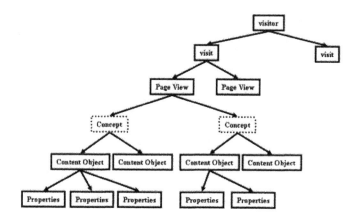

Fig. 1. Customer Interaction Model

The concepts themselves may be related through a domain specific ontology. For example an online movie retailer may have content objects related to films, actors, directors, producers, choreographer, etc. Using such an ontology within the web usage mining process or indeed during the deployment of web usage mining results remains a challenge.

There is also an important temporal dimension to the model. People change and so do their tastes. Previous preferences may be less relevant to current requirements. Also, within a visit, users get distracted as they navigate though a web site and get exposed to the breadth of information available, making earlier page views less relevant to the users' current needs. Other temporal effects include seasonality of purchases and the context of the visit based of life-events such as births, deaths, graduation etc.

Note that the model above is general in the sense that it encompasses interactions between a visitor and a business in non-electronic channels too, though the same depth of data is not available in non-electronic channels, where data generated is generally limited to visitor transactions only.

2.2 Data Sources from Online Interaction

In web usage mining, the focus is generally on visitor-centred analysis of the data collected though in certain circumstances visit based analysis is more appropriate, especially given the well documented issues with visitor identification in web data [10]. From a web measurement perspective, visit-based analytics is also useful to discover visit specific process bottlenecks that result in the abandonment of the visit.

From a knowledge generation perspective, the ultimate aim is to gain insights into customer behaviour so as to improve the customer experience and profitability. Central to this analysis is the collection of data associated with customer preferences. The data used as input to the web usage mining algorithm for knowledge generation may be sourced in disparate ways. Data can be collected by explicitly asking the user for the information or implicitly by recording user behaviour (Figure 2).

In the context of the web, the most commonly available data is web logs[2] that document visitor navigation through the web site. This data is collected implicitly and can provide insights into user interests based on the frequency with which certain content is accessed, the time spent on the content, the order in which content is navigated or simply on the fact that certain content was accessed while other content was not accessed.

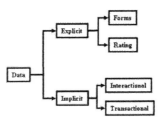

Fig. 2. Data Collection for Customer Insight

Another form of implicit data collection is transactional in nature. These data represent actual purchases made by the customer. Once again the assumption made here is that the user only purchases products that are of interest to them.

There are two main forms of explicit data collection on the web. The first is the filling of forms. These may be forms filled by users to register for a service or on-line surveys and competitions. The other explicit data collection technique is content or

---

[2] More recently, alternatives to web server logs, based on JavaScript and applets, have been proposed that alleviate a number of data quality issues with web server logs. The nature of the data is generally the same as that stored in web logs and so the following discussion is just as valid for data collected using these alternatives techniques.

product rating on a web site. This can involve form-filling or selecting check boxes, to provide feedback information. As explicit data collection requires additional effort from the customer, all non-essential data items are generally not reliable as customers tend to input incorrect data due to privacy concerns. Also rankings are inherently subjective in nature and may not be reliable for use in group behavioural analytics.

3 Web Measurement

Attempts to measure activity on a web site date back to the development of the earliest web sites. The first form of measurement was the embedding of counters on web pages that displayed the number of times that a web page was requested from the server. As web sites became more complex, the counters used by web sites became less attractive as measures of activity on web sites. Other than simply the increased complexity of the web environment, counters in themselves did not provide any useful knowledge that could be used by web site owners to enhance their services or even gain insights into site performance.

The second generation of web measurement tools used web server logs to produce more detailed statistics. These tools, often referred to as web log analysis tools, typically parsed the log files generated by the web server and produced static graphical reports showing the activity by day, time of day, top page accesses, least accessed pages, server error code distributions, most commonly used browsers used to access the web site etc. The analysis provided by these tools, was generally focussed on hits (components of pages) served by the server, and while useful for site administrators to improve site performance, were not useful from the perspective of gaining insights into user behaviour. These tools generally did not warehouse the data from which the statistics were produced and nor did they provide systematic filtering and visit/visitor identification techniques so as to provide visitor centric analysis[3].

More recently, the focus of the analytics has shifted to visitor behaviour. Tools used for this type of analysis are often referred to as Web analytics tools. The approach taken by these tools is that a web site can be considered to be successful when the objectives of its owner are satisfied. The objectives can be to: convert site visitors into consumers, convert site users into repeat visitors, increase the sale of a product, deliver specific information, or increase the hit on an ad banner. The success metrics are established relative to the definition of success.

This approach to analysis is based on the fact that activity on a web site can be decomposed into a succession of steps [2,9,19]. The effectiveness of the web site is computed based on the ability to satisfy each step. If a site provides easy access to information or a service in a specific step, it means that the user can easily go through to the next step. In a similar approach Spiliopoulou et al. defines three kinds of access [18]: access to an action page (which guides to an objective), access to a target page (the objective is achieved) and access to others pages.

---

[3] Later versions of software from web log analysis vendors such as WebTrends and NetGenesis did provide high-end analytical tools that had this functionality, but for the classification presented in this paper we classify the high end products as web analytics products.

A way to distinguish the different steps (or activity on the site) is to use additional knowledge about the content of the site. Teltzrow et al. [19] proposed associating a service concept with each page. Each concept corresponds to a specific step in the buying process. The metrics can be computed based on the access or not of the different concepts. Spiliopoulou et al. [18] used a service-based concept hierarchy to model all components of the site, where the model helps to distinguish the different kinds of pages.

Besides the classic measures that compute the ratio of site visitors who buy something on the site, some others metrics have been proposed for measuring the success of retail sites. Berthon et al. [2] provide a list of metrics aimed at evaluating different aspects of the website's effectiveness:

- Ability to make surfers aware of its Web site (awareness efficiency);
- Ability to convert aware surfers into surfers who accesses the web site (locatability/ attractability efficiency);
- Ability to convert surfers who accesses the site into visitors (contact efficiency);
- Ability to convert visitors in consumers (conversion efficiency); and the
- Ability to convert consumers into loyal customers (retention efficiency).

Lee proposes micro-conversion rates [9] inspired by the online buying process. These statistics describe the websites effectiveness for each step of the buying process:

- look-to-click rate: number of product links followed / number of products impressions;
- click-to-basket rate: number of products placed in basket / number of products displayed;
- basket-to-buy rate: number of products purchased / number of basket placements;
- look-to-buy rate: number of products purchased / number of product Impressions.

3.1 Emerging Standards in Web Measurement

A sign of maturity of a field is the development and adoption of industry standards. The ABC international standards working party (IFABC, International Federation of Audit Bureaux[4]) has developed a set of rules and definitions that are the effective world-wide standard for Web audits[5]. Definitions and rules specific to the Internet industry in the UK and Ireland are controlled and developed by JICWEBS, the Joint Industry Committee for Web Standards. The three most important concept definitions from ABCe are:

1. Unique User, defined as "The total number of unique combinations of a valid identifier. Sites may use (i) IP+User-Agent, (ii) Cookie and/or (iii) Registration ID."

---

[4] http://www.ifabc.org/
[5] http://www.abce.org.uk

2. Session, defined as "a series of *page impressions* served in an unbroken sequence from within the site to the same *user*."

3. Page Impression, defined as "a file or a combination of files sent to a valid *user* as a result of that *user*'s request being received by the server."

From a web analytics perspective there is an additional side-effect of the adoption of the ABCe standard as it provides industry standard data cleaning guidelines. These industry standards specify heuristics for visit and visitor identification, spider and other automated access identification and rules for filtering out of invalid visitor traffic (automated accesses and web server error codes). While the metrics specified by ABCe are useful from a traffic audit perspective, web analytics aims to dig deeper into web data with regards to understanding the customer behaviour. However, as the data used in web analytics is the same as that used in generating a web traffic audit, standard data cleaning processes imply that the quality of the knowledge generated will have a standard interpretation.

3.2 Scenario Development and Measurement

In this section we propose a new approach to deploying web mining for web measurement. This approach is based around the use of customer interactional scenarios and the monitoring of customer behaviour against these expected scenarios.

For most businesses, the web is just another low-cost, medium for interacting with their customers. Customer interactions on traditional channels are always aimed at providing some service, which is achieved through a business process. The completion of the process results in value for the customer as well as the business. The web is no different in this respect and thus the key processes that the customer is expected to complete are the value generators for the business and have a direct impact on the return on investment in web infrastructure. The processes and the benefits of customers completing these processes are dependent on the business model and hence the development of the processes requires interaction with business and domain experts, who describe these processes using scenarios that typical customers would be expected to follow when using the web channel.

These processes can range from registration processes on a portal, product purchasing on a retail site, mortgage applications on a financial services site, a pedagogical session of an e-learning site, job applications on a recruitment site or even searching for a dealer or booking a test drive on an automobile manufacturer's site. These key processes for the business are where ROI is generated.

The aim of the analysis is to provide abandonment rates and to identify site usability bottlenecks causing abandonment of the process. The starting point for the analysis is the definition of the process in terms of the various stages that constitute it. The most common and well understood process is that of the purchasing process in the context of a retailer. Customers enter the site, browse products (including searching for products using local search facilities), put products in the shopping basket, enter the checkout area and finally, depending on the site design go through a couple of payment and delivery stages, prior to completing the checkout and the corresponding purchase process.

The domain expert then specifies subsections of the web site that are associated with the different stages of the process to be analysed. These different stages define a process that the visitors to the web site are expected to follow during a visit or indeed across a number of visits as they progress through the customer lifecycle of engage, transact, fulfil and service. The resulting metrics provide insights into how successfully the business has converted visitors to their site from one stage to the next, the number of clicks it has taken visitors to move through the various stages of the process and transitions from one stage to another are tracked to identify process bottlenecks.

In addition to the definition of the process, the domain expert can also provide more domain knowledge in the form of taxonomies defined on the content or product pages at each stage of the process. These taxonomies can then be used to drill into high level metrics as shown in Table 1-3, to discover actual navigational pathway at various levels of generalisation within the taxonomy using sequence discovery algorithms such Capri [3].

Depending on the complexity of the product and indeed the process, the process may be completed within a single visit or across multiple visits. Indeed even for simple products, most customer tend to compare prices across multiple retailers prior to making a purchase, resulting in a purchasing process spanning across multiple visits. The key to analysing processes that span across visits is deciding when to treat a particular visitor as having abandoned the process as opposed to still being a valid prospect. Understanding customer behaviour within each stage is key to defining the abandonment event. Four key metrics of behaviour are used to profile visitor behaviour[6] within each stage of the process. These are the frequency of visits, recency of visit, the time spent in the visit and the average time between visits. If the recency of a visit by a visitor falls outside the confidence interval defined on the average time between visits, we can assume the prospect to have abandoned the process.

Consider a process consisting of four stages. Table 1 shows the number of visitors in each stage of the process, calculated from data collected from an online retailer site. Note that these numbers do not signify a conversion rate of 2%. Not all visitors in stages 1, 2 and 3 have as yet abandoned the process. There are still valid prospects in the process. As time goes on, these prospects will either transition to later stages in the process or abandon the process as described below.

Table 2 shows the metric values characterising intra-stage visitor behaviour.

Table 1. Visitors in Stage

Stage	Number of Visitors
1	123087
2	32272
3	23154
4	3764

---

[6] Recency, frequency and monetary value-based profiling of customer behaviour is an established technique in database marketing. On the web, in non-retail contexts, the use of duration as opposed to monetary value is often used. Recency is defined as the time elapsed since the last visit by a visitor.

Table 2. Visitor Behaviour in Stage

Stage	Number of Visits	Number of Visitors	Average Recency	Average Time Between Visits	Average Time in Stage
1	1-2	113534	33.35	16.17	9.80
1	3-4	6302	34.60	21.34	37.24
1	5+	3251	28.52	40.49	44.76
2	1-2	30040	32.98	21.41	10.74
2	3-4	1814	22.62	21.34	37.24
2	5+	418	20.88	33.58	42.90
3	1-2	22086	30.94	21.50	11.18
3	3-4	920	26.61	25.07	39.54
3	5+	148	22.39	38.56	44.17
4	1-2	3764	-	-	10.77

We can see from the table that as the number of visits within a stage grows, so does that average time between the visits while the recency of visits is actually decreasing. Also, note that the amount of time spent in the stage increase quite dramatically when the number of visits increases to over two visits. Finally, the average recency of visitors in Stage 1 with less than five visits is much higher than the average time between visits, suggesting that a large proportion of these visitors have abandoned the process. A similar conclusion can be reached for visitors in Stages 2 and 3 who have only made one or two visits within the stage. Stage 4 denotes completion of the process.

Table 3. Visits to Stage

Stage	Visits to Stage	Number of Visitors	Average Time to Stage
1	1-2	123015	0.83
2	1-2	27675	1.54
2	3-4	2444	10.89
2	5+	2132	25.19
3	1-2	20219	1.55
3	3-4	1565	10.50
3	5+	1352	25.46
4	1-2	3305	2.41
4	3-4	215	10.57
4	5+	242	28.57

Finally, Table 3 shows metrics related to the behaviour of a visitor to get to a stage in the process. Once again we can use the confidence interval defined on average time to stage to get a measure of how likely it is that visitors that in Stage i are likely to transition to Stage i+1. As can be seen from Table 3, the average time to stage values are quite low compared to the average time in stage values in Table 2, suggesting that the majority of visitors that are still in Stages 1, 2 and 3, have probably abandoned the process.

4 Knowledge Generation for Personalisation

A number of research groups have taken a more technology oriented view of web usage mining than the definition in Section 2. Joshi et al. [6] outline three operations of interest for web mining:

- Clustering (finding grouping of users and pages, for example);
- Associations (for example, which pages tend to be requested together); and
- Sequential analysis (the order in which pages are accessed, for example)

Perkowitz and Etzioni [14] on the other hand view web mining as principally generating knowledge for automatic personalisation, defined as the provision of recommendations that are generated by applying data mining algorithms to combined data on behavioural information on users and the structure and content of a web space.

Given our broader perspective on web usage mining, we class these applications as being knowledge generation applications that can provide the models required for various business applications. For example, we now describe the deployment of web usage mining results within the context of personalisation and later present our platform for personalisation called Concerto.

From the perspective of knowledge generation for personalisation, the decision as to whether to use visit based or visitor-based analysis is based on whether or not the recommendation engine uses user history (profiles) as input to the recommendation generation algorithm. When planning for personalisation it is not uncommon to consider two main types of visitors to the site (see Figure 3). These are, first time visitors and return visitors. The key distinction between these types of visitors is the non-availability or availability of prior knowledge about the user. With on-line privacy concerns and ensuing legislation the need to opt-in to personalisation services means that even return visitors that have not opted-in could potentially have to be treated as anonymous, first-time visitors. Additionally, visitor identification in the absence of a requirement to log onto the site is based on heuristics and while the use of persistent cookies does alleviate the problem to a certain extent, it is still fraught with inaccuracies. These issues are increasing the focus on the use of visit based analytics for personalisation.

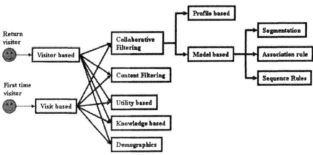

Fig. 3. Personalisation Approaches

A number of classifications of recommendation technologies have been provided in literature [4,16,17,20]. For the purposes of this discussion we use the classification provided by [4]. Figure 3 shows this classification. Of these different approaches to personalisation, collaborative-filtering is by far the most popular approach. Scalability issues related to traditional, profile-based collaborative filtering, has led to research into model-based collaborative filtering approaches. The pros and cons of using models as opposed to individual profile based approaches are akin to those of using greedy learning algorithms in machine learning as opposed to lazy learning algorithms.

Web usage mining can be used to generate the knowledge used in model-based collaborative filtering. Web usage mining techniques commonly used for this purpose include association rule discovery, sequence rule discovery [12] and segmentation [11]. The deployment of the knowledge generated through the use of web mining for personlisation is essentially a real-time scoring application of the knowledge.

4.1 Measuring Personalisation Effectiveness

An ideal method for evaluating the benefit of personalization is to compute business metrics such as those presented in Section 3 of this paper with and without the use of personalization and to compare the results obtained in these two situations. If personalization has been effective, the results should show that, with personalisation switched on, the goals of site owner are satisfied to a greater extent.

Peyton [15] correctly points out that a comparison based on different periods of time is not the best choice, because it introduces some external factors that can distort the validity of the inference made. For example, some periods are more favourable to buyers than others or people can be influenced by fashion, etc. A more robust comparison is achieved through the creation and use of a control group as commonly done in database marketing. Users of this group get no personalized content, while other users receive personalized content. A lift in the metrics can then be attributed solely to the effect of personalization. Of course, the selection of an unbiased sample for the control group is essential for the true value of the personalization to be measured. A similar approach is also appropriate when comparing two alternatives personalisation techniques/approaches.

Yang [21] uses knowledge about expected outcomes, in their approach to evaluating personalisation. The knowledge describes the activities of users when they are influenced by a good, a bad or an irrelevant personalisation system. The knowledge allows a decision to be made on the quality of the personalisation.

Kim [8] provides empirical results on personalisation, using behavioural data as well as structural data. They use decision tree techniques to identify customers with a high propensity to purchase recommendations, and measure the uptake of these recommendations to this sub-group. Their results show that finding customers who are likely to buy recommended products and then recommending the products to them produces high-quality recommendations.

The approaches described above evaluate the effectiveness of personalisation from the site owner perspective. Some others studies evaluate the effect of personalisation from the users perspective. The success of a site can be measured by evaluating if the visitor expectations are satisfied. This kind of study is based on the collection of the opinion of visitors about the site. For instance, Alpert et al. [1] and Karat et al. [7] propose some studies to understand the value of personalisation for users (or customers) and underline which personalization features they like better. Their studies involved the participation of a sample of users (of the ibm.com web site) that accept to be observed during their interaction with the web site prototype (based on scenarios or not), and to fill in questionnaires. The down side of these types of usability studies is the difficulties in selecting a representative group of users, and the expense of the exercise.

5   Concerto: A Foundation for Flexible Personalization

In this section we describe a platform for deploying the results of web mining knowledge, within the context of personalisation, developed in the authors laboratory. The aim of this section is to highlight architectural issues associated with the deployment of web mining results in a highly scalable environment.

Figure 3 shows the various approaches to generating recommendations. Each of these techniques has advantages and disadvantages and are more suited to certain types of context. For example, profile based recommendations can only work for visitors with a history in the form of ranked items and who are behaving in a manner predictable from their past behaviour, while utility based techniques require the user to set up a utility function etc.

Recognising the fact that no one approach to recommendation generation works well all the time, the authors have developed a foundation for using multiple recommendation engines in concert, called Concerto. The key to the development of such a foundation is the scalability of the system - as delivering personalised content at the cost of delaying delivery of content to the end user is not acceptable.

Figure 4 shows the key components of Concerto. The session manager is responsible for maintaining the state of current, active visits on the web site. The session manager extracts certain contextual attributes such as the date/time and touch point of the visit and passes the user click stream (list of page views accessed by the visitor, within the current visit) along with the contextual attributes to the recommendation manager. The recommendation manager is in charge of generating useful recommendations, which it achieves by making asynchronous calls to all the live recommendation advisors. Each advisor is a separate recommendation engine, possibly using different knowledge sources, recommendation paradigms and parameter settings to generate recommendations. Communication between the recommendation manager and the recommendation engines occurs through topics/queues and a timeout is used to ensure that no single recommendation advisor delays the delivery of recommendations to the user. The administrator of Concerto sets this timeout.

The Recommendation Manager collates recommendations from multiple recommendation advisors and ranks them based on the context assembled. It has a highly pluggable architecture, making it straightforward to add new recommendation advisor components that utilise different paradigms.

A number of recommendation advisor components have been developed based on sequential knowledge and segmentation knowledge. Additional components based on content filtering and profile based collaborative filtering are also being implemented.

As a side-product of deploying Concerto on a web site, web usage data can be collected as an alternative to parsing web logs. This data is uploaded into a visitor centric star schema for future analysis using a web usage mining tool. Within the context of personalisation, the data can be used to generate models for model–based collaborative filtering as well as to evaluate the effectiveness of personalisation itself through tracking of user responses to personalised content.

Personalisation architectures needs to be scalable with respect to the number of recommendation engines used as well as the number of concurrent users that can be serviced by the system. To meet this scalability challenge, Concerto has an application server based architecture, effectively decoupling the scalability of the software from the constraints of the server machine as seen in client-server applications. Application servers provide some of the basic plumbing required to build enterprise applications, including load balancing, caching, message-queuing and management, security and session management.

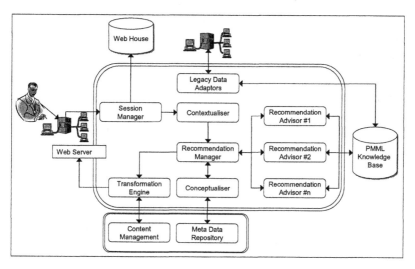

Fig. 4. The Concerto Personalization Platform

5.1 The Role of Standards in Concerto

As can be seen from Figure 4, providing a scalable personalisation experience to site visitors requires a complex infrastructure consisting of at least a Content Management System (CMS), a knowledge base, tools for generating the knowledge and recommendation engines for generating the list of content appropriate for a visitor to the site. The complexity of the technology involved and the various modes of deployment can result in an integration nightmare. In this section we highlight some of the standards that are appearing in industry that can contribute to a reduction in the required integration effort. Note that these standards are not specifically aimed at personalisation systems, however, they lend themselves to these systems and the authors have found there use within Concerto to provide substantial benefits. This section also aims to highlight the advantages of considering the use of standards within deployment architectures for web mining in general, using the personalisation context as a use case. Note that this section does not aim to provide an exhaustive list of standards for use in personalisation. It only covers those standards that have been or planned to be used within Concerto.

The Predictive Modelling Markup Language[7] (PMML) is an XML based standard developed by the Data Mining Group with the aim of aiding model exchange between different model producers and between model producers and consumers. Most data mining vendors have their own proprietary representations for knowledge discovered using their algorithms. PMML provides the first standard representation that is adhered to by all the major data mining vendors. Being XML based, models represented in PMML can be easily parsed, manipulated and used by automated tools. Using PMML as the knowledge representation for knowledge that can be used by Concerto, decouples the software used for model generation and that for deploying the knowledge in real-time for recommendation generation.

A related standard is the Java Data Mining API[8] that provides a standard API for data mining engines. JDM supports the building, testing and applying of models as well as the management of meta-data related to these activities. JDM aims to do for data mining what JDBC did for database systems, i.e. to decouple the code that uses data mining from the provider of the data mining service. While not directly related to personalisation, model-based recommendation engines can be viewed as real-time scoring engines and hence their application can be viewed as the real-time scoring of data. Conformance of these engines to the JDM API could add value thorough the effective decoupling of the personalisation infrastructure from the recommendation engine service provision. JDM API also supports the export of knowledge to PMML.

The use of a domain ontology within the web usage mining and personalisation context provides the promise of the discovery and application of deeper domain knowledge to recommendation generation and hence improved personalisation. The representation of such ontologies in an XML standard provides the basis for the exchange and deployment of this knowledge across sectors. Web Ontology Language (OWL)[9] is a standard currently being developed for this purpose.

The Simple Object Access Protocol[10] (SOAP) is an open standard for the interchange of structured data, and facilitates communication between heterogeneous systems. In Concerto, we provide a SOAP interface to the recommendation manager. The objective of this was to make Concerto easily deployable within existing web infrastructure. Organisations looking to deploy Concerto can do so through the SOAP

---

[7] http://www.dmg.org
[8] http://www.jcp.org/jsr/detail/73.jsp
[9] http://www.w3.org/2001/sw/WebOnt
[10] http://www.w3.org/tr/soap/

interface without any concerns of compatibility of their existing web site infrastructure.

Finally, standards such as J2EE[11], EJB, JNDI and JMS provide the basis for deploying personalisation components in a scalable and open manner. In the Concerto architecture, the use of queues and topics along with message driven bean technology, to communicate asynchronously makes it straightforward to add new recommendation engines, in a scalable fashion, to Concerto without affecting the rest of the Concerto architecture.

5.2   Concerto Deployment Architectures

Concerto provides two main approaches to deployment within a web infrastructure. These are the deployment as a service and the deployment as the content infrastructure. Concerto also provides a third option for deployment, as an Intermediary. This approach to deployment is a low cost mechanism for evaluating the effectiveness of the deployed web usage mining knowledge using a control group based approach, prior to actual deployment. The use of this approach for final deployment is possible but not recommended as the loose coupling with the customer web site while attractive from the speed of implementation perspective is not reliable and can lead to unreliable service with regard to the presentation of content. We now briefly present each of these approaches to deployment.

5.2.1   Concerto as a Service
Concerto provides a SOAP and Java interface to its Recommendation Manager. This enables Concerto to be deployed as a service to the corporate web site (Figure 5). In this deployment, the current web site continues to be the touch point to the visitor. When a visitor request is received by the content management system or server side script, the CMS or script initiates a call to Concerto using either SOAP or RMI/IIOP, depending on the technology on which the content infrastructure is based.

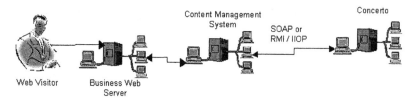

Fig. 5. Deploying Concerto as a Service

Concerto can be used as a service in two modes: Stateless and Stateful. The key difference between these modes is whether the responsibility for maintaining state within the customer interaction is on Concerto or on the web site using it as a service. The call to Concerto from the web site includes all the contextual attributes of the

---

[11] http://java.sun.com/j2ee/

visitor that are available and the current request (for stateful mode) or the complete current visit (for stateless mode).

From the perspective of scalability clearly the stateless mode is more scalable. However, Concerto cannot be used for data collection when it is deployed as a stateless service.

5.2.2 Concerto as Content Infrastructure

This deployment is shown in Figure 4 and represents the most highly integrated deployment of Concerto. The visitor request to the web site is received by the front controller servlet in Concerto and delivery of the content is also managed by Concerto. In this mode of deployment, Concerto interacts with the content management system through an adapter to access content objects while the templating is handled by Concerto itself. Depending on the requirement of the advisors Concerto may make two calls to the CMS, one for meta-data and the other for content that needs to be delivered to the visitor based on the explicit request and the recommended objects.

This deployment of Concerto is most closely coupled with the web site of the business and is most appropriate where the web site is currently being (re)developed so that the use of Concerto is built into the design of the web site.

5.2.3 Concerto as an Intermediary

In this mode of deployment (Figure 6), Concerto receives the request directly from the visitor through a proxy server and it in turn makes an HTTP request to the business's web site for content while at the same time requesting the Recommendation Manager to generate a recommendation pack. The content returned from the web site is manipulated using embedded tags within the content to integrate the recommended content into the page prior to delivery to the visitor.

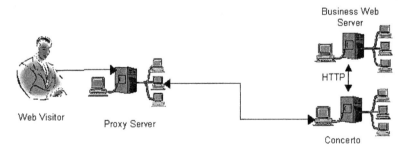

Fig. 6. Concerto Deployment as an Intermediary

Especially in cases where the current web site has been deployed in the form of a set of server side scripts rather than a content management system that orchestrates content in real-time, this mode of deploying is an attractive option as it requires minimal changes to the existing web site. However, the overhead of handling the recommendations and transforming them into content lies on Concerto which may involve the integration of meta-data about the content within the Concerto deployment.

Additionally, this deployment architecture is particularly useful for carrying out evaluation of the recommendation engines using control groups as outlined in Section 4.2 prior to deployment with a real-time environment. Here the control group continues to access the business web site as previously, getting no personalised content. The target group on the other hand is directed to the proxy server and hence receives personalised content. A comparison of metrics generated for the two groups provides empirical evidence of the expected ROI from the deployment of the recommendation engine.

Table 4 below provides a comparison of the pros and cons of the three alternative deployments of Concerto.

Table 4. Concerto Deployment Options

Deployment Architecture	Advantages	Disadvantages
Service	Existing web site retains control of customer interaction	Changes need to be made to templates to incorporate recommended content Changes need to be made to web site to incorporate call to Concerto When deployed as a stateless service Concerto cannot be used for improved data collection
Content Infrastructure	Increased data quality of collected click stream data	Existing web site loses control on interaction
Intermediary	Minimal Integration required with existing web site Quick turnaround for prototype	The proxy needs to be configured based on the idiosyncrasies of the current web site Existing web site loses control on interaction Concerto requires meta-data about the content infrastructure of the site to ensure the validity of recommended content on the orchestrated page

6 Concluding Comments and Future Challenges

In this paper we suggested that web usage mining has to date failed to have an impact on industry due to failings at the deployment stage of web usage mining projects and hence the delivery of a return on investment in the technology. We discussed the two key application areas for web usage mining technology with specific reference to the deployment of results within the analysis of business processes and the personalisation of web interactions.

The application of web usage mining to the generation of useful insights into customer behaviour and the relationship between these behaviours and the completion of key business processes that generate value for the business remains a challenge that needs to be addressed. If the use of this technology in web measurement is to have a real impact, we need to be able to use the technology in the context of key business processes and provide real solutions to business bottlenecks.

A number of challenges also remain to be addressed with regard to the deployment of web usage mining results for personalisation of web interactions. Current recommendation technologies assume that the users' context is always the same. That is, every visitor to a web site has behaviour that is predictable based on a single profile generated based on all previous visit behaviours. This of course is not the case. For example, the goal of the visit may be different based on the time of visit. A visit by the visitor during office hours may have very different characteristics to a visit during the evening or when shopping for a gift. There is a need to provide a flexible basis for recommendation generation using different paradigms and knowledge chosen based on the context of the user. This of course would require the context of the user to be specified prior to the visit beginning, a highly unlikely event.

A challenge for the web mining community is to see if they can infer the context of the visit from the visitors' behaviour. If this is possible, then the next challenge lies in the flexible deployment of knowledge discovered on context specific behaviour. The Concerto platform provides the basis for such deployment, with the multiple recommendation engines and the use of the recommendation manager to choose which recommendation engines to invoke for a particular visit or indeed part of a visit.

The use of multi-agent/hybrid recommendation engines will also be key for integration of knowledge discovered from the disparate data sources specified in Section 2.1. Current systems tend to work specifically with one of the data sources at a time. For example, most collaborative filtering systems assume the existence of product rankings and web usage mining based systems usually only work with visit click streams. Integration of this data can be achieved through the use of some heuristics. Alternatively, knowledge discovered from each of these sources can be integrated at the time of deployment, as is the case in Concerto. This of course raises its own challenges regarding the integration of recommendations generated by the individual recommendation engines.

Another challenge is the currency of knowledge deployed. How often must this knowledge be updated? The application of any changes to a web site is bound to affect user behaviour. The deployment of recommendation engines is no different in this respect and you would expect user behaviour to alter in response to the new behaviour of the web site. The key question is how these changes in behaviour can be monitored so as to identify the need for new knowledge to be discovered and deployed on the site.

All the above challenges point to another key gap in current research in web mining deployment - the systematic evaluation of the recommendation paradigms. Nakagawa *et al.* recently published initial results comparing the effectiveness of deploying association rule and sequence rule knowledge based recommendation engines based on certain site characteristics [13]. There is a need for more systematic evaluation based on the characteristics of visitors as well as a visit. This will help in the development of more knowledge based integration of multiple recommendation engines, ultimately leading to improved recommendation generation.

Another challenge is the incorporation of domain knowledge that may be available on the web content of the web site, such as domain ontologies. The importance of this challenge is increasing with the web content becoming more dynamic in nature and the dependence of recommendation technologies on deeper understanding of the content it is required to recommend. The use of such knowledge not only has the ability to increase the breadth of the recommendations generated but also the serendipity of recommendations generated.

No discussion on future challenges of data mining or web related technologies is complete without a discussion on issues regarding the scalability of the technology.

Scalability in this context includes the knowledge generation itself but more specifically, refers to the generation of recommendations in an environment where the number of concurrent users and related behavioural knowledge is ever increasing. As more context aware recommendation platforms are developed, the complexity of the recommendation generation process is bound to increase. It is however essential that the time taken to generate the recommendations and deliver the personalised content to the visitor is not adversely affected as a visitor is not going to find slow content delivery acceptable. The use of an application server based architecture as in the case of Concerto is the type of thought that must go into the development of general deployment engines for web usage mining knowledge, whether deployed on the web or in other customer touch points such as call centres.

Integration of deployment infrastructure into an organisations existing infrastructure is the key to successful deployment. The development of standards to support this integration is also encouraging and the use of these standards and indeed the enhancement and proposing of new useful standards that aid integration remains another challenge.

Acknowledgements. The work for this paper was partially supported by the European Commission's Marie Curie Grant No. HPMT-2000-00049 'PERSONET'. The authors would also like to acknowledge the contribution of Ken McClure and Miguel Alvarez to the implementation of Concerto.

References

1. Alpert S., Karat J., Karat C.-M., Brodie C., and Vergo J., "User attitudes regarding a user-adaptive e-commerce Web Site", In User Modeling and User-Adapted Interaction 13: 373-396, 2003.
2. Berthon P., Pitt L. and Watson Richard. The world wide web as advertising medium: toward an understanding of conversion efficiency, In the Journal of Advertising Research, vol. 36, issue 1, pp. 43-54.
3. Büchner, A.G., Baumgarten, M., Anand, S. S., Mulvenna, M. D., and Hughes, J. G. Navigation Pattern Discovery from Internet Data, B. Masand, M. Spiliopoulou (eds.) Advances in Web Usage Analysis and User Profiling, Lecturer Notes in Computer Science, Springer-Verlag, 2000.
4. Burke, R. Hybrid Recommender Systems: Survey and Experiments, To appear in User Modeling and User-Adapted Interaction.
5. Cooley, R., Tan, P-N., Srivastava, J. Discovery of Interesting Usage Patter s from Web Data, Web Usage Analysis and User Profiling, In Lecture Notes in Artificial Intelligence, Brij Masand, Myra Spiliopoulou (Eds.), pp. 163-182, 2000.
6. Joshi, A., Joshi, K., Krishnapuram, R., On mining Web Access Logs, in Proceedings of the ACM-SIGMOD Workshop on Research Issues in Data Mining and Knowledge Discovery, 2000, pp. 63-69
7. Karat C.-M., Brodie C., Karat J., Vergo J., and Alpert S., "Personalizing the user experience on ibm.com", in IBM Systems Journal, vol. 42, no. 4, 2003.
8. Kim, J.K., Cho, Y. H., Kim, W. J., Kim, J. R. and Suh, J. H., A Personalized Recommendation Procedure for Internet Shopping Support, Electronic Commerce Research and Applications, Vol. 1, No. 3-4, pp301-313, 2002

9. Lee J., Podlaseck M., Schonberg E., Hoch R., and Gomory S. Analysis and Visualization of Metrics for Online Merchandising, In Lecture Notes in Computer Science, Springer-Verlag Heidelberg, ISSN: 0302-9743, Volume 1836 / 2000, January 2000.
10. Mobasher, B., R. Cooley and J. Srivastava Data Preparation for Mining World Wide Web Browsing Patterns, in the Journal of Knowledge and Information Systems, Vol. 1, No. 1, 1999.
11. Mobasher, B., Dai, H., Luo, T., Sung, Y., Nakagawa, M. and Wiltshire, J. Discovery of Aggregate Usage Profiles for Web Personalization, in Proceedings of the Web Mining for E-Commerce Workshop (WebKDD'2000), held in conjunction with the ACM-SIGKDD Conference on Knowledge Discovery in Databases (KDD'2000), August 2000, Boston.
12. Mobasher, B., Dai, H., Luo, T., Nakagawa, M. Using Sequential and Non-Sequential Patterns for Predictive Web Usage Mining Tasks. In Proceedings of the IEEE International Conference on Data Mining (ICDM'2002), Maebashi City, Japan, December, 2002
13. Nakagawa, M. and Mobasher, B. Impact of Site Characteristics on Recommendation Models Based On Association Rules and Sequential Patterns, In Proceedings of the IJCAI'03 Workshop on Intelligent Techniques for Web Personalization, Acapulco, Mexico, August 2003
14. Perkowitz M., Etzioni O., "Towards adaptive Web sites: Conceptual framework and case study". Artificial Intelligence 2000; 118: 245-275
15. Peyton L. Measuring and Managing the Effectiveness of Personalization, In Proceedings of the 5th International conference on Electronic commerce, 2003, Pittsburgh, Pennsylvania.
16. Resnick, P. and Varian, H. R.: 1997, 'Recommender Systems'. Communications of the ACM, 40 (3), 56-58.
17. Schafer, J. B., Konstan, J. and Riedl, J.: 1999, 'Recommender Systems in E-Commerce'. In: EC '99: Proceedings of the First ACM Conference on Electronic Commerce, Denver, CO, pp. 158-166.
18. Spiliopoulou M. and Pohle C. Data Mining for Measuring and Improving the Success of Web Sites, Data Mining and Knowledge Discovery, 5:85-114, 2001.
19. Teltzrow M. and Berendt B. Web-Usage-Based Success Metrics for Multi-Channel Businesses. In Proceedings of the Fifth WEBKDD workshop: Webmining as a Premise to Effective and Intelligent Web Applications (WEBKDD'2003), Washington, DC, USA, August 27, 2003.
20. Terveen, L. and Hill, W: 2001, 'Human-Computer Collaboration in Recommender Systems'. In: J. Carroll (ed.): Human Computer Interaction in the New Millennium. New York: Addison-Wesley.
21. Yang, Y. and Padmanabhan, B. On Evaluating Online Personalization, In proceedings of the Workshop on Information Technology and Systems (WITS 2001), pages 35-41, December 2001.

Mining the Web to Add Semantics to Retail Data Mining

Rayid Ghani

Accenture Technology Labs
161 N Clark St, Chicago, IL 60601
Rayid.Ghani@accenture.com

Abstract. While research on the Semantic Web has mostly focused on basic technologies that are needed to make the Semantic Web a reality, there has not been a lot of work aimed at showing the effectiveness and impact of the Semantic Web on business problems. This paper presents a case study where Web and Text mining techniques were used to add semantics to data that is stored in transactional databases of retailers. In many domains, semantic information is implicitly available and can be extracted automatically to improve data mining systems. This is a case study of a system that is trained to extract semantic features for apparel products and populate a knowledge base with these products and features. We show that semantic features of these items can be successfully extracted by applying text learning techniques to the descriptions obtained from websites of retailers. We also describe several applications of such a knowledge base of product semantics that we have built including recommender systems and competitive intelligence tools and provide evidence that our approach can successfully build a knowledge base with accurate facts which can then be used to create profiles of individual customers, groups of customers, or entire retail stores.

1 Introduction

Most of the research on the Semantic Web has focused on the basic technologies that are required to make the Semantic Web a reality. Techniques for Ontology Generation, Ontology Mediation, Ontology Population, and Reasoning from the Semantic Web have all been the major areas of focus. While this research has been promising, there has not been a lot of work aimed at showing the effectiveness and impact of the Semantic Web on business problems. This paper focuses on the applications of these techniques and argues that the presence of semantic knowledge can not only result in improved business applications, but also enable new kinds of applications. We present a case study that uses Web and Text Mining techniques to add semantics to pre-existing databases. The augmentation of semantics to existing product databases that retailers current have results in exists for a retailer would enable new kinds of applications that data mining algorithms would be ideally suited for.

Current Data Mining techniques usually do not automatically take into account the semantic features inherent in the data being "mined". In most data

B. Berendt et al. (Eds.): EWMF 2003, LNAI 3209, pp. 43–56, 2004.

mining applications, a large amount of transactional data is analyzed without a systematic method for "understanding" the items in the transactions or what they say about the customers who purchased those items. The majority of algorithms used to analyze transaction records from retail stores treat the items in a market basket as objects and represent them as categorical values with no associated semantics. For example, in an apparel retail store transaction, a basket may contain a shirt, a tie and a jacket. When data mining algorithms such as association rules, decision trees, neural networks etc. are applied to this basket, they completely ignore what these items "mean" and the semantics associated with them. Instead, these items could just be replaced by distinct symbols, such as A, B and C or with apple, orange and banana for that matter, and the algorithms would produce the same results. The semantics of particular domains are injected into the data mining process in one of the following two stages: In the initial stage where the features to be used are constructed e.g. for decision trees or neural networks, feature engineering becomes an essential process that uses the domain knowledge of experts and provides it to the algorithm . The second instance where semantics are utilized is in interpreting the results. Once association rules or decision trees are generated and A and B are found to be correlated, the semantics are then used by humans to interpret them. Both of these methods of injecting semantics have been proved to be effective but at the same time are very costly and require a lot of human effort.

In many domains, semantic information is implicitly available and can be automatically extracted. In this paper, we describe a system that extracts semantic features for apparel products and populates a knowledge base with these products and features. We use apparel products and show that semantic features of these items can be successfully extracted by applying text learning techniques to the product names and descriptions obtained from websites of retailers. We also describe several applications of such a knowledge base of product semantics including recommender systems and competitive intelligence and provide evidence that our approach can successfully build a knowledge base with accurate facts which can then be used to create profiles of individual customers, groups of customers, or entire retail stores.

The work presented in this paper was motivated by discussions with CRM experts and retailers who currently analyze large amounts of transactional data but are unable to systematically understand the semantics of an item. For example, a clothing retailer would know that a particular customer bought a shirt and would also know the SKU, date, time, price, size, and color of a particular shirt that was purchased. While there is some value to this data, there is a lot of information not being captured that would facilitate understanding the tastes of the customer and enable a variety of applications. For example, is the shirt flashy or conservative? How trendy is it ? Is it casual or formal? These "softer" attributes that characterize products and the people who buy them tend not to be available for analysis in a systematic way.

In this paper, we describe our work on a system capable of inferring these kinds of attributes to enhance product databases. The system learns these attributes by applying text learning techniques to the product descriptions found on retailer web sites. This knowledge can be used to create profiles of individuals that can be used for recommendation systems that improve on traditional collaborative filtering approaches and can also be used to profile a retailer's positioning of their overall product assortment, how it changes over time, and how it compares to their competitors. Although the work described here is limited to the apparel domain and a particular set of features, we believe that this approach is relevant to a wider class of data mining problems and that extracting semantic clues and using them in data mining systems can add a potentially valuable dimension which existing data mining algorithms are not explicitly designed to handle.

2   Related Work

There has been some work in using textual sources to create knowledge bases consisting of objects and features associated with these objects. Craven et al.[3], as part of the WebKB group at Carnegie Mellon University built a system for crawling the Web (specifically, websites of CS departments in universities) and extract names of entities (students, faculty, courses, research projects, departments) and relations (course X is taught by faculty Y, faculty X is the advisor of student Y, etc.) by exploiting the content of the documents, as well as the link structure of the web. This system was used to populate a knowledge base in an effort to organize the Web into a more structured data source but the constructed knowledge base was not used to make any inferences. Recently, Ghani et al. [6] extended the WebKB framework by creating a knowledge base consisting of companies and associated features such as address, phone numbers, employee names, competitor names etc. extracted from semi-structured and free-text sources on the Web. They applied association rules, decision trees, relational learning algorithms to this knowledge base to infer facts about companies. Nahm & Mooney [11] also report some experiments with a hybrid system of rule-based and instance-based learning methods to discover soft-matching rules from textual databases automatically constructed via information extraction.

3   Overview of Our Approach

At a high level, our system deals with text associated with products to infer a predefined set of semantic features for each product. These features can generally be extracted from any information related to the product but in this paper, we only use the descriptions associated with each item. The features extracted are then used to populate a knowledge base, which we call the product semantics knowledge base. The process is described below.

1. Collect information about products
2. Define the set of features to be extracted
3. Label the data with values of the features

4. Train a classifier/extractor to use the labeled training data to now extract features from unseen data
5. Extract Semantic Features from new products by using the trained classifier/extractor
6. Populate a knowledge base with the products and corresponding features

4 Data Collection

We constructed a web crawler to visit web sites of several large apparel retail stores and extract names, urls, descriptions, prices and categories of all products available. This was done very cheaply by exploiting regularities in the html structure of the websites and manually writing wrappers[1]. We realize that this restricts the collection of data from websites where we can construct wrappers and although automatically extracting names and descriptions of products from arbitrary websites would be an interesting application area for information extraction or segmentation algorithms[14], we decided to take the manual approach. The extracted items and features were placed in a database and a random subset was chosen to be labeled.

5 Defining the Set of Features to Extract

After discussions with domain experts, we defined a set of features that would be useful to extract for each product. We believe that the choice of features should be made with particular applications in mind and that extensive domain knowledge should be used. We currently infer values for 8 kinds of attributes for each item but are in the process of identifying more features that are potentially interesting. The features we use are Age Group, Functionality, Price point, Formality, Degree of Conservativeness, Degree of Sportiness, Degree of Trendiness, and Degree of Brand Appeal. More details including the possible values for each feature are given in Table 1.

The last four features (conservative, sportiness, trendiness, and brand appeal) have five possible values 1 to 5 where 1 corresponds to low and 5 is the highest (e.g. for trendiness, 1 would be not trendy at all and 5 would be extremely trendy).

6 Labeling Training Data

The data (product name, descriptions, categories, price) collected by crawling websites of apparel retailers was placed into a database and a small subset (600 products) was given to a group of fashion-aware people to label with respect to each of the features described in the previous section. They were presented with the description of the predefined set of features and the possible values that each feature could take (listed in Table 1).

---

[1] In our case, the wrappers were simple regular expressions that took the html content of web pages into account and extracted specific pieces of information

Table 1. Details of features extracted from each product description

Feature Name	Possible Values	Description
Age Group	Juniors, Teens, GenX, Mature, All Ages	For what ages is this item most appropriate?
Functionality	Loungewear, Sportswear, Eveningwear, Business Casual, Business Formal	How will the item be used?
Pricepoint	Discount, Average, Luxury	Compared to other items of this kind is this item cheap or expensive?
Formality	Informal , Somewhat Formal, Very Formal	How formal is this item?
Conservative	1(gray suits) to 5 (Loud, flashy clothes)	Does this suggest the person is conservative or flashy?
Sportiness	1 to 5	
Trendiness	1 (Timeless Classic) to 5 (Current favorite)	Is this item popular now but likely to go out of style? or is it more timeless?
Brand Appeal	1(Brand makes the product unappealing) to 5 (high brand appeal)	Is the brand known and makes it appealing?

7 Verifying Training Data

Since the data was divided into disjoint subsets and each subset was labeled by a different person, we wanted to make sure that the labeling done by each expert was consistent with the other experts and there were no glaring errors. One way to do that would be to now swap the subsets for each person and ask the other labelers to repeat the process on the other set. Obviously, this can get very expensive and we wanted to find a cheaper way to get a general idea of the consistency of the labeling process. For this purpose, we decided to generate association rules on the labeled data. We pooled all the data together and generated association rules between features of items using the apriori algorithm[1]. The particular implementation that we used was [2]. By treating each product as a transaction (basket) and the features as items in the basket, this scenario becomes analogous to the traditional market-basket analysis. For example, a product with some unique ID, say Polo V-Neck Shirt, which was labeled as Age Group: Teens, Functionality: Loungewear, Pricepoint: Average, Formality: Informal, Conservative: 3, Sportiness: 4, Trendiness:4, Brand Appeal: 4 becomes a basket with each feature value as an item. By using Apriori algorithm, we can derive a set of rules which relate multiple features over all products that were labeled. We ran apriori with both single and two-feature antecedents and consequents. Table 2 shows some sample rules that were generated.

By analyzing the association rules, we found a few inconsistencies in the labeling process where the labelers misunderstood the features. As we can see from Table 2, the association rules match our general intuition e.g. Apparel items labeled as informal were also labeled as sportswear and loungewear. Items with average prices did not have high brand appeal - this was probably because items

Table 2. Sample Association Rules

Rule	Support	Confidence
Informal <- Sportswear	24.5%	93.6%
Informal <- Loungewear	16.1%	82.3%
Informal <- Juniors	12.1%	89.4%
PricePoint=Ave <- BrandAppeal=2	8.8%	79.0%
BrandAppeal=5 <- Trendy=5	16.3%	91.2%
Sportswear <- Sporty=4	9.0%	85.7%
AgeGroup=Mature <- Trendy=1	9.4%	78.8%

with high brand appeal are usually more expensive. An interesting rule that was discovered was that items that were labeled as belonging to Mature Age group were also labeled as being not trendy at all.

Using association rules over the entire labeled data proved to be very useful in verifying the consistency of the labeling process done by several different labelers and we believe would be a useful tool for data verification in general where the labeling is performed by multiple people.

8   Training from the Labeled Data

We treat the learning problem as a traditional text classification problem and create one text classifier for each "semantic feature". For example, in the case of the Age Group feature, we classify the product into one of five classes (Juniors, Teens, GenX, Mature, All Ages). The initial algorithm used to perform this classification was Naive Bayes and a description is given below.

8.1   Naive Bayes

Naive Bayes is a simple but effective text classification algorithm[10,9]. Naive Bayes defines an underlying generative model where, first a class is selected according to class prior probabilities. Then, the generator creates each word in a document by drawing from a multinomial distribution over words specific to the class. Thus, this model assumes each word in a document is generated independently of the others given the class. Naive Bayes forms maximum a posteriori estimates for the class-conditional probabilities for each word in the vocabulary V from labeled training data D. This is done by counting the frequency that word w_t occurs in all word occurrences for documents d_i in class c_j, supplemented with Laplace smoothing to avoid probabilities of zero:

$$\Pr(w_t|c_j) = \frac{1 + \sum_{i=1}^{|\mathcal{D}|} N(w_t, d_i)\Pr(c_j|d_i)}{|V| + \sum_{s=1}^{|V|}\sum_{i=1}^{|\mathcal{D}|} N(w_s, d_i)\Pr(c_j|d_i)}, \tag{1}$$

where $N(w_t, d_i)$ is the count of the number of times word w_t occurs in document d_i, and where $\Pr(c_j|d_i) \in \{0, 1\}$ as given by the class label.

At classification time we use these estimated parameters by applying Bayes' rule to calculate the probability of each class.

$$\Pr(c_j|d_i) \propto \Pr(c_j)\Pr(d_i|c_j)$$
$$= \Pr(c_j) \prod_{k=1}^{|d_i|} \Pr(w_{d_{i,k}}|c_j). \tag{2}$$

8.2 Incorporating Unlabeled Data Using EM

In our initial data collection phase, we collected names and descriptions of thousands of women's apparel items from websites. Since the labeling process was expensive, we only labeled about 600 of those, leaving the rest as unlabeled. Recently, there has been much recent interest in supervised learning algorithms that combine information from labeled and unlabeled data. Such approaches include using Expectation-Maximization to estimate maximum a posteriori parameters of a generative model [12], using a generative model built from unlabeled data to perform discriminative classification [7], and using transductive inference for support vector machines to optimize performance on a specific test set [8]. These results have shown that using unlabeled data can significantly decrease classification error, especially when labeled training data are sparse.

For the case of textual data in general, and product descriptions in particular, obtaining the data is very cheap. A simple crawler can be build and large amounts of unlabeled data can be collected for very little cost. Since we had a large number of product descriptions that were collected but unlabeled, we decided to use the Expectation-Maximization algorithm to combine labeled and unlabeled data for our task.

Expectation-Maximization. If we extend the supervised learning setting to include unlabeled data, the naive Bayes equations presented above are no longer adequate to find maximum a posteriori parameter estimates. The Expectation-Maximization (EM) technique can be used to find locally maximum parameter estimates.

EM is an iterative statistical technique for maximum likelihood estimation in problems with incomplete data [4]. Given a model of data generation, and data with some missing values, EM will locally maximize the likelihood of the parameters and give estimates for the missing values. The naive Bayes generative model allows for the application of EM for parameter estimation. In our scenario, the class labels of the unlabeled data are treated as the missing values.

EM is an iterative two-step process. Initial parameter estimates are set using standard naive Bayes from just the labeled documents. Then we iterate the E- and M-steps. The E-step calculates probabilistically-weighted class labels, $\Pr(c_j|d_i)$, for every unlabeled document using Equation 2. The M-step estimates new classifier parameters using all the documents, by Equation 1, where $\Pr(c_j|d_i)$

is now continuous, as given by the E-step. We iterate the E- and M-steps until the classifier converges.

9   Experimental Results

In order to evaluate the effectiveness of the algorithms described above for building an accurate knowledge base, we calculated classification accuracies using the labeled product descriptions and 5 fold cross-validation. The evaluation was performed for each attribute and the table below reports the accuracies. The first row in the table (baseline) gives the accuracies if the most frequent attribute value was predicted as the correct class. The experiments with Expectation-Maximization were run with the same amount of labeled data as Naive Bayes but with an additional 3500 unlabeled product descriptions.

Table 3. Classification accuracies for each attribute using 5 fold cross-validation. Naive Bayes uses only labeled data and EM uses both labeled and unlabeled data.

Algorithm	Age Group	Functionality	Formality	Conservative	Sportiness	Trendiness	Brand Appeal
Baseline	29%	24%	68%	39%	49%	29%	36%
Naive Bayes	66%	57%	76%	80%	70%	69%	82%
EM	78%	70%	82%	84%	78%	80%	91%

Looking at Table 3, we can see that Naive Bayes outperforms our baseline for all the attributes. Using unlabeled data and combining it from the initially labeled product descriptions with EM helps improve the accuracy even further. To get a qualitative and intuitive feel for the performance of these algorithms and for the effectiveness of our approach, Table 4 gives a list of words which had high weights for some of the features that we used the naive bayes classifier to extract. There words were selected by scoring all the words according to their log-odds-ratio scores and picking the top 10 words. Looking at the words gives us a qualitative and intuitive idea of what type of words are indicative of each attribute and verifies our initial hypothesis that the marketing language associated with product does correspond to these softer attributes that we are trying to infer.

9.1   Results on a New Test Set

The results reported earlier in Table 3 are extremely encouraging but are indicative of the performance of the algorithms on a test set that follows a similar distribution as the training set. Since we first extracted and labeled product descriptions from a retail website and then used subsets of that data for training and testing (using 5 fold cross-validation), the results may not hold for test data that is drawn from a different distribution or a different retailer.

Table 4. For each class, the table shows the ten words that are most highly weighted by one of our learned models. The weights shown represent the weighted log-odds ratio of the words given the class.

Conservative=5(high)	Conservative=1(low)	Formality=Informal	Somewhat Formal
lauren	rose	jean	jacket
ralph	special	tommy	fully
breasted	leopard	jeans	button
seasonless	chemise	denim	skirt
trouser	straps	sweater	lines
jones	flirty	pocket	york
sport	spray	neck	seam
classic	silk	tee	crepe
blazer	platform	hilfiger	leather

agegroup=juniors	Functionality=Loungewear	Functionality=Partywear	Sportiness=5(high)
jrs	chemise	rock	sneaker
dkny	silk	dress	camp
jeans	kimono	sateen	base
tee	calvin	length:	rubber
collegiate	klein	skirt	sole
logo	august	shirtdress	white
tommy	lounge	open	miraclesuit
polo	hilfiger	platform	athletic
short	robe	plaid	nylon
sneaker	gown	flower	mesh

Brand Appeal=5(high)	Trendiness=1(low)
lauren	lauren
ralph	seasonless
dkny	breasted
kenneth	trouser
cole	pocket
imported	carefree
	ralph
	blazer
	button

The results we report in Table 5 are obtained by training the algorithm on the same labeled data set as before but testing it on a small (125 items) new labeled data set collected from a variety of retailers. As we can observe, the results are consistently better than baseline and in some cases, even better than in Table 3. This results enables us to hypothesize that our system can be applied to a wide variety of data and can adapt to different distributions of test sets using the unlabeled data.

Table 5. Classification accuracies when trained on the same labeled data as before but tested on a new set of test data that is collected from a new set of retailers

Algorithm	Age Group	Functionality	Formality	Conservative	Sportiness	Trendiness	Brand Appeal
Naive Bayes	83%	45%	61%	70%	81%	80%	87%

10 Applications

The knowledge base (KB) constructed by labeling unseen products has several applications. In this section, we describe some concrete applications that we have developed. The KB can be used to create profiles of individuals that can be used for recommender systems that improve on traditional collaborative filtering approaches and can also be used to profile a retailer's positioning of their overall product assortment, how it changes over time, and how it compares to their competitors.

10.1 Recommender Systems

Being able to analyze the text associated with products and map it to the set of predefined semantic features in real-time gives us the ability to create instant profiles of customers shopping in an online store. As the shopper browses products in a store, the system running in the background can extract the name and description of the items and using the trained classifiers, can infer semantic features of that product. This process can be used create instant profiles based on viewed items without knowing the identity of the shopper or the need to retrieve previous transaction data. This can be used to suggest subsequent products to new and infrequent customers for whom past transactional data may not be available. Of course, if historical data is available, our system can use that to build a better profile and recommend potentially more targeted products. We believe that this ability to engage and target new customers tackles one of the challenges currently faced by commercial recommender systems [13] and can help retain new customers.

We have built a prototype of a recommender system for women's apparel items by using our knowledge base of product semantics. More details about the recommender system can be found in [5].The knowledge base is populated with thousands of items and their associated semantic attributes inferred by the learning algorithm described in earlier sections. Our system monitors the browsing behavior of user browsing a retailer's website and in real-time, extracts names and descriptions of products that they browse. The description text is then passed through our learned models and the semantic attributes of the products are inferred. For each product browsed, our system calculates $P(A_{i,j}|Product)\forall i,j$, where $A_{i,j}$ is the jth value of the ith attribute. The attributes are the semantic features described in Table 1 and the possible values for each attribute are also listed in the table. The user profile is constructed by combining these probabilities for each product browsed: User Profile =

$$\Pr(U_{i,j}|PastNItems) = \frac{1}{N}\sum_{k=1}^{N}\Pr(A_{i,j}|Item_k) \tag{3}$$

The user profile is stored in terms of probabilities for each attribute value which allows us flexibility to include mixture models in future work in addition to being more robust to changes over time.

As the user browses products, the system compares the evolving profile against the products in the knowledge base, which has products classified into the same taxonomy of semantic features, and recommends the closest matching ones. Currently, we give equal weight to all products browsed when constructing the profile. In future work, we plan to experiment with different weighting schemes such as weighting recent items more than older ones.

There are two prevalent approaches to building recommender systems : Collaborative Filtering and Content-based. Collaborative Filtering systems work by collecting user feedback in the form of ratings for items in a given domain and exploit similarities and differences among profiles of several users to recommend an item. It recommends other items bought by people who also bought the current item of interest and completely ignores "what" the current item of interest was. Collaborative Filtering approaches suffer from two main problems: the "sparsity" problem that most customers do not browse or buy most products in a store and the "New Item" problem that a new product cannot be recommended to any customer until it has been browsed by a large enough number of customers. On the other hand, content-based methods provide recommendations by comparing representations of content contained in an item to representations of content that interests the user. A main criticism of content-based recommendation systems is that the recommendations provided are not very diverse. Since the system is powered solely by the user's preferences and the descriptions of the items browsed, it tends to recommend items "too" similar to the previous items of interest.

This type of recommender system improves on collaborative filtering as it would work for new products which users haven't browsed yet and can also present the user with explanations as to why they were recommended certain products (in terms of the semantic attributes). We believe that our system also performs better than standard content-based systems. Although content-based systems also use the words in the descriptions of the items, they traditionally use those words to learn one scoring function. For example, a classical content-based recommendation engine takes the text from the descriptions of all the items that user has browsed or bought and learns a model (usually a binary target function: "recommend" or "not recommend"). In contrast, our system changes the feature space from words (thousands of features) to the eight semantic attributes. This still enables us to recommend a wide variety of products unlike most content-based systems. Another potential advantage of our system is its ability to suggests products across categories (i.e. apparel styles may be predictive of furniture, for example) which content-based systems are not able to do.

Since our goal was not to build the best recommendation system but rather to demonstrate the potential of a knowledge base of product semantics, we did not explore many approaches to building a user's profile. In future work, we plan to tackle the cases where a user's profile consists of a number of separate profiles. For example, if a user is looking for something for herself and also for her son, our system should be able to recognize that the items that the user is buying or browsing are inherently different. This could be done through mixture models where we construct a profile using a mixture of different profiles. Another potential solution is to monitor the users profile as they browse more and more products. Since each product can be though of as a point in an n-dimensional Euclidean space (where n is the number of features, in our case, 8), we can calculate the distance of a new product from the current profile of the user. If a new product is "very" different from the current profile of the user (using thresholds based on cross-validation), it can be placed in a separate profile or treated as an outlier. We also plan to conduct user studies to validate the effectiveness of such a recommendation system based on these intermediate-level semantic features.

10.2   Store Profiling

Product recommendations are just one application that we have built so far. We also have a prototype that profiles retailers to build competitive intelligence applications. For example, by closely tracking the product offerings we can notice changes in the positioning of a retailer. We can track changes in the industry as a whole or specific competitors and compare it to the performance of retailers. By profiling their aggregate offerings, our system can enable retailers to notice changes in the positioning of product lines by competitor retailers and manufacturers. This ability to profile retailers enables strategic applications such as competitive comparisons, monitoring brand positioning, tracking trends over time, etc.

10.3   Demand Forecasting

An important problem every retailer faces is demand forecasting. Using historical sales data, retailers can forecast the sales for each product for some period in the future. While this process is relatively simple for products that don't change over time or where the product cycles are long, it becomes difficult in the case of fast-changing inventory. For example, forecasting the sales of Heinz ketchup can be done by analyzing the sales of the same product in the past. In contrast, a skirt that was sold last season doesn't sell anymore and the sales data for that skirt is not comparable with the new product lines for the coming season. Having the semantic attributes of products lets retailers compare products and create simlarities between them so that the historical sales data can be leveraged to make predictions about the future.

11   Conclusions and Future Work

We described our work on a system capable of inferring semantic attributes of products enabling us to enhance product databases for retailers. The system learns these attributes by applying supervised and semi-supervised learning techniques to the product descriptions found on retailer web sites. One of the main assumptions we make is the descriptions associated with the products accurately convey the semantic attributes. We believe that this assumption is justified because in most cases these descriptions are written by marketers to position the product in the consumer's mind in a manner that implicitly suggests these softer attributes. The system can be bootstrapped from a small number of labeled training examples utilizes the large number of cheaply obtainable unlabeled examples (product descriptions) available from retail websites.

In the prototype we have built at Accenture Technology Labs, we currently have several applications for this type of a knowledge base. We use it to create profiles of individuals that can be used for recommendation systems that improve on traditional collaborative filtering approaches. The ability to infer the semantics of products can also be used to profile a retailer's positioning of their overall product assortment, how it changes over time, and how it compares to their competitors. Although the work described here is limited to the apparel domain and a particular set of features, we believe that this approach is relevant to a wider class of data mining problems. We believe that by going beyond the immediately available data, such as the fact that a customer is looking at or bought a product, and paying attention to what these products mean, we can increase the effectiveness of data mining applications.

References

1. R. Agrawal, H. Mannila, R. Srikant, H. Toivonen, and A. I. Verkamo. Fast discovery of association rules. In U. Fayyad, G. Piatetsky-Shapiro, P. Smyth, and R. Uthurusamy, editors, *Advances in Knowledge Discovery and Data Mining, AAAI Press/The MIT Press*, pages 307–328, 1996.
2. C. Borgelt. apriori. http://fuzzy.cs.Uni-Magdeburg.de/~borgelt/.
3. M. Craven, D. DiPasquo, D. Freitag, A. McCallum, T. Mitchell, K. Nigam, and S. Slattery. Learning to construct knowledge bases from the world wide web. *Artificial Intelligence*, 118(1-2):69–114, 2000.
4. A. P. Dempster, N. M. Laird, and D. B. Rubin. Maximum likelihood from incomplete data via the EM algorithm. *Journal of the Royal Statistical Society, Series B*, 39(1):1–38, 1977.
5. R. Ghani and A. E. Fano. Building recommender systems using a knowledge base of product semantics. In *Proceedings of the Workshop on Recommendation and Personalization in ECommerce at the 2nd International Conference on Adaptive Hypermedia and Adaptive Web based Systems*, 2002.
6. R. Ghani, R. Jones, D. Mladenic, K. Nigam, and S. Slattery. Data mining on symbolic knowledge extracted from the web. In *Workshop on Text Mining at the Sixth ACM SIGKDD International Conference on Knowledge Discovery and Data Mining*, 2000.

7. T. Jaakkola and D. Haussler. Exploiting generative models in discriminative classifiers. In *Advances in NIPS 11*, 1999.
8. T. Joachims. Transductive inference for text classification using support vector machines. In *Machine Learning: Proceedings of the Sixteenth International Conference*, 1999.
9. D. D. Lewis. Naive (Bayes) at forty: The independence assumption in information retrieval. In *Machine Learning: ECML-98, Tenth European Conference on Machine Learning*, pages 4–15, 1998.
10. A. McCallum and K. Nigam. A comparison of event models for naive Bayes text classification. In *Learning for Text Categorization: Papers from the AAAI Workshop*, pages 41–48, 1998. Tech. rep. WS-98-05, AAAI Press.
11. U. Y. Nahm and R. J. Mooney. Text mining with information extraction. In *AAAI 2002 Spring Symposium on Mining Answers from Texts and Knowledge Bases*, 2002.
12. K. Nigam, A. McCallum, S. Thrun, and T. Mitchell. Text classification from labeled and unlabeled documents using EM. *Machine Learning*, 39(2/3):103–134, 2000.
13. J. Schafer, J. Konstan, and J. Riedl. Electronic commerce recommender applications. *Journal of Data Mining and Knowledge Discovery*, 5:115–152, 2000.
14. K. Seymore, A. McCallum, and R. Rosenfeld. Learning hidden Markov model structure for information extraction. In *Machine Learning for Information Extraction: Papers from the AAAI Workshop*, 1999. Tech. rep. WS-99-11, AAAI Press.

Semantically Enhanced Collaborative Filtering on the Web

Bamshad Mobasher, Xin Jin, and Yanzan Zhou

Center for Web Intelligence
School of Computer Science, Telecommunication, and Information Systems
DePaul University, Chicago, Illinois, USA
{mobasher,xjin,yzhou}@cs.depaul.edu

Abstract. Item-based Collaborative Filtering (CF) algorithms have been designed to deal with the scalability problems associated with traditional user-based CF approaches without sacrificing recommendation or prediction accuracy. Item-based algorithms avoid the bottleneck in computing user-user correlations by first considering the relationships among items and performing similarity computations in a reduced space. Because the computation of item similarities is independent of the methods used for generating predictions, multiple knowledge sources, including structured semantic information about items, can be brought to bear in determining similarities among items. The integration of semantic similarities for items with rating- or usage-based similarities allows the system to make inferences based on the underlying reasons for which a user may or may not be interested in a particular item. Furthermore, in cases where little or no rating (or usage) information is available (such as in the case of newly added items, or in very sparse data sets), the system can still use the semantic similarities to provide reasonable recommendations for users. In this paper, we introduce an approach for semantically enhanced collaborative filtering in which structured semantic knowledge about items, extracted automatically from the Web based on domain-specific reference ontologies, is used in conjunction with user-item mappings to create a combined similarity measure and generate predictions. Our experimental results demonstrate that the integrated approach yields significant advantages both in terms of improving accuracy, as well as in dealing with very sparse data sets or new items.

1 Introduction

The continued growth and increasing complexity of Web-based applications, from e-commerce, to Web services, to dynamic content providers; has led to a proliferation of personalization tools on a variety of sites. Personalized services, such as recommender systems, help engage visitors, turn casual browsers into customer, or help visitor to more effectively locate pertinent information. Collaborative filtering (CF) [25,14,5,11] is one of the most successful and widely used technologies in personalization and recommender systems.

Traditionally, CF-based systems compare a representation of an active user's preferences (such as explicit ratings on items or implicit navigational patterns)

B. Berendt et al. (Eds.): EWMF 2003, LNAI 3209, pp. 57–76, 2004.
© Springer-Verlag Berlin Heidelberg 2004

with the historical records of past users to find the k most similar *neighbors* of the active user. These historical records are then used to predict the preference value of the active user on a particular, yet to be rated or visited, item; or to recommend the top N items in which the user may be interested. Since the focus of such systems is on comparing the correlations or similarities among users, they are often referred to as *user-based collaborative filtering* systems.

Despite their success and popularity, traditional CF-based techniques suffer from some well-known limitations [24]. One of the critical limitations is the lack of scalability of the underlying memory-based k-nearest-neighbor approach which requires that the neighborhood formation phase be performed as an online process. For very large data sets this may lead to unacceptable latency for providing recommendations. The scalability problems are further accentuated when collaborative filtering is used in the context of Web usage data. In this case, users' browsing patterns are used to implicitly obtain measures of content preference. For frequent visitors the size of user or session vectors tends to be much larger than in the case of e-commerce purchase patterns. Performing user-user similarity computations in this context further degrades the system performance.

Another important limitation of CF-based systems emanates from the sparse nature of the underlying datasets. As the number of items in the database increases, the density of each user record with respect to these items will decrease. This, in turn, will decrease the likelihood of a significant overlap of visited or rated items among pairs of users, resulting in less reliable computation of correlations, and thus less reliable predictions.

Finally, a significant shortcoming of such systems is their inability to provide recommendations or predictions for new or recently added items: a user's rating on a new item cannot be compared with the ratings of other users on the same item. Furthermore, the system can never generate predictions for new items which have not yet been visited or rated by (a sufficient number of) other users. This problem is often referred to as the "new item problem".

A number of optimization strategies have been proposed and employed to remedy the scalability and sparsity problems associated with collaborative filtering. These strategies include similarity indexing [1] to reduce real-time search costs, and dimensionality reduction methods based on Latent Semantic Indexing (LSI) to alleviate the data sparsity in the user-item mappings [24,22]. Other approaches have focused on model-based techniques which use machine learning techniques, such as unsupervised clustering of user records [19] or supervised classification models [5]. These approaches separate the offline tasks of creating user models from the real-time task of recommendation generation, thus improving scalability. However, this is sometimes at the cost of lower recommendation accuracy.

In the context of click-stream and e-commerce data, Web usage mining [26] techniques, such as clustering and association rule discovery, that rely on offline pattern discovery from user transactions, have been studied as an underlying mechanism for personalization and recommender systems [16,17,18]. Such techniques generally provide both a computational advantage, as well as better recommendation effectiveness, than traditional CF-based techniques, particularly in the context of click-stream data. For a recent survey of personalization based on Web usage mining see [21].

There has also been a growing body of work in enhancing collaborative filtering by integrating data from other sources such as content and user demographics [6,20,2,15]. Content-oriented approaches, in particular, can be used to address the "new item problem" discussed above. Generally, in these approaches, keywords are extracted from the content of Web pages and are used to recommend other pages or items to a user, not only based on user ratings or visit patterns, but also (or alternatively) based on the content similarity of these pages to other pages already visited by the user. Keyword-based approaches, however, are incapable of capturing more complex properties of, or relationships among, objects at a deeper semantic level. Unstructured keyword-based representations often result in a substantial amount of noise resulting in reduced recommendation accuracy.

Recently, a new class of *item-based* CF algorithms has been proposed to deal with the scalability problems in user-based CF algorithms [23,8]. Item-based CF algorithms avoid the bottleneck in user-user computations by first considering the relationships among items. Rather than finding user neighbors, the system tries to find k similar items that are rated (or visited) by different users in some similar way. Then, for a target item, predictions can be generated, for example, by taking a weighted average of the target user's item ratings (or weights) on these neighbor items. Thus, these algorithms alleviate the scalability problem that exists in user-based CF algorithms, because the similarity computations are performed in the smaller space of the items, and because often the item-item comparisons can be performed offline. At the same time, CF algorithms have been shown to achieve prediction accuracies that are comparable to or even better than user-based CF algorithms.

Item-based CF algorithms still suffer from the problems associated with data sparsity, and they still lack the ability to provide recommendations or predictions for new or recently added items. However, the item-based CF framework provides the necessary ingredients to seamlessly incorporate other sources of evidence about items (in addition to item ratings or weights). This flexibility comes from the fact that the computation of item similarities is independent of the methods used for generating predictions or recommendations, thus multiple knowledge sources, including structured semantic information about items, can be used for performing the similarity computations.

In this paper, we introduce an approach for semantically enhanced collaborative filtering in which structured semantic knowledge about items, extracted automatically from the Web based on domain-specific reference ontologies, is used in conjunction with user-item ratings (or weights) to create a combined similarity measure for item comparisons. In contrast to previous approaches to hybrid content-collaborative systems that enhance *user based* CF [2,15], we integrate semantic knowledge into the *item-based* CF framework. The integration of semantic similarities for items with rating (or usage-based) similarities provides two primary advantages. First, the semantic attributes for items provide additional clues about the underlying reasons for which a user may or may not be interested in particular items (something that is hidden behind the rating values in the usual context). This, in turn, allows the system to make inferences based on this additional source of knowledge, resulting in improved recommendation accuracy and coverage. Secondly, in cases where little or no rating (or usage) information is available (such as in the case of newly added items, or in very sparse data sets), the system can still use the semantic similarities to provide reasonable recommendations for users. These claims are verified by our experimental results, on two different data sets.

The rest of this paper is organized as follows. In Section 2, we provide the necessary background information on the item-based collaborative filtering framework. In Section 3, we discuss our semantically enhanced approach. In this section we first discuss the problem of ontology-based extraction of class instances in a particular domain and the structured representation of the extracted semantic attributes for items. We then present our approach for combining semantic and rating (or usage) similarity of items to generate predictions. In Section 4, we discuss the characteristics of our experimental data sets and present our experimental evaluation of the proposed approach. Finally, we conclude with a summary of our findings and some directions for future work.

2   Background on Item-Based Collaborative Filtering

In a collaborative filtering (CF) scenario, generally we start with a list of m users $U = \{u_1, u_2, \ldots, u_m\}$, a list of n items $I = \{i_1, i_2, \ldots, i_n\}$, and a mapping between user-item pairs and a set of weights. The latter mapping can be represented as a $m \times n$ matrix M. In the traditional CF domain the matrix M usually represents user ratings of items, thus the entry $M_{r,j}$ represents a user u_r's rating on item i_j. In this case, the users' judgments or preferences are explicitly given by matrix M. Collaborative filtering can also be used in the context of Web usage data. In that case, the set U may represent user sessions, some of which may belong to the same user who has visited the site multiple times. For usage data, generally, the entry $M_{r,j}$ represents an implicit weight associated with an item (e.g., page or product) i_j in a user session u_r. This weight may be binary (representing the existence or non-existence of the item in the user session), or it may be based on the amount of time spent on the particular item during the session.

For a given active user (also called the *target user*) u_a, the task of a CF system is to (1) predict $M_{a,t}$ for a given *target item* i_t which has not already been visited or rated by u_a; or (2) recommend a set of items that may be interesting to user u_a.

In user-based CF algorithms, first a set of k nearest neighbors of the target user are computed. This is performed by computing correlations or similarities between user records (rows of the matrix M) and the target user. Then, different methods can be used to combine the neighbors' item ratings (or weights) to produce a prediction value for the target user on unrated (or unvisited) items. As noted in the introduction, a major problem with this approach is the lack of scalability: the complexity of the system increases linearly as a function of the number of users which, in large-scale e-commerce sites, could reach tens of millions.

In contrast, *item-based* CF algorithms attempt to find k similar items that are co-rated (or visited) by different users similarly. This amounts to performing similarity computations among the columns of matrix M. Thus, item-based CF algorithms avoid the bottleneck in user-user computations by first considering the relationships among items. For a target item, predictions can be generated by taking a weighted average of the target user's item ratings (or weights) on these neighbor items.

2.1   Finding Similar Items (Item Neighbors)

The first step in computing the similarity of two items i_p and i_q (column vectors in the data matrix M) is to identify all the users who have rated (or visited) both items. Many measures can be used to compute the similarity between items. The most common approach, when dealing with Web usage data, is to use the standard cosine similarity between two vectors:

$$sim(i_p, i_q) = \frac{\sum\limits_{k=1}^{m} M_{k,p} \times M_{k,q}}{\sqrt{\sum\limits_{k=1}^{m} (M_{k,p})^2 \times \sum\limits_{k=1}^{m} (M_{k,q})^2}}$$

where $M_{k,p}$ represents the weight associated with item i_p in the session (or user) vector k.

For ratings data, however, variances in user ratings styles must be taken into account. For example, in a movie rating scenario, with a rating scale between 1 and 5, some users may give a rating of 5 to many movies they consider to be "good"; while other more "strict" raters may only give a rating of 5 to those movies they consider "perfect". To offset the difference in rating scales, the data can be normalized to focus on rating variances (deviations from the mean ratings) on co-rated items. For our purposes, when dealing with ratings data, we adapt the *Adjusted Cosine Similarity* measure introduced by Sarwar et al. [23]:

$$sim(i_p, i_q) = \frac{\sum\limits_{k=1}^{m} (M_{k,p} - \overline{M_k}) \times (M_{k,q} - \overline{M_k})}{\sqrt{\sum\limits_{k=1}^{m} (M_{k,p} - \overline{M_k})^2 \times \sum\limits_{k=1}^{m} (M_{k,q} - \overline{M_k})^2}}$$

where $M_{k,p}$ represents the rating of user k on item i_p, and $\overline{M_k}$ is the average rating value of user k on all items.

2.2   Computing Predictions

After computing the similarity between items, we select a set of k most similar items to the target item and generate a predicted value for the target item. We use a *weighted sum* as follows.

$$M_{a,t} = \frac{\sum\limits_{j=1}^{k} (M_{a,j} \times sim(i_j, i_t))}{\sum\limits_{j=1}^{k} sim(i_j, i_t)}$$

Here, $M_{a,t}$ denotes the prediction value of target user u_a on target item i_t. Only the k most similar items (k nearest neighbors of item i_t) are used to generate the prediction.

Despite their effectiveness, item-based CF algorithms still suffer from the problems associated with data sparsity, and they still lack the ability to provide recommendations or predictions for new or recently added items. To deal with these problems, we introduce an approach for semantically enhanced collaborative filtering in which structured semantic knowledge about items, extracted automatically from the Web, is used in conjunction with user-item ratings (or weights) to create a combined similarity measure for item comparisons. This approach is discussed in the next section.

3   Using Semantic Knowledge to Enhance Collaborative Filtering

In this section, we first discuss the issue of extracting structured semantic attributes from the Web to populate instances of domain-specific ontology classes corresponding to items. We then present our approach to integrate the extracted semantic knowledge into the item-based collaborative filtering framework.

3.1   Extracting Domain Semantics from the Web

In order to obtain semantic information about items used in the collaborative filtering process, we must extract domain-level structured objects as semantic entities contained within Web pages on one or more Web sites. This task involves the automatic extraction and classification of objects of different types into classes based on an underlying reference domain ontology.

An ontology provides a set of well-founded constructs that define significant concepts and their semantic relationships. An example of an ontology is a relational schema for a database involving multiple tables and foreign keys semantically connecting these relations. Such constructs can be leveraged to build meaningful higher level knowledge in a particular domain. Domain ontologies for a Web site usually include concepts, subsumption relations between concepts (concept hierarchies), and other relations among concepts that exist in the domain represented by the Web site. In this paper, we do not directly deal with the problems of automatic ontology acquisition and learning. Rather, we assume the existence of a pre-defined reference ontology for a specific domain based on which the semantic attributes of items can be extracted. Our goal is to use this semantic knowledge about items together with item ratings (or weights

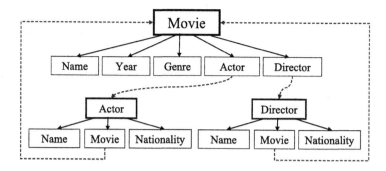

Fig. 1. Portion of the ontological representation for a movie Web site

in the context of Web usage data) to create a combined similarity measure for item-based collaborative filtering.

The problem of extracting instances of the ontology classes from Web pages is an interesting problem in its own right and has been studied extensively. This process can be viewed as the classification of objects embedded in one or more Web pages into classes specified as part of a reference ontology. For example, in [10] a text classifier is learned for each "semantic feature" based on a small manually labeled data set. First Web pages are extracted from different Web sites that belong to a similar domain, and then the semantic features are manually labeled. This small labeled data set is fed into a learning algorithm as training data to learn the mappings between Web objects and concept labels. Craven et al. [7] adopt a combined approach of statistical text classification and first-order text classification in recognizing concept instances. In that study, the learning process is based on both page content and linkage information. The problems and issues related to using ontologies in the context of Web mining has been discussed in [3].

In our approach, we have used domain-specific wrapper agents that use text mining and heuristic rules to extract class and attribute instances from Web sites based on a pre-specified reference ontology. At the present time, we do not use a general ontology representation language, such as DAML+OIL [12]. Rather, we represent the ontology classes as part of the schema for a relational database. Our simple representation scheme does not take into account complex relationships among classes (such as inheritance), but is adequate for specifying the attributes associated with classes (relations). Our wrapper agents use the relational schema for classes and simple heuristics based on textual cues to extract attribute values and populate instances of these classes (tuples). In the future, we intend to extend our work by incorporating more general ontology languages that can capture (and allow reasoning with) a richer set of structural relationships among classes and objects. The implementation details of the wrapper agents is beyond the scope of the present work and will be discussed elsewhere.

As an example, let us consider a movie Web site such as the Internet Movie Database (www.imdb.com). This Web site includes a collection of pages containing information about movies, actors, directors, etc. A collection of pages describing a specific movie might include attribute information such as the movie title, genre, actors, director, etc. These represent the attributes associated with a class that represents movies in our reference ontology. A domain ontology for this site may contain the classes **Movie, Actor** and **Director** along with their attributes. In our representation, some of the attributes represent properties of a given class and others represent reference slots corresponding to other classes. For instance, the "Actor" attribute of the **Movie** class represents a reference to the class (relation) **Actor** and, in the relational representation, is specified as a foreign key in the **Movie** relation. Figure 1 depicts the class **Movie** and its attributes. An actor or director's attribute information may include name, filmography (a set of movies), gender, nationality, etc. The dotted arrows in attributes such as "Actor" and "Director" indicated that they represent references to other classes in the ontology. The collection of Web pages in the site represent a group of embedded objects that are the instances of these classes.

In order to facilitate the computation of item similarities, generally, the extracted class instances will need to be converted into a vector representation. In our case, the values of semantic attributes associated with class instances are collected into a relational table whose rows represent the n items, and whose columns correspond to each of the extracted attributes. Additional preprocessing tasks, such as normalization and discretization (for continuous attributes), can be performed on the data in order to provide a uniform representation. This process generally results in the addition of attributes, for example, representing different intervals in a continuous range, or representing each unique discrete value for categorical attributes in the original data. The final result is a $n \times d$ matrix S, where d is the total number of unique semantic attributes. We call this matrix the *semantic attribute matrix*.

3.2   Integrating Semantic Similarity with Collaborative Filtering

As noted earlier, the item-based CF framework provides a computational advantage over user-based approaches, since item similarities can be computed offline, prior to the online task of generating recommendations. But, this framework also provides another important advantage. Since the computation of item similarities is independent of the methods used for generating predictions or recommendations, other sources of evidence about items (in addition to item ratings or weights) can be used for performing the similarity computations.

The integration of semantic similarities for items with rating (or usage-based) similarities provides two primary advantages. First, the semantic attributes for items provide additional clues about the underlying reasons for which a user may or may not be interested in particular items (something that is hidden behind the rating values in the usual context). This, in turn, allows the system to make inferences based on this additional source of knowledge, possibly improving the accuracy of recommendations. Secondly, in cases where little or no rating (or usage) information is available (such as in the case of newly added items, or in very sparse data sets), the system can still use the semantic similarities to provide reasonable recommendations for users.

In the following we describe our approach for integrating semantic similarities into the standard item-based collaborative filtering framework. Our approach involves first performing latent semantic analysis on the semantic attribute matrix obtained using the process described in Section 3.1. This is necessary in order to reduce noise and to collapse highly correlated attributes. We then compute item similarities, both based on the reduced semantic attribute matrix, as well as based on the user-item ratings (or usage) matrix. Finally, we use a combined similarity measure, as a linear combination of the two similarities to perform item-based collaborative filtering.

Using Latent Semantic Analysis on Semantic Attributes. Latent Semantic Indexing (LSI) [4] is a dimensionality reduction technique which is widely used in information retrieval (IR). Many IR applications have shown that performing latent semantic analysis, including in document indexing, can improve the accuracy of information retrieval. Given a term-document frequency matrix, LSI is used to decompose it into two matrices of reduced dimensions and a diagonal matrix of singular values. Each dimension in the reduced space is a latent variable (or factor) representing groups of highly correlated index terms. Reducing the dimensionality of the original matrix reduces the amount of noise in the data as well as its sparsity, thereby, improving retrieval based on the computation of similarities between the indexed documents and user queries. Here we apply this idea to create a reduced dimension space for the semantic attributes associated with items.

Singular Value Decomposition (SVD) is a well known technique used in LSI to perform matrix decomposition. In our case, we perform SVD on the semantic attribute matrix $S_{n \times d}$ by decomposing it into three matrices:

$$S_{n \times d} = U_{n \times r} \bullet \Sigma_{r \times r} \bullet V_{r \times d}$$

where U and V are two orthogonal matrices; r is the rank of matrix S, and Σ is a diagonal matrix of size $r \times r$, where its diagonal entries contain all singular values of matrix S and are stored in decreasing order. One advantage of SVD is that it provides the best lower rank approximation of the original matrix S [4]. We can reduce the diagonal matrix Σ into a lower-rank diagonal matrix $\Sigma_{k \times k}$ by only keeping k ($k < r$) largest values. Accordingly, we reduce U to U' and V to V'. Then the matrix $S' = U' \bullet \Sigma' \bullet V'$ is the rank-k approximation of the original matrix S.

In the above process, U' consists of the first k columns of the matrix U corresponding to the k highest order singular values. In the resulting semantic attribute matrix, S', each item is, thus, represented by a set of k latent variables, instead of the original d attributes. This results in a much less sparse matrix, improving the results of similarity computations, as well as the computational cost associated with the process. Furthermore, the generated latent variables represent groups of highly correlated attributes in the original data, thus potentially reducing the amount of noise associated with the semantic information. As we will illustrate in the next section, performing latent semantic analysis on the semantic space, generally leads to substantial gains in prediction accuracy based on the semantic attributes.

Predictions Based on a Combined Similarity Measure. The semantic similarity measure $SemSim(i_p, i_q)$, for a pair of items i_p and i_q, is computed using the standard vector-based cosine similarity on the reduced semantic space. This process can be viewed as multiplying the matrix S' by its transpose and normalizing each corresponding row and column vector by its norm. This results in a $n \times n$ square matrix in which an entry i, j corresponds to the semantic similarity of items i and j.

Similarly, we compute item similarities based on the user-item matrix M. As noted in Section 2, in the case of usage data, we use the cosine similarity measure. In the case of ratings data (such as movie ratings) we employ the adjusted cosine similarity in order to take into account the variances in user ratings. We denote the rating (or usage) similarity between two items i_p and i_q as $RateSim(i_p, i_q)$.

Finally, for each pair of items i_p and i_q, we combine these two similarity measures to get $CombinedSim$ as their linear combination:

$$CombinedSim(i_p, i_q) = \alpha \cdot SemSim(i_p, i_q) + (1 - \alpha) \cdot RateSim(i_p, i_q)$$

where α is a *semantic combination parameter* specifying the weight of semantic similarity in the combined measure. If $\alpha = 0$, then $CombinedSim(i_p, i_q) = RateSim(i_p, i_q)$, in other words we have the standard item-based filtering. On the other hand, if $\alpha = 1$, then only the semantic similarity is used which, essentially, results in a form of content-based filtering. Finding the appropriate value for α is not a trivial task, and is usually highly dependent on the characteristics of the data. We choose the proper value by performing sensitivity analysis for particular data sets in our experimental section below.

In order to compute predicted ratings or recommendations, we use the weighted sum approach discussed in Section 2. Specifically,

$$M_{a,t} = \frac{\sum\limits_{j=1}^{k} (M_{a,j} \times CombinedSim(i_j, i_t))}{\sum\limits_{j=1}^{k} sim(i_j, i_t)},$$

where, $M_{a,t}$ denotes the prediction value of target user u_a on target item i_t.

4   Experimental Evaluation

In this section we compare the semantically enhanced and standard item-based collaborative filtering in the context of two different data sets. In the first case, we focus our attention to the traditional context in which collaborative filtering is used, namely that of item ratings. For this purpose we choose the domain of movies and user's ratings of these movies. Secondly, we apply our approach to Web usage data. Specifically, we have chosen a real estate Web site containing information about various residential properties. While these data sets are quite different, the experimental results in this section demonstrate that the integrated approach yields advantages both in terms of improving accuracy, as well as in resolving some of the shortcomings associated with traditional approaches.

In each case, the data set was divided into random training and test sets. The training sets were used to build the models while the test sets were used to generate and evaluate recommendations. To assure statistical accuracy, this process was repeated five times for different random partitionings of the data. Unless otherwise specified, all of the results reported in this section represent averages over the five folds.

4.1   Data Sets and Evaluation Metrics

For the movie data set we used the ratings data from the MovieLens recommendation system (www.movielens.org). This data set contains 100,000 ratings on 1682 movies from 943 users. Each user has rated 20 or more movies with a rating scale of 1 to 5. We used our own wrapper agent to extract movie instances from the Internet Movie Database (www.imdb.com) based on the movie ontology depicted in Figure 1. Specifically, each instance was populated with semantic attributes, including movie title, release year, director(s), cast, genre, and plot.

The extracted instances were then converted into a binary table in standard spreadsheet format, where each row represents a movie, and each column represents a unique attribute value. For attributes involving continuous data types (such as "price" and "year") we performed discretization to generate a set of intervals as attributes. Similarly, for attributes involving a concept hierarchy, each concept node was represented as a unique attribute. This process resulted in a table representing each movie as an attribute vector with 2762 dimensions. Prior to computing the semantic similarity among movies, singular value decomposition was performed on the data, using different SVD dimensions, resulting in the corresponding semantic similarity matrices. The generated similarity matrices where then used in our experiments along with the rating similarities among movies, computed from the original ratings data.

To measure the accuracy of the recommendations we computed the standard *Mean Absolute Error* (MAE) between ratings and predictions in the test data sets. Specifically, given the set of actual/predicted rating pairs $\langle a_i, p_i \rangle$ for all the n movies in the test set, the MAE is computed as:

$$MAE = \frac{\sum_{i=1}^{n} |a_i - p_i|}{n}.$$

Note that lower MAE values represent higher recommendation accuracy. In this case, the ratings are based on a discrete scale of 1 (lowest) to 5 (highest). Thus, the maximum possible value for MAE is 4 (indicating a maximum possible error on all predictions).

In the case of the real estate data, we started with the raw Web usage data from the server logs of a local affiliate of a national real estate company. The primary function of the Web site is to allow prospective buyers visit various Web pages containing information related to some 300 residential properties. The portion of the Web usage data during the period of analysis contained approximately 24,000 user sessions from 3800 unique users. The preprocessing phase for this data was focused on extracting a full record for each user of properties she visited. This required performing the necessary aggregation operations pageviews

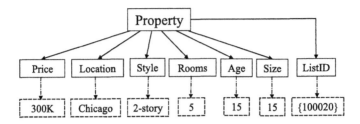

Fig. 2. Portion of the ontology for the class "Property" in the real estate Web site

in order to treat a property as the atomic unit of analysis. In addition, the visit frequency for each user-property pair was recorded, since the number of times a user comes back to a property listing is a good measure of that user's interest in the property. Finally, the data was filtered to limit the final data set to those users that had visited at least three properties. In our final data matrix, each row represented a user vector with properties as dimensions and visit frequencies as the corresponding dimension values.

To automatically extract semantic information about the properties, we used a reference ontology for the domain depicted in Figure 2. In this case, our ontology only contained a single class called "property." The figure only shows a subset of the attributes associated with "property" that were used for computing semantic similarities. An example of an instance of this class is also depicted in Figure 2 (dotted arrows show the mapping between each attribute and the corresponding attribute value in the extracted instance). Using a wrapper agent based on this reference ontology, the attribute values for each property instance were extracted directly from pages related to that property on the Web site. The discretization and normalization process described above for the movie data was also applied in this case resulting in final set of 120 unique attribute dimensions for each property vector. We then applied singular value decomposition to generate different semantic similarity matrices that were used in our experiments.

In contrast to the movie data set, this usage data does not involve item ratings. Thus, the standard MAE measure is not the appropriate approach for determining the accuracy of predictions. Instead we use the notion of *hit ratio* in the context of top-N recommendations. For each user, we randomly held one visited property as test data and used the rest as training data. The recommendation algorithm generates the top N recommended properties in the test set. If the previously held property appears in the recommendation set, this is considered a *hit*. We defined the Hit Ratio as the total number of hits divided by the total number of users in the test set.

It should be noted that the hit ratio increases as the value of N (number of recommendations) increases. Thus, in our experiments, we pay especial attention to a smaller number of recommendations (between 1 and 10) that result in good hit ratios.

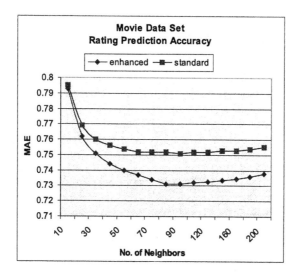

Fig. 3. Prediction accuracy for semantically enhanced recommendations v. standard item-based collaborative recommendations

4.2 Experiments with Movie Ratings Data

Figure 3 depicts the prediction accuracy of our semantically enhanced recommendations in contrast to those produced by standard item-based collaborative filtering. Here the MAE has been plotted with respect to the number of neighbors (similar items) in the k-nearest-neighbor algorithm. In both cases, the MAE converges between 80 and 100 neighbors, however, the semantically enhanced approach results in an overall improvement in accuracy.

A more telling picture emerges when we compare the range of values for the semantic combination parameter α. Recall that α is the parameter determining the degrees to which the semantic and rating similarities are used in the generation of neighbors. When $\alpha = 0$, then only semantic similarity among items is used, while $\alpha = 1$ represents the other side of the spectrum where only rating similarity is used (i.e., standard item-based recommendations). Figure 4 serves two purposes. First, it shows the impact of α on MAE, and secondly, it shows the impact of performing singular value decomposition (in this case, 100 dimensions) on the semantic data prior to computing similarities.

Applying SVD provides a two-fold advantage. On the one hand, SVD generally results in much better computational performance during tasks such as similarity computations or clustering. On the other hand, as clearly indicated by these results, it results in a general improvement in recommendation accuracy (most likely due to a reduction in noise). In the SVD case, the optimum value of α is around 0.40 which is also the point at which performing SVD has the largest impact. Note that at $\alpha = 1$, results for SVD-100 and no SVD are the same, since in that case the semantic similarity matrix is not taken into account. Interestingly, the results also show that in this data set using only semantic at-

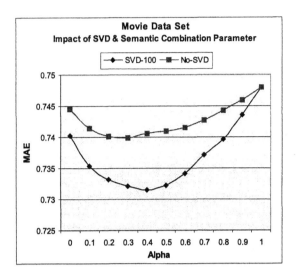

Fig. 4. Impact of the semantic combination parameter and SVD-based dimensionality reduction on recommendation accuracy

tributes ($\alpha = 0$) results in recommendations whose quality are in par with (or better) than recommendations based on rating similarities. However, it is clear that the combination of semantic and rating similarities provides an advantage over both of these boundary conditions.

As noted earlier, one of the problems associated with traditional collaborative filtering algorithms emanate from the sparsity of data sets to which they are applied. This sparsity has a negative impact on the accuracy and predictability of recommendations. This is one area in which, we believe, the integration of semantic knowledge with ratings data can provide significant advantage. To test this hypothesis, we created multiple training/test data sets in which the proportion of the training data to the complete ratings data set was changed from 90% to 10%. These proportions have a direct correspondence with the level of sparsity in the ratings data. In the case of each of the combination parameter values, we created five random training and test data sets and computed average MAE's over the five folds. We then computed the average improvement in MAE achieved by the semantically enhanced method over the standard item-based CF approach.

Figure 5 depicts these results for the SVD-100 data using a combination parameter $\alpha = 0.4$. While the overall recommendation accuracy drops as the proportion of training data is reduced (not shown), the results indicate that, generally, for sparser data sets, the semantic approach achieves larger improvements. As might be expected, this improvement starts to converge to 0 for very sparse data sets. This is because for very small training sets, neither approach can generate a reasonable number of recommendations. However, for up to a training ratio of 30%, the semantic approach provides improvements of up to 20% in MAE scores.

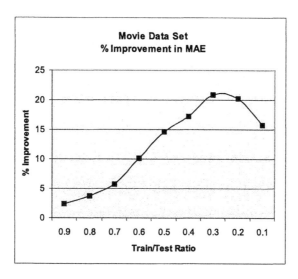

Fig. 5. Improvement in MAE for different test/train ratios (using 100 SVD dimensions and $\alpha = 0.4$)

As a final experiment with the movie data set, we focused our attention on another common problem with CF-based approaches, namely, the "new item" ("cold start") problem: since there are no ratings for new items, standard item-based algorithm cannot find item neighbors using rating similarity and fail to give predictions. Our goal here was to determine the degree to which semantic information from the domain can help produce accurate recommendations in the absence of any available ratings data for new items.

To achieve this goal we chose all movies which only received one rating and held these ratings as the test data. The actual movies in the selected data set were predominantly those that were very recently released (relative to the last date captured by the data). Thus, the sample closely modeled the conditions under which newly added items are considered for recommendation. In the training data, these movies received no ratings at all, and thus they were considered to be "new items". We compared our algorithm to a baseline algorithm, in which each user's average rating from training data was used as the prediction for "new items" in test data. These results are depicted in Figure 6. They show that, at all neighbor size levels, our algorithm can provide more accurate predictions than the baseline case.

4.3 Experiments with Real Estate Usage Data

As our first experiment with the Reality data, we compared the hit ratio of the semantically enhanced approach at different combination parameters for both the complete data set and the 40-dimension SVD data set. These results are depicted in Figure 7. In this case we only focused on the Top 10 recommendations generated by the algorithm.

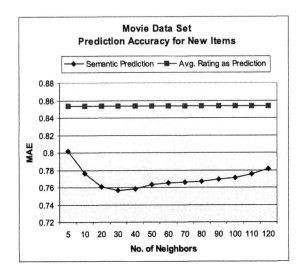

Fig. 6. Using semantically enhanced predictions for new (previously unrated) items

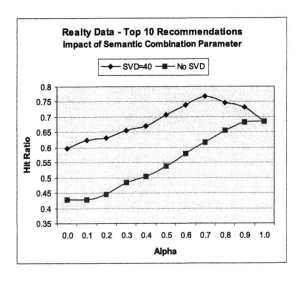

Fig. 7. Impact of semantic combination parameter for the top 10 recommendations in the real estate usage data

The results suggest similar conclusions to those observed in the movie data set. First, in general, singular value decomposition has an even more dramatic impact in this case; more so when the focus is shifted to the semantic information (α close to 0) as opposed to usage data. In fact, we see that in this data set, without performing SVD on the semantic attribute matrix, the combined approach does not improve accuracy when compared to pure usage-based recom-

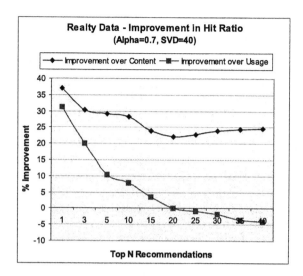

Fig. 8. Improvement of the semantically enhanced recommendations over content-only and usage-only recommendations

mendations. This may be an indication that many different attributes contribute to the type of property in which visitors show interest. Applying SVD results in a smaller number of latent factors by combining multiple attributes. These factors, individually, may be more predictive in determining user interests than the more fine grained attributes. As can be seen, with SVD the semantic approach results in significant improvements over both usage-only and content-only recommendations, particularly at a combination parameter $\alpha = 0.7$.

Next, we measured the hit ratio improvement achieved by our algorithm (with semantic combination parameter $\alpha = 0.7$), over the two boundary cases when only usage-based similarity ($\alpha = 1$) or only semantic similarity ($\alpha = 0$) are used to generate recommendations. Figure 8 depicts these results. The combined similarity measure achieved between 20% to 37% improvement over the semantic-only recommendations (i.e., over pure content-based filtering). In the case of usage-based recommendations, we observe that with recommendation sets of size less than 20, the combined approach always achieved better Hit Ratio. The improvement is particularly significant for small values of N. Indeed, in real situations, we are interested in few, but accurate recommendations, and this is precisely where the semantically enhanced approach seems to provide the most advantage.

5   Conclusions and Future Work

In this paper we have extended the item-based collaborative filtering framework by integrating structured semantic information about items for similarity computations. We have used domain-specific reference ontologies to automatically extract such features from the Web and populate class instances. Our enhanced similarity measure combines domain-based semantic item similarities with item similarities based on the user-item mappings. Our experimental results show that the semantically enhanced approach improves the prediction accuracies, while maintaining the computational advantages of item-based CF. In the context of Web usage and e-commerce data, the improvements are even more significant, particularly when focusing on a small number of recommendations.

The application of latent semantic analysis to the extracted semantic features, which reduces noise in the data, further improves the results when the hybrid approach is compared to usage-only or semantic-only recommendations. Furthermore, we have experimentally shown that, for new, unrated items, our approach can produce reasonably accurate recommendations, thus alleviating the "new item problem" associated with standard collaborative filtering. Our experiments also suggest that the integrated approach provides better quality predictions in the face of very sparse ratings or usage data.

An interesting area of current and future work is to use the characteristics of the domain together with machine learning techniques to automatically determine the semantic combination parameter (i.e., the degree to which the semantic similarity is combined with the item similarities based on ratings or usage). We will also further study the impact of using other approaches for measuring semantic similarities which take into account the structure of the underlying domain ontologies. Of particular relevance in this context is the work of Ganesan et al. [9] on using hierarchical structures in computing similarities, and that of Hotho et al. [13] on ontology-based text clustering.

References

1. C. C. Aggarwal, J. L. Wolf, and P. S. Yu. A new method for similarity indexing for market data. In *Proceedings of the 1999 ACM SIGMOD Conference*, Philadelphia, PA, June 1999.

2. C. Basu, H. Hirsh, and W. Cohen. Recommendation as classification: Using social and content-based information in recommendation. In *Proceedings of the the 15th National Conference on Artificial Intelligence (AAAI 98)*, Madison, WI, July 1998.

3. B. Berendt, A. Hotho, and G. Stumme. Towards semantic web mining. In *Proceedings of the First International Semantic Web Conference (ISWC02)*, Sardinia, Italy, June 2002.

4. M.W. Berry, S.T. Dumais, and G.W. O Brien. Using linear algebra for intelligent information retrieval. *SIAM Review*, 37:573–595, 1995.

5. D. Billsus and M.J. Pazzani. Learning collaborative information filters. In *Proceedings of the International Conference on Machine Learning*, Madison, WI, 1998.

6. M. Claypool, A. Gokhale, T. Miranda, P. Murnikov, D. Netes, and M. Sartin. Combining content-based and collaborative filters in an online newspaper. In *Proceedings of the ACM SIGIR '99 Workshop on Recommender Systems: Algorithms and Evaluation*, Berkeley, California, August 1999.

7. M. Craven, D. DiPasquo, D. Freitag, A. McCallum, T. Mitchell, K. Nigam, and S. Slattery. Learning to construct knowledge bases from the world wide web. *Artificial Intelligence*, 118(1-2):69–113, 2000.

8. M. Deshpande and G. Karypis. Item-based top-n recommendation algorithms. *ACM Transactions on Information Systems*, 22(1):1–34, 2004.

9. P. Ganesan, H. Garcia-Molina, and J. Widom. Exploiting hierarchical domain structure to compute similarity. *ACM Transactions on Information Systems*, 21(1):63–94, 2003.

10. R. Ghani and A. Fano. Building recommender systems using a knowledge base of product semantics. In *Proceedings of the Workshop on Recommendation and Personalization in E-Commerce, at the 2nd Int'l Conf. on Adaptive Hypermedia and Adaptive Web Based Systems*, Malaga, Spain, May 2002.

11. J. Herlocker, J. Konstan, A. Borchers, and J. Riedl. An algorithmic framework for performing collaborative filtering. In *Proceedings of the 22nd ACM Conference on Research and Development in Information Retrieval (SIGIR'99)*, Berkeley, CA, August 1999.

12. I. Horrocks. Daml+oil: A reasonable web ontology language. In *Proceedings of the 8th International Conference on Extending Database Technology*, pages 2–13, Prague, Czech Republic, March 2002. Springer-Verlag.

13. A. Hotho, A. Maedche, and S. Staab. Ontology-based text clustering. In *Proceedings of the IJCAI-2001 Workshop Text Learning: Beyond Supervision*, Seattle, WA, August 2001.

14. J. Konstan, B. Miller, D. Maltz, J. Herlocker, L. Gordon, and J. Riedl. Grouplens: Applying collaborative filtering to usenet news. *Communications of the ACM*, 40(3), 1997.

15. P. Melville, R.J. Mooney, and R. Nagarajan. Content-boosted collaborative filtering. In *Proceedings of the SIGIR2001 Workshop on Recommender Systems*, New Orleans, LA, September 2001.

16. B. Mobasher, R. Cooley, and J. Srivastava. Automatic personalization based on web usage mining. *Communications of the ACM*, 43(8):142–151, 2000.

17. B. Mobasher, H. Dai, T. Luo, and M. Nakagawa. Effective personalization based on association rule discovery from web usage data. In *Proceedings of the 3rd ACM Workshop on Web Information and Data Management (WIDM01)*, Atlanta, Georgia, November 2001.

18. B. Mobasher, H. Dai, and M. Nakagawa T. Luo. Discovery and evaluation of aggregate usage profiles for web personalization. *Data Mining and Knowledge Discovery*, 6:61–82, 2002.

19. M. O'Conner and J. Herlocker. Clustering items for collaborative filtering. In *Proceedings of the ACM SIGIR Workshop on Recommender Systems*, Berkeley, CA, August 1999.

20. M. Pazzani. A framework for collaborative, content-based and demographic filtering. *Artificial Intelligence Review*, 13(5-6):393–408, 1999.

21. D. Pierrakos, G. Paliouras, C. Papatheodorou, and C.D. Spyropoulos. Web usage mining as a tool for personalization: A survey. *User Modeling and User-Adapted Interaction*, 13:311–372, 2003.

22. B. Sarwar, G. Karypis, J. Konstan, and J. Riedl. Application of dimensionality reduction in recommender systems–a case study. In *Proceedings of the WebKDD 2000 Workshop at the ACM-SIGKDD Conference on Knowledge Discovery in Databases (KDD'00)*, August 2000.

23. B. Sarwar, G. Karypis, J. Konstan, and J. Riedl. Item-based collaborative filtering recommendation algorithms. In *Proceedings of the 10th International WWW Conference*, Hong Kong, May 2001.

24. B. M. Sarwar, G. Karypis, J. Konstan, and J. Riedl. Analysis of recommender algorithms for e-commerce. In *Proceedings of the 2nd ACM E-Commerce Conference (EC'00)*, Minneapolis, MN, October 2000.

25. U. Shardanand and P. Maes. Social information filtering: Algorithms for automating 'word of mouth'. In *Proceedings of the Computer-Human Interaction Conference (CHI95)*, Denver, CO, May 1995.

26. J. Srivastava, R. Cooley, M. Deshpande, and P. Tan. Web usage mining: Discovery and applications of usage patterns from web data. *SIGKDD Explorations*, 1(2):12–23, 2000.

Mapping Documents onto Web Page Ontology

Dunja Mladenić[1,2] and Marko Grobelnik[1]

[1] J.Stefan Institute, Ljubljana, Slovenia
{Dunja.Mladenic, Marko.Grobelnik}@ijs.si,
http://www-ai.ijs.si/{DunjaMladenic, MarkoGrobelnik}/
[2] Carnegie Mellon University, Pittsburgh, PA, USA
Dunja.Mladenic@cs.cmu.edu,
http://www.cs.cmu.edu/d̃unja/

Abstract. The paper describes an approach to automatically mapping Web pages onto ontology using document classification based on the Yahoo! ontology of Web pages. Techniques developed for learning on text data are used here on the hierarchical classification structure (ontology of Web documents). The high number of features is reduced by taking into account the hierarchical structure and using feature subset selection developed for the Naive Bayesian classifier. We focus on data sets with many features that also have a highly unbalanced class distribution. Documents are represented as word-vectors that include word sequences of up to five consecutive words. Based on the hierarchical structure the problem is divided into subproblems, each representing one on the categories included in the Yahoo! hierarchy. The resulting model is a set of independent classifiers, each used to predict the probability that a new document is a member of the corresponding category represented as a node in the hierarchy. Our example problem is automatic document categorization where we want to identify documents relevant for the selected category. Usually, only about 1%-10% of examples belong to the selected category. Experimental evaluation on real-world data shows that the proposed approach gives good results. Our experimental comparison of eleven feature scoring measures show that considering data and algorithm characteristics significantly improves the performance.

1 Introduction

Web page ontology can be defined in different ways depending on the objective of the ontology. This Chapter addresses ontology of Web documents, where the documents themselves are organized in a content hierarchy, with more general nodes placed closer to the root of the hierarchy. Each node is labeled by a set of keywords describing the content of documents that are placed in the node. Each document is described by a one-sentence summary including a hyperlink that points to the actual Web document located somewhere on the Web. As manual construction and maintenance of such an ontology is time consuming, we have addressed a related subproblem of automatically assigning a set of the most relevant nodes from the existing ontology to a new text document.

B. Berendt et al. (Eds.): EWMF 2003, LNAI 3209, pp. 77–96, 2004.

For this task we have adopted text mining methods in particular using machine learning classification algorithm Naive Bayes on text data, where the data is obtained from the publicly available Web page ontology Yahoo [1]. The classification algorithm is applied on word-vector representation of Web documents, where each word from the document (also referred to as an example) corresponds to a vector component (usually referred to as a feature). In general, features used to describe examples are not necessarily all relevant and beneficial for the task in hands. Additionally, a high number of features may slow down the process while giving similar results as obtained with a much smaller feature subset. Feature subset selection is commonly used when classifying text data, since most text data is characterized by several tens of thousands of features. Moreover, our experiments show that using the proposed feature subset selection improves the performance of our approach enabling better mapping of Web pages on the existing ontology.

Architecture of the system is described in Section 2. Section 3 describes the process of constructing word sequences that are used for describing content of text documents. Section 4 gives description of the process used to select subsets of words using several known and some new scoring measures. Data characteristics are given in Section 5. Experimental comparison of the tested measures on real-world data is given in Section 6. The results are discussed in Section 7.

2   Architecture of the System

Input to our system is an ontology of Web documents, where the ontology contains only hyperlinks to the Web documents while the documents themselves are located all over the Web. The ontology is organized as a content hierarchy, with more general nodes placed closer to the root of the hierarchy (see Section 5 for data description). The ontology itself is represented with a set of Web documents located at the ontology site, here referred to as Yahoo Web documents. For each ontology node there is a Yahoo Web document containing:

- the node name - a set of keywords describing the content of documents that are placed in the node,
- a set of hyperlinks to the other ontology nodes,
- a set of hyperlinks to the actual Web documents with a short content description for each of them.

Output of the system is a model represented as a set of classifiers. The model is used for inserting a new Web document into the ontology, so that for a new Web document it returns a ranked list of the best fitting ontology nodes. If the top node in the ranked list has very low score (low probability that the new documents belongs to it), this indicates the need for extending the ontology. The whole system consists of four phases, as shown in Figure 1:

feature construction used to transform the text document given in html format to word-vectors as described in Section 3,

subproblem definition that takes the documents organized into ontology and forms a set of weighted training examples for each ontology node

feature selection used to reduce dimensionality of the training examples, this is specific to each node

classifier construction that for each node takes the set of associated training examples and constructs a classifier

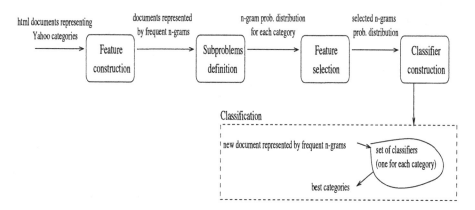

Fig. 1. Arichitecture of the system for automatically mapping documents onto an existing ontology.

The documents organized in the existing ontology are used as training examples for the classifier construction that models the mapping of documents into different parts of the ontology. The **feature construction phase** takes html documents, generates new features (word sequences) and represents each html document as a word-vector of that features. In the **subproblem definition phase** a binary classification problem is defined for each node in the ontology (hierarchy). Each problem is handled separately, applying **feature selection** and **classifier construction**. The final model consists of a set of classifiers, one for each ontology node. The model is used for classification (mapping) of a new document onto a set of nodes, so that we get a subset of the ontology nodes ranked according to the probability that the new document should be mapped onto each of them.

The classifier construction is performed using the Naive Bayesian classifier base on the multinomial event model as suggested in [2] Notice that the product goes over all word sequences that occur in the representation of document Doc.

$$P(C|Doc) = \frac{P(C)\Pi_{W_j \in Doc}P(W_j|C)^{TF(W_j,Doc)}}{\sum_i P(C_i)\Pi_{W_l \in Doc}P(W_l|C_i)^{TF(W_l,Doc)}}$$

Where $P(W_j|C)$ is the conditional probability here estimated using Laplace probability estimate, $TF(W_j, Doc)$ is the frequency of word W_j in document Doc. Notice that using word sequences instead of only single words means even stronger violation of the feature independence assumption used in the Naive Bayesian classifier.

3   Using Word Sequences

In our approach, each document is represented as a word-vector, where one vector component referred to as a feature, reflects the number of occurrences of a word or a word sequence in the document. Features are generated using an algorithm [3] similar to the Apriori algorithm [4] used for association rule generation.

We use word sequences, also known as n-grams, to form the new features. We generate features that represent up to five words (1-grams, 2-grams, ...5-grams) occurring in a document as a sequence (eg. 'machine learning', 'world wide web'). We interleaved this feature generation with the feature selection using "stop-list" with common English words and removal of infrequent features. First we remove words contained in the "stop-list" (eg. a, the, for, each, at, will, be) enabling some features that represent a word sequence to actually capture longer sequences. For instance, 'Word for Windows' that is represented as a 2-gram 'Word Windows' or 'winners will be posted at the end of each two-week period' that is represented as a 5-gram 'winners posted end two-week period'. We additionally reduce the high number of features by pruning infrequent features. Infrequent features are here defined as features (word sequences) that occur less than 4 times. By using word sequences we can capture some characteristic word combinations and also increase the number of features. For example, in the whole Yahoo hierarchy (without a top category *'Regional'*) that we use for automatic document categorization the number of features has increased from 317,522 features representing single words (before removing infrequent features) to 1,410,303 features (before removing infrequent features) representing word sequences containing 1 or 2 words.

The process of feature generation is performed in passes over documents, where *i-grams* are generated in the *i*-th pass only from the candidate features of length *i-1* generated in the previous pass. This process is similar to the large *k-itemset* generation used in association rules algorithm [4]. In Figure 2 we give Algorithm for the generation of new features. In the first pass all single words not contained in the "stop-list" and having sufficient frequency (here we check for term frequency > 3) are taken LargeNGramSet. Word sequences of size 2 up to MaxNGramSize (here we take MaxNGramSize = 5) are generated using several pruning criteria. In each pass, all documents are checked one by one using a window NGramQueue to get a sequence of words. Before the next word is added to the window (a window is moved one word to the right) the word is checked for being a proper word (not a number or a special symbol), for not being in the "stop-list" StopWordSet and for being included in the current set of word sequences LargeNGramSet. The window is reset when the next word is not a proper word or is not included in the set of word sequences generated so far.

Variables used in Algorithm in Figure 2:

Input variables:

MinNGramOcc - minimal occurrences of N-Gram to become large N-Gram
MaxNGramSize - maximal size of N-Grams

StopWordSet - set of stop words (language dependent)
DocVec - vector of documents (DocVec[1], ..., DocVec[|DocVec|])
SymVec - vector of document lexical symbols (SymVec[1], ..., SymVec[|SymVec|])

Temporary variables:
Sym - lexical symbol in document (possible value types: word, number, symbol)
CandNGramMap - mapping from candidate N-Gram to its occurrence counter
NGramQueue - queue (window) of last NGramSize words (excluding StopWordSet)

Output variables:
LargeNGramSet - set of large N-Grams (occurring $\geq$ MinNGramOcc times)

Algorithm (C like pseudo-code):

```
1.   LargeNGramSet = all single words in DocVec, not in StopWordSet and
2.   occurring ≥ MinNGramOcc times;
3.   for NGramSize = 2 to MaxNGramSize do {
4.     CandNGramMap=[];
5.     for SymVec = DocVec[1] to DocVec[|DocVec|] do {
6.       NGramQueue=[];
7.       for Sym = SymVec[1] to SymVec[|SymVec|] do {
8.         if (TypeOf(Sym)==word){
9.           if (Sym not in StopWordSet){
10.            if Sym in LargeNGramSet then {
11.              if (|NGramQueue|+1==NGramSize){
12.                if (Concatenated(NGramQueue) in LargeNGramSet){
13.                  NGramQueue.Push(Sym);
14.                  CandNGramMap[Concatenated(NGramQueue)]++;
15.                  NGramQueue.Pop();
16.                    } else {NGramQueue.Push(Sym); NGramQueue.Pop();}
17.                } else {NGramQueue.Push(Sym);}
18.              } else {NGramQueue=[];}
19.            } /* if (Sym not in StopWordSet) */
20.          } else {NGramQueue=[];}
21.        }; /* for Sym */
22.      }; /* for SymVec */
23.      LargeNGramSet += {NGram:CandNGramMap[NGram] ≥ MinNGramOcc};
24.    };
25.    return LargeNGramSet;
```

Fig. 2. Algorithm for the generation of features representing word sequences (n-grams). Please notice that `NGramQueue` is a queue and not a stack. The generated features are used in enriched bag-of-words document representation.

For illustration, we show in Figure 3 the accumulated number of features during the described process of feature generation on Yahoo documents that compose the whole Yahoo hierarchy. The left hand-side graph shows for each pass of the *i-gram* generation the influence of the number of included Yahoo documents to the number of new features. For example, in the first pass (the lowest curve in the left hand-side of Figure 3) about 100,000 features are generated after including 20,000 documents, about 200,000 features after including 30,000 documents and about 320,000 features after including all 49,600 documents. After reducing the number of features by pruning infrequent features we get about 70,000 features representing single words (1-grams) to start with in the second pass over documents. In the second pass (the steepest curve in the left hand-side of Figure 3) all pairs of words (2-grams) that appear in the documents and consist of words included in the set of 1-grams are added. As can be seen from Figure 3, the second pass adds many infrequent features resulting with more than 1,400,000 features that after pruning infrequent features reduce to about 200,000 features. We stop with 5-grams since, in the fifth pass only about 10,000 features are added (the almost flat curve in the left hand-side of Figure 3) and about 6,000 of them are deleted as infrequent features. The right hand-side graph in Figure 3 shows the same process of feature generation over time. Influence of pruning infrequent features after each pass is even more evident here. It can be also clearly seen that the highest number of features is added in the second pass where 2-grams are generated, while in the fifth pass the curve showing the increasing number of features is almost flat (the right most part of the right hand-side graph in Figure 3).

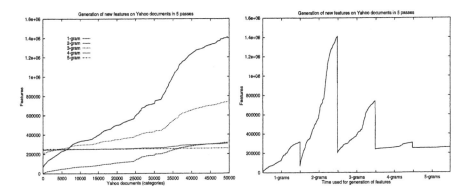

Fig. 3. Influence of included Yahoo documents to the accumulated number of features (left hand-side graph) and the process of feature generation (right hand-side graph). Notice that the two graphs represent the same results in two different ways. At the end of each pass over documents all the features that occur less than 4 times are deleted.

4   Selecting Subset of Words

Selecting subset of words to be used to describe content of documents is based on the idea of selecting subset of features commonly used in machine learning. When dealing with text data, we can easily have several tens of thousands of different words (features). Thus the whole process of feature subset selection is simplified by the assumption of feature independence. In this way the solution quality is traded for the time needed to find a solution, justified by the large number of features usually present in text data. Basically, a scoring is applied to each feature and the features are sorted according to the assigned score. Then, a predefined number of the best features is taken to form the feature subset.

Scoring of individual features can be performed using some of the measures used in machine learning for instance, *Information gain* used in decision tree induction [5]. In our comparison eleven feature scoring measures were included. Information gain was included as the well known measure successfully used in some text-learning experiments. *Expected cross entropy* used in text-classification experiments [6] is similar to Information gain. The difference is that instead of calculating average over all possible feature values, only the value denoting that word occurred in a document is considered. Our experiments show that this means an important difference in the resulting performance. *Mutual information* used in text-classification experiments [7] is similar to *Cross entropy for text* with the latter additionally taking into account word probability. These two measures and a very simple frequency measure proposed in [7] were reported to work well on text data. This third measure is calculated either as the number of documents that contain word W referred to as document frequency $DF(W)$ or as the number of occurrences of word W referred to as *Term frequency* $TF(W)$. This measure requires the stop words removal. We use the second definition: $Freq(W) = TF(W)$. *Odds ratio* is commonly used in information retrieval, where the problem is to rank out documents according to their relevance for the positive class value using occurrence of different words as features [8].

$$OddsRatio(W) = \log \frac{P(W|pos)(1 - P(W|neg))}{(1 - P(W|pos))P(W|neg)}$$

Where $P(W|pos)$ is the conditional probability of word W occurring in documents belonging to the target content category and $P(W|neg)$ is the conditional probability of word W occurring in the other documents.

Our experiments show that *Odds ratio* is especially suitable to be used in a combination with the Naive Bayesian classifier for our kind of problems. We propose four variants of *Odds ratio*, to test if the results are sensitive to some modifications in the formula. As a baseline method we used random scoring method defined to score each word by a random number.

5   Data Description

Data sets used in our experiments were generated from the Yahoo! hierarchy of Web pages as described in [9] and present five out of the fourteen sub-hierarchies that can be formed from the top level ontology nodes: *'Arts and Humanities'*, *'Entertainment'*, *'Computers and Internet'*, *'Education'*, *'References'*.

5.1   Web Page Ontology

The categories in Yahoo! ontology of Web pages are human constructed and designed for human Web browsing. Documents that are already classified and used to build the hierarchy are Web documents, making the hierarchy biased toward human knowledge areas that are represented in Web documents. For example, one of the most general categories named *'Bussines and Economy'* is over-represented including more than a third of all documents, while the other category that appears at the same level of the hierarchy named *'Social Science'* includes less than 1% of all documents. Our approach to mapping Web pages onto ontology is not limited to the Yahoo! hierarchy and can be used on some of the other text hierarchies that are not Web-oriented.

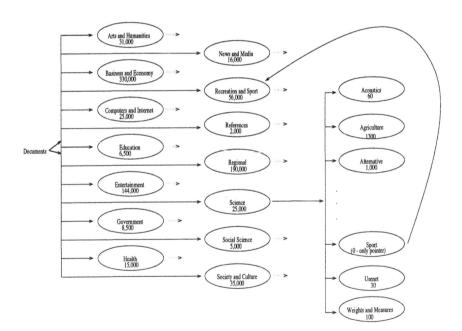

Fig. 4. Top level of the Yahoo categorization with the first level of subcategories in *'Science'* category. Approximate number of documents in each category is given under the category name (eg. 25,000 documents are classified under *'Science'*). The data is taken from the Yahoo site in UK & Ireland, November 1997.

The Yahoo! hierarchy when we obtained it (excluding subcategory *'Regional'*) was built on approximately a million Web documents located on Internet all around the world. We refer here to these documents as *actual Web documents*. Hyperlinks to those documents are organized in about 50,000 *Yahoo Web documents*. Each Yahoo document represents one of the included categories with the more general categories closer to the root of the hierarchy. The category is denoted by keywords, describing category content, that appear on the path from the root of the hierarchy to the node representing the category. For instance, *'Sport'* a subcategory of *'Science'* in Figure 4 is named *'Science: Sport'* and in our approach assigned two keywords: *Science, Sport*. In other words, a more specific category is named by adding a keyword to the name of the more general category directly connected to it (one level higher in the hierarchy).

Yahoo documents are connected with hyperlinks forming a hierarchical structure that can be represented as a directed acyclic graph (or a tree with additional connections between some of its nodes). For the sake of simplicity, we will talk about the tree and remind on additional connections only when needed. Each Web document classified in the Yahoo hierarchy appears only once, but there can be several connections in the hierarchy (hyperlinks between Yahoo documents) leading to it. For example, the Yahoo document representing *'Sport'*, a subcategory of *'Science'* includes a hyperlink to the top category *'Recreation and Sport'* (see Figure 4). In this way, the user still has the impression of a tree structure that nicely matches our intuition about the hierarchical organization of categories. Some nodes at the bottom of the hierarchy contain mostly hyperlinks to the actual Web documents, while the other nodes contain mostly or even only (eg. *'Science: Sport'* in Figure 4) hyperlinks to other Yahoo Web documents (nodes in the hierarchy). There are currently fourteen top level Yahoo categories each named by only one keyword. Figure 4 shows them with the approximate number of actual Web documents each category is based on. Each of the top categories is further represented with a hierarchical structure of more specific categories. As an example we show in Figure 4 the part of the first-level subcategories in *'Science'* top category ranging from *'Acoustics'* (named *'Science: Acoustics'* and assigned two keywords *Science, Acoustics*) to *'Weights and Measures'* (named *'Science: Weights and Measures'* and assigned two keywords *Science, Weights and Measures*).

5.2   Data Sets Used in Our Experiments

We have defined the problem as predicting document category based on the documents that are already categorized into a Web page ontology. Each data set is given as a classification hierarchy of text documents, with the more general categories closer to the root of the hierarchy. Each category is denoted by keywords, describing category content. More specific category is named by adding a keyword to the name of the more general category that is one level higher in the hierarchy.

The data was obtained from the publicly accessible Yahoo Web site. Table 1 gives data set characteristics including information about the number of nodes in the hierarchy, the number of features showing also how many features represent different length word sequences, the number of examples (documents), the average distance between nodes measured as the average number of connections between any two nodes in the hierarchy and the average number of features in positive documents. The average number of features in positive documents is calculated as the average over the defined subproblems. Features are generated for word sequences (n-gram) of length up to fice consequtice words as described in Section 3.

Table 1. Data set characteristics for five data sets formed from the five top Yahoo categories. The problem is document categorization based on the hierarchy of categories and the corresponding documents. For each data set we give (from left to right) its name, the number of included content categories, the number of features (word sequences and their length), the number of examples (actual Web document the category is based on), the average distance between two nodes in the hierarchy, the average number of features in positive examples (average number of word sequences in all the documents belonging to one category).

Yahoo dataset	# categories (nodes)	# features (1-grams+...+5-grams)	# examples (Web docs)	Avg. node distance	Avg. pos. features
'Entertainment'	8,081	30,998 (15,144+11,211+ 2,970+1,059+505)	79,011	7.56	60
'Arts and Humanities'	3,085	11,473 (7,380+3,538+ 463+75+17)	27,765	6.59	65
'Computers and Internet'	2,652	7,631 (5,049+2,276+ 261+38+7)	23,105	6.77	55
'Education'	349	3,198 (1,919+1,061+ 184+28+6)	5,406	4.54	100
'References'	129	928 (701+196+ 28+3+0)	1,995	4.29	45

More specifically, the following data sets are used in our experiments. *'Entertainment'* having 8,081 nodes with an average distance 7.56 between them, 30,998 features consisting of 15,144 1-grams, 11,211 2-grams, 2,970 3-grams, 1,059 4-grams, 505 5-grams and 79,011 actual Web documents. *'Arts and Humanities'* having 3,085 nodes with an average distance 6.59 between them, 11,473 (7,380+3,538+463+75+17) features and 27,765 actual Web documents. *'Computers and Internet'* having 2,652 nodes with an average distance 6.77 between them, 7,631 (5,049+2,276+261+38+7) features and 23,105 actual Web documents. *'Education'* having 349 nodes with an average distance 4.54 between them, 3,198 (1,919+1,061+184+28+6) features and 5,406 actual Web documents. *'References'* having 129 nodes with an average distance 4.29 between them, 928 (701+196+28+3+0) features and 1,995 actual Web documents.

From the data characteristics given in Table 1 it can be seen that the number of unique words (1-grams) varies from 701 for *'References'* to 15,144 for *'Entertainment'*. The set of negative examples is the same for all subproblems in one data set. The set of positive examples changes for each of the subproblems. For most of the subproblems the probability of positive class value is < 0.1, meaning that we have a problem with unbalanced class distribution.

In order to model a hierarchy of content categories and handle a large number of categories we generate a binary classification model for each of the hierarchy nodes (leaf or non-leaf) by collecting word probabilities from all the documents in and below the node (see [10,11] for more information). These documents are taken as positive examples while all the other documents in the hierarchy are used as negative. This means that the most classifiers are induced from highly unbalanced class distribution with only about 1%-10% of positive examples. Since each classifier competes with the other classifiers, it is important that a classifier identifies documents belonging to its category. Thus we say that our problem has asymmetric misclassification costs given only implicitly in the problem. By asymmetric misclassification costs we mean that one of the class values (positive) is the target class value for which we want to get predictions and we prefer false positive over false negative.

6   Experimental Results

In our experiments we compare different feature scoring measures and observe the influence of the number of selected features to the system performance. Since we have a set of classifiers, the number of selected features is determined relatively to the classifier category size expressed by the number of features in positive examples. We refer to this relative number of features as *Vector size*. In this way, a classifier for a larger category is using more features than a classifier for some smaller category, while both classifying the same testing example. Reported results are averaged over 5 repetitions using hold-out testing on independent set of 500 (300 for the two smaller data sets) randomly selected testing examples. In order to enable operational usage of the system on larger data sets we include the pruning mechanisms described in [12]. Result is speed up of the classification process, since for each document classification, not all but only promising categories are considered (85%-95% of all categories are pruned).

To evaluate the results we use Precision, Recall and F_2-measure as commonly used evaluation measures for text data [13]. $F-measure$ is a combination of Precision P and Recall R commonly used in information retrieval $F_\beta = \frac{(1+\beta^2)P \times R}{\beta^2 P + R}$. The relative importance of each is expressed with the value of parameter β. We report average Precision and Recall per document calculated for the fixed probability threshold (experimentally set to 0.95 [12]). Precision can be seen as the classification accuracy calculated only for positive examples, while Recall is the proportion of positive examples the system recognized as positive (values in

Table 2. Comparison of feature scoring measures for the problem of keyword prediction on five data sets formed from the Yahoo hierarchy. For each data set, the compared feature scoring measures are sorted according to their performance in F2-measure. The values of F1-measure, Precision and Recall are given for better understanding. We give averages with standard errors calculated over 5 runs.

Dom. name	Scoring measure	Average on keyword assignment			
		F1-measure	F2-measure	Precision	Recall
Ent.	**Odds ratio**	**0.48 ± 0.006**	**0.59 ± 0.007**	**0.44± 0.006**	**0.80 ± 0.006**
	Term frequency	0.39 ± 0.003	0.49 ± 0.12	0.41± 0.006	0.71 ± 0.010
	Cross entropy Txt	0.29 ± 0.007	0.39 ± 0.007	0.35± 0.003	0.69 ± 0.007
	Mutual info. Txt	0.25 ± 0.005	0.27 ± 0.006	0.57± 0.007	0.38 ± 0.007
	Information gain	0.27 ± 0.008	0.22 ± 0.004	0.86± 0.005	0.21 ± 0.006
	Random	0.002± 0.001	0.002± 0.001	0.99± 0.006	0.001± 0.007
Arts.	**Odds ratio**	0.46 ± 0.003	**0.59 ± 0.005**	**0.40± 0.002**	**0.83 ± 0.006**
	Term frequency	**0.47 ± 0.007**	**0.58 ± 0.008**	**0.48± 0.003**	**0.77 ± 0.009**
	Cross entropy Txt	0.32 ± 0.003	0.44 ± 0.004	0.33± 0.004	0.75 ± 0.008
	Mutual info. Txt	0.31 ± 0.005	0.35 ± 0.004	0.56± 0.007	0.46 ± 0.006
	Information gain	0.25 ± 0.006	0.21 ± 0.005	0.94± 0.002	0.20 ± 0.004
	Random	0.0051± 0.001	0.001± 0.001	0.99± 0.001	0.001± 0.001
Comp.	**Odds ratio**	0.46 ± 0.006	**0.60 ± 0.006**	**0.40± 0.007**	**0.84 ± 0.005**
	Term frequency	**0.48 ± 0.008**	**0.58 ± 0.007**	**0.50± 0.004**	**0.74 ± 0.005**
	Cross entropy Txt	0.37 ± 0.007	0.49 ± 0.008	0.35± 0.004	0.75 ± 0.007
	Mutual info. Txt	0.36 ± 0.003	0.38 ± 0.003	0.62± 0.005	0.45 ± 0.005
	Information gain	0.21 ± 0.005	0.17 ± 0.005	0.94± 0.005	0.15 ± 0.005
	Random	0.01 ± 0.001	0.01 ± 0.001	0.99 ± 0.001	0.004± 0.001
Edu.	**Term frequency**	**0.48 ± 0.007**	**0.55 ± 0.007**	**0.57± 0.010**	**0.65 ± 0.010**
	Odds ratio	0.33 ± 0.008	**0.48 ± 0.008**	**0.36± 0.010**	**0.81 ± 0.005**
	Mutual info. Txt	0.40 ± 0.004	0.46 ± 0.007	0.48± 0.010	0.59 ± 0.010
	Cross entropy Txt	0.32 ± 0.009	0.46 ± 0.007	0.28± 0.010	0.82 ± 0.006
	Information gain	0.13 ± 0.007	0.11 ± 0.006	0.98± 0.002	0.11 ± 0.006
	Random	0.01 ± 0.002	0.01 ± 0.002	0.99± 0.001	0.003± 0.002
Ref.	**Odds ratio**	**0.53 ± 0.006**	**0.64 ± 0.006**	**0.51± 0.007**	**0.81 ± 0.008**
	Cross entropy Txt	0.52 ± 0.008	**0.60 ± 0.010**	**0.62± 0.003**	**0.71 ± 0.010**
	Mutual info. Txt	0.52 ± 0.010	0.55 ± 0.010	0.73± 0.010	0.60 ± 0.020
	Term frequency	0.50 ± 0.010	0.53 ± 0.010	0.78± 0.005	0.57 ± 0.010
	Information gain	0.25 ± 0.007	0.22 ± 0.007	0.99± 0.002	0.21 ± 0.006
	Random	0.07 ± 0.006	0.06 ± 0.005	0.99± 0.001	0.05 ± 0.005

[0..1]). If testing example is originally assigned to several categories, all these categories are taken as correct and compared to the set of predicted categories. We perform this comparison in two ways: (1) keyword prediction taking into account proximity to the correct category using keywords assigned to each category and (2) category prediction requesting prediction of the correct category.

Additional to Precision and Recall we report F_2-measure that is a combination of the two, commonly used when we care more about Recall than about

Table 3. Comparison of feature scoring measures for the problem of category prediction on five data sets formed from the Yahoo hierarchy. For each data set, the compared feature scoring measures are sorted according to their performance in F2-measure. The values of F1-measure, Precision and Recall are given for better understanding. We give averages with standard errors calculated over 5 runs.

Dom. name	Scoring measure	Average on category prediction			
		F1-measure	F2-measure	Precision	Recall
Ent.	**Odds ratio**	**0.29± 0.002**	**0.30 ± 0.003**	**0.41 ± 0.004**	**0.34 ± 0.003**
	Term frequency	0.24± 0.003	0.27 ± 0.003	0.38 ± 0.003	0.34 ± 0.003
	Mutual info. Txt	0.22± 0.004	0.23 ± 0.004	0.57 ± 0.006	0.29 ± 0.007
	Information gain	0.25± 0.002	0.20 ± 0.003	0.87 ± 0.002	0.17 ± 0.002
	Cross entropy Txt	0.15± 0.002	0.18 ± 0.002	0.29 ± 0.005	0.28 ± 0.005
	Random	0.001± 0.0001	0.001± 0.0002	0.99 ± 0.007	0.001±0.0002
Arts.	**Odds ratio**	**0.29± 0.002**	**0.32 ± 0.004**	**0.36 ± 0.005**	**0.38 ± 0.004**
	Term frequency	0.28± 0.002	0.29 ± 0.003	0.43 ± 0.004	0.34 ± 0.003
	Mutual info. Txt	0.24± 0.005	0.25 ± 0.005	0.56 ± 0.006	0.31 ± 0.007
	Cross entropy Txt	0.18± 0.002	0.22 ± 0.003	0.27 ± 0.005	0.32 ± 0.006
	Information gain	0.21± 0.002	0.17 ± 0.002	0.93 ± 0.003	0.15 ± 0.002
	Random	0.0012± 0.0001	0.001± 0.0003	0.99 ± 0.006	0.001±0.0002
Comp.	**Odds ratio**	**0.30± 0.002**	**0.33 ± 0.002**	**0.36 ± 0.009**	**0.57 ± 0.005**
	Term frequency	0.27± 0.003	0.26 ± 0.002	0.45 ± 0.003	0.27 ± 0.003
	Mutual info. Txt	0.25± 0.003	0.24 ± 0.004	0.60 ± 0.006	0.26 ± 0.006
	Cross entropy Txt	0.19± 0.005	0.21 ± 0.004	0.28 ± 0.004	0.27 ± 0.002
	Information gain	0.19± 0.007	0.14 ± 0.006	0.94 ± 0.004	0.12 ± 0.005
	Random	0.001± 0.0003	0.001± 0.0002	0.99 ± 0.001	0.001± 0.0002
Edu.	**Mutual info. Txt**	**0.40± 0.006**	**0.45 ± 0.009**	**0.52 ± 0.010**	**0.53 ± 0.010**
	Odds ratio	0.32± 0.005	**0.43 ± 0.005**	**0.36 ± 0.009**	**0.57 ± 0.010**
	Term frequency	**0.40± 0.010**	**0.42 ± 0.010**	**0.57 ± 0.010**	**0.45 ± 0.020**
	Cross entropy Txt	0.2 ± 0.006	0.26 ± 0.004	0.23 ± 0.010	0.37 ± 0.005
	Information gain	0.09± 0.003	0.07 ± 0.002	0.97 ± 0.003	0.07 ± 0.002
	Random	0.01± 0.001	0 ± 0.001	0.99 ± 0.002	0.001± 0.001
Ref.	**Odds ratio**	**0.37± 0.007**	**0.42 ± 0.009**	**0.46 ± 0.009**	**0.51 ± 0.012**
	Mutual info. Txt	0.34± 0.005	0.32 ± 0.005	0.69 ± 0.015	0.32 ± 0.006
	Term frequency	0.28± 0.007	0.26 ± 0.070	0.72 ± 0.007	0.26 ± 0.007
	Cross entropy Txt	0.23± 0.005	0.22 ± 0.005	0.50 ± 0.003	0.23 ± 0.005
	Information gain	0.20± 0.003	0.16 ± 0.002	0.99 ± 0.002	0.14 ± 0.002
	Random	0.05± 0.006	0.04 ± 0.005	0.99 ± 0.001	0.04 ± 0.004

Precision. Tables 2 and 3 give results of the comparison (1) and (2) respectively. We observe performance (F2-measure) for the best performing number of selected features that is in most cases vector size 1 (meaning select as many features as there are features that occur in positive examples). To get an idea about the actual number of the used features, vector size 1 means in average over categories: on 'Entertainment' 58 out of 30,998 features (0.2%), on 'Arts and Humanities' 65 out of 11,473 features (0.7%), on 'Computers and Internet' 42 out of 7,631 features (0.62%), on 'Education' 85 out of 3,198 features (2.7%), on 'References' 49 out of 928 features (5.3%). Additionally to the value

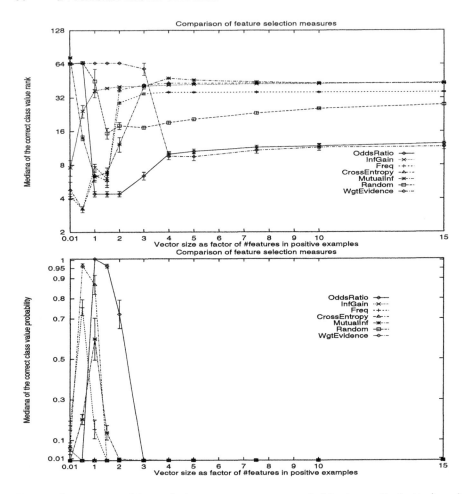

Fig. 5. Comparison of (upper) the correct category rank (the lower the better) and (lower) probability for different feature scoring measures on *'Reference'*.

of F_2-measure, we give values of Precision, Recall and F_1-measure. F_1-measure is included to show how the same feature scoring measures would compare in case we would have a problem where Precision and Recall are equally important. As we can see from Tables 2 and 3, there would not be much difference, Odds ratio and Term frequency would remain the best.

On all data sets Odds ratio is among the best performing measures (see Tables 2 and 3) and the best performance is achieved when only a small number of features is used. For instance, in Table 2 on *'Computers and Internet'* Odds ratio achieves F_2-measure of 0.60, Precision of 0.40 and Recall of 0.84, meaning that 40 % of document predicted positive are positive and that 84% of all positive documents are identified. This is consistent with the results reported in text-learning on the problem of predicting clicked hyperlinks from the set of visited Web documents [14] where the feature selection based on Odds ratio achieved the best results. Similar observation regarding the number of features is reported on text categorization in [7] , where the reduction of up to 90% in the number of features resulted in either an improvement or no loss in the system performance. Observation of standard error on all five data sets confirms that the best performing measures are significantly better than the other tested measures.

Additionally, we report two non-standard but intuitive measures: rank and probability assigned to the correct category. For each testing example we observe a list of categories each assigned a probability as a result of consulting the corresponding subproblem classifier. Sorting categories according to that probability gives ranking that we use to get the rank of the correct category. If there are more correct categories, the one with the highest predicted probability is considered. To get summary results over the testing examples we give median rather than mean, since some of the testing examples are rather non-typical of their category, containing eg., a welcome page or only one sentence asking for language preference or an error message or a page giving redirection.

Rank and probability obtained in the same experiments show that Odds ratio is again the best or one of the two best performing measures. Cross entropy for text and Term frequency achieved similar results as Odds ratio on two out of the five data sets. Information gain performed similar as Random. Tables giving the detailed results of rank and probability can be found in [10]. Standard errors confirm that the results are significant. Observation of the average number of considered categories during the classification shows that Odds ratio is considering about 3 times less categories than Cross entropy for text and about 2 times less categories than Term Frequency.

For illustration of the influence of the number of selected features we show graphs for 'Reference'. Figure 5 gives median for the correct category rank and probability on 'Reference'. It can be seen that the best performance in rank and probability is achieved by Odds ratio and Cross entropy for text using relatively small number of features (vector size 0.5-1.5). For instance, on 'References' the mediana of the correct category rank is 3.8 the mediana of the correct category probability over 0.99, ie. the half of the testing examples are assigned rank up to 3.8 and probability > 0.99 for the correct category. For larger feature subsets the rank became insensitive to the additional features, while the probability is almost 0.

To show the efficiency of the used scoring measure we give in Figure 6 the influence of the relative number of selected features to the number of categories considered in classification. For Random scoring and Information gain this number grows with the growing number of selected features (vector size). For the other measures, the number of considered categories is mostly stable when using more features (eg., using ≥ 50 features for 'Reference'). Odds ratio is the second best in the low number of considered categories and this is also one of the best performing measures. Cross entropy for text that is also among the best performing measures is the worst in the number of considered categories.

There is no significant difference in the performance between Odds ratio and any of its four variants we tested. This shows that the most important charac-

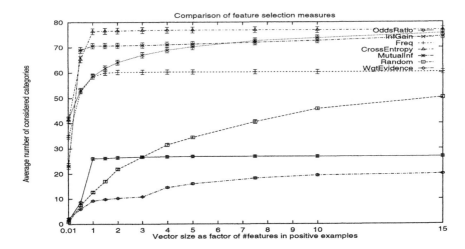

Fig. 6. Comparison of the number of considered categories (the lower the better) for different feature scoring measures on *'Reference'*.

teristics of Odds ratio are included in its variants. It also shows that we didn't get any significant improvement by including probability of word occurrence (Weighted Odds ratio) nor by including features characteristic for negative examples (Conditional Odds ratio).

7   Discussion

Mapping Web pages onto ontology is addressed here on a problem where text Web documents are organized into content hierarchy. There is some related work on automatic categorization of text documents. Koller and Sahami [6] proposed an approach to hierarchically classifying documents. They used the Reuters dataset that 'does not have a predetermined hierarchical classification structure', so they 'identified labels that tend to subsume other labels, and used those as the higher level topics'. In their hierarchy all documents are placed at the bottom of the hierarchy in tree leaves. Documents are represented as Boolean word-vectors with features representing words selected using greedy algorithm that eliminates features one by one using Cross entropy measure. They compared several learning algorithms and learn document category from the hierarchical structure, dividing classification task into a set of smaller problems corresponding to the splits in the classification hierarchy nodes. They give results on three domains each having a 3-level hierarchy that is based on up to 1,000 documents and the biggest having 12 nodes. McCallum et al. also developed an approach for learning from class hierarchies based on shrinkage [15] and reported results on the two bottom layers of the Yahoo hierarchy. However, there approach does not address the problem of documents being placed in any hierarchy node. Rather they used the same assumption as used in [6] that all the documents are places in the leaves.

The Yahoo data we are using here is much bigger, have predetermined hierarchical classification structure with document not necessarily placed only in the hierarchy leaves. This means that some documents sitting in the non-leaf nodes are too general to be classified into any of the existing leaf nodes. A classifier using these non-leaf documents should consider classification into any of the hierarchy nodes (not only leaf nodes). We use the Yahoo hierarchy for two learning problems: *assign categories* and *assign a set of keywords* to a document. For a new document, the learned model returns for each category (and the corresponding set of keywords) from in the text hierarchy the probability that the document is its member. One possibility is to use 'flattened' approach and generate one huge classifier with many class values, each value corresponding to one category. Additionally to the high number of class values, a large number of features is needed in order to cover all the variety of the large number of documents included in different categories. As pointed out in [6], an alternative idea is to split the whole problem into subproblems and use a local feature subset selection on each subproblem. We use the hierarchical structure to define subproblems each corresponding to the individual Yahoo category. For each of the subproblems, a classifier is constructed that predicts the probability for a document to be a member of the corresponding category and thus to be characterized by the corresponding set of keywords.

In our experiments with Naive Bayes the best performing feature scoring measures are Odds ratio and its variants, while the worst are Random and Information gain. The other perform comparable or worse than Odds ratio and better than Information gain. A closer look to the highly scored features by Odds ratio and by Information gain explains the huge difference in their performance and poor performance of Information gain. It also indicates how important is to consider data set and algorithm characteristics. In related work, Brank et al. [16] report that on Reuters data set, feature selection using Odds ratio indeed improves the classification results of Naive Bayes but it does not help SVM-classifier, which performs better than Naive Bayes. Testing this on our data set is an interesting problem for future work.

Yang and Pedersen [7] give experimental comparison of five measures for feature selection in text categorization on word-vectors representing documents. Their experiments confirm our observation that a rather small feature subset should be used since it gives either better or as good results as large feature subset or all the features. We also agree in the observation that a simple frequency of a feature (used after stop words removal and calculated either using term or document frequency) achieves very good results. Our results disagree in the performance of Information gain. Information gain was one of the best performing measures on problems addressed by Yang and Pedersen [7], while we found it performing poorly (similar to random) on our data. The reason for that we find in the difference in our data and classification algorithms. Their data set is defined to include one class value for each category, while we split the problem into subproblems each corresponding to one category and having binary-valued class. The result of learning is in our case a set of specialized classifiers instead of one huge classifier including the union of features characteristic for different categories. The other important issue is the used classification algorithm. Yang and Pedersen [7] used k-Nearest Neighbor and Linear Least Square Fit mapping. The specific of the Naive Bayesian classifier we are using is that it considers only features that occur in a classification document. This means that highly scored features should be features that will probably occur in new documents.

Poor performance of Information gain can be explained by its symetric treatment of class values. Here we have unbalanced class distribution and also highly unbalanced feature value distribution. When calculating feature score we observe two values for each feature (word sequence): occurs or does not occur in a document. The prior probability that a word sequence occurs in a document $P(W)$ is rather small. Most of the features selected by Information gain are features with the majority feature value ($P(\overline{W})$ is high). If $P(\overline{W}) >> P(W)$ then the high value of Information gain in most cases means that the second part $P(\overline{W}) \sum_i P(C_i|\overline{W}) \log \frac{P(C_i|\overline{W})}{P(C_i)}$ of the Information gain formula is high. In other words, knowing that W does not occur in a document brings useful information about the class value. Intuitively, when classifying a new document, a better classification results are expected if the classification is based on words that occur in a document. It is possible that absence of some words in a document is very informative and this is taken into account by the new feature scoring measure we named Conditional Odds ratio. The problem is that the classification based mostly on the absence of words is usually harder and requires larger feature subset than the classification based on word occurrences. Cross entropy for text makes distinction between the feature values and achieves good results in our experiments. Odds ratio and its variants achieve better results than Cross entropy for text mainly due to favoring features characteristic for positive examples (high $P(W|'pos')$). The other tested measures make no distinction between the class values. Moreover, Information gain makes no distinction between the feature values (it is using feature absence). Since we have unbalanced class distribution with over 90% of examples having negative class value, most of the features are characteristic for negative examples. This means that most of the features highly scored by Information gain are either informative when they do not occur in a document or they are characteristic for negative class value (just the opposite of Odds ratio!).

8   Conclusions

In analysis of our experiments of document categorization using Naive Bayes, we have observed that the best performing feature scoring measures makes difference between the class values. The best results are achieved by Odds ratio that assumes that a problem has a binary-valued class and one of the class values is the target class value (asymmetric misclassification costs). The next group of measures achieving good results all favor common features (Cross entropy for text, Term frequency). Mutual information for text differs from Cross entropy for text only in not favoring frequent features and achieves worse results. Information gain differs from Cross entropy for text only in using feature absence as well as feature presence and achieves poor results.

Our conclusion is that in general the most important characteristics of a good feature scoring measure for text are: favoring common features and considering data and algorithm characteristics. For learning algorithms that make difference between feature presence and absence, such as the Naive Bayesian classifier used here, it is important that a scoring measure also makes this difference. For the data sets with binary-valued class where one class value is the target class value, the most important characteristics of a good feature scoring measure is to make difference between the class values and favor features characteristic for the target class value. In this case, favoring common features is not an important issue. Namely, Weighted odds ratio that favors common features is not performing better than Odds ratio.

Instead of using a filtering approach to feature selection that ignores the learning algorithm or using the wrapper approach that uses the learning algorithm as a 'black-box', we suggest that data and algorithm characteristics are studied in advance. We applied the Naive Bayesian classifier to the data sets that have an unbalanced class and feature value distribution and asymmetric misclassification costs, where the minority class value is the target class value. Experimental comparison of different feature scoring measures used in feature selection shows that Odds ratio achieves the best results. Our classifier uses the same conditional probability as used in Odds ratio for scoring the features. In this way, the selected features are features expected to have the greatest influence to the posterior probability of class values returned by the Naive Bayesian classifier.

More precisely, let us consider data and algorithm characteristics to see which features should be selected. In our case the majority class value is negative ($P(neg) > P(pos)$). If we want to identify the positive documents then for such documents the Naive Bayesian classifier should assign higer probability to the positive class than to the negative class value ($P(pos|Doc) > P(neg|Doc)$). Based on the formula of Naive Bayes (see Section 2), we can see that this can be achieved only if the inside product is higher for the positive class value than for the negative class value ($\Pi_{W_j \in Doc} P(W_j|pos)^{TF(W_j, Doc)} > \Pi_{W_j \in Doc} P(W_j|neg)^{TF(W_j, Doc)}$). At the same time, Odds ratio favors words that are more common in positive documents that in negative documents ($P(W_j|pos) > P(W_j|neg)$). Having many such words selected for learning means, that we have good chances to get the above mentioned product in the classifier higher for the positive than for the negative class value. Thus our suggestion is to use Odds ratio for feature selection when using the Naive Bayesian classifier for modeling the documents.

Moreover, our experiments suggest that we should select as many best features as there are features that occur in the positive examples. Closer look to the features sorted according to Odds ratio show that this approximately means simply select all the features that occur in positive examples without performing any feature scoring. In general, we can conclude that on such problems with unbalanced class distribution and asymmetric misclassification costs, features characteristic for the positive examples should be selected.

References

1. Filo D., Y.J.: Yahoo! inc. In: http://www.yahoo.com/docs/pr/. (1997)
2. McCallum, A., N.K.: A comparison of event models for naive bayes text classifiers. In: Proceedings of the AAAI-98 Workshop on Learning for Text Categorization. (1998)
3. Mladenić, D., G.M.: Word sequences as features in text-learning. In: Proceedings of the Seventh Electrotechnical and Computer Science Conference ERK'98, Slovenia: IEEE section. (1998)
4. Agrawal R., Mannila H., S.R.T.H.V.A.: Fast discovery of association rules. In: Advances in Knowledge Discovery and Data Mining, U.M. Fayyad, G. Piatetsky-Shapiro, P. Smyth, R. Uthurusamy (Eds.). (1996)
5. Quinlan, J.: Constructing Decision Tree. Morgan Kaufman Publishers (1993)
6. Koller, D., S.M.: Hierarchically classifying documents using very few words. In: Proceedings of the 14th International Conference on Machine Learning ICML97. (1997)
7. Yang, Y., P.J.: A comparative study on feature selection in text categorization. In: Proceedings of the 14th International Conference on Machine Learning ICML97. (1997) 412–420
8. van Rijsbergen C.J., Harper D.J., P.M.: The selection of good search terms. Information Processing and Management **17** (1981) 77–91
9. Mladenić, D., G.M.: Feature selection on hierarchy of web documents. Journal of Decission support systems **35** (2003) 45–87
10. Mladenić, D.: Machine learning on non-homogeneous, distributed text data. In: PhD thesis, University of Ljubljana, Slovenia, http://www.cs.cmu.edu/~TextLearning/pww/PhD.html. (1998)
11. Mladenić, D.: Turning yahoo into an automatic web-page classifier. In: Proceedings of the 13th European Conference on Aritficial Intelligence ECAI'98. (1998)
12. Grobelnik M., M.D.: Efficient text categorization. In: Proceedings of the ECML-98 Workshop on Text Mining. (1998)
13. Lewis, D.: Evaluating and optimizating autonomous text classification systems. In: Proceedings of the 18th Annual International ACM-SIGIR Conference on Recsearch and Development in Information Retrieval. (1995)
14. Mladenić, D.: Feature subset selection in text-learning. In: Proceedings of the 10th European Conference on Machine Learning ECML98. (1998)
15. McCallum A., Rosenfeld R., M.T.N.A.: Improving text classification by shrinkage in a hierarchy of classes. In: Proceedings of the 15th International Conference on Machine Learning (ICML-98), Morgan Kaufmann, San Francisco, CA (1998)
16. Brank J., Grobelnik M., M.F.N.M.D.: Interaction of feature selection methods and linear classification models. In: Proceedings of the ICML-2002 Workshop on Text Learning, Sydney: The University of New South Wales (2002)

Mining Web Sites Using Wrapper Induction, Named Entities, and Post-processing

Georgios Sigletos[1,2], Georgios Paliouras[1],
Constantine D. Spyropoulos[1], and Michalis Hatzopoulos[2]

[1] Institute of Informatics and Telecommunications, NCSR "Demokritos",
P.O. BOX 60228, Aghia Paraskeyh, GR-153 10, Athens, Greece
{sigletos, paliourg, costass}@iit.demokritos.gr
[2] Department of Informatics and Telecommunications, University of Athens,
TYPA Buildings, Panepistimiopolis, Athens, Greece
{sigletos, mike}@di.uoa.gr

Abstract. This paper presents a new framework for extracting information from collections of Web pages across different sites. In the proposed framework, a standard wrapper induction algorithm is used that exploits named entity information that has been previously identified. The idea of post-processing the extraction results is introduced for resolving ambiguous fields and improving the overall extraction performance. Post-processing involves the exploitation of two additional sources of information: field transition probabilities, based on a trained bigram model, and confidence scores, estimated for each field by the wrapper induction system. A multiplicative model that is based on the product of those two probabilities is also considered for post-processing. Experiments were conducted on pages describing laptop products, collected from many different sites and in four different languages. The results highlight the effectiveness of the new framework.

1 Introduction

Information extraction (IE) is a form of shallow text processing that involves the population of a predefined template with relevant fragments directly extracted from a text document. This definition is a simplified version of the much harder free-text IE task examined by the Message Understanding Conferences (MUC) [1, 2]. Despite its simplicity, though, it has gained popularity in the past few years, due to the proliferation of the World Wide Web (WWW) and the need to recognize relevant pieces of information within the Web chaos. For example, imagine a shopping comparison agent that visits various vendor sites, extracts laptop descriptions and presents the results to the user.

Extracting information from Web sites is typically handled by specialized extraction rules, called *wrappers*. Wrapper induction [3] aims to generate wrappers, by mining highly structured collections of Web pages that are labeled with domain-specific information. At run-time, wrappers extract information from unseen collections of pages and fill the slots of a predefined template. These collections are

B. Berendt et al. (Eds.): EWMF 2003, LNAI 3209, pp. 97–112, 2004.
© Springer-Verlag Berlin Heidelberg 2004

typically built by querying an appropriate search form in a Web site and collecting the response pages, which commonly share the same content format.

A central challenge to the wrapper induction community is IE from pages across multiple sites, including unseen sites, by a single trained system. Pages collected from different sites usually exhibit multiple hypertext markup structures, including tables, nested tables, lists, etc. Current wrapper induction research relies on learning separate wrappers for different structures. Training an effective site-independent IE system is an attractive solution in terms of *scalability*, since any domain-specific page could be processed, without relying heavily on the hypertext structure.

In this paper we present a new approach to IE from Web pages across different sites. The proposed method relies on using domain specific *named entities*, identified within Web pages by a named entity recognizer tool. Those entities are embedded within the Web pages as XML tags and can serve as a page-independent common markup structure among pages from different sites. A standard wrapper induction system can be trained and exploit the additional textual information. Thus, the new system relies more on page-independent named-entity markup tags for inducing delimiter-based rules for IE and less on the hypertext markup tags, which vary among pages from multiple sites.

We experimented with STALKER [4], which performs extraction from a wide range of Web pages, by employing a special formalism that allows the specification of the output multi-place schema for the extraction task. However, information extraction from pages across different sites is a very hard problem, due to the multiple markup structures that cannot be described by a single formalism. In this paper we suggest the use of STALKER for *single-slot* extraction, i.e. extraction of isolated field instances, from pages across different sites.

A further contribution of this paper is a method for post-processing the system's extraction results in order to disambiguate fields. When applying a set of single-slot extraction rules to a Web page, one cannot exclude the possibility of identical or overlapping textual matches within the page, among different rules. For instance, rules for extracting instances of the fields *cdromSpeed* and *dvdSpeed* in pages describing laptop products may overlap or exactly match in certain text fragments, resulting in ambiguous fields. Among those predicted fields, the correct choice must be made.

To deal with the issue of ambiguous fields, two sources of information are explored: *transitions* between fields, incorporated in a bigram model, and *confidence scores*, generated by the wrapper induction system. Deciding upon the correct field can be based on information from either the trained bigram model and/or the confidence score. A multiplicative model that combines these two sources of information is also presented and compared to each of the two components.

The rest of this paper is structured as follows: Section 2.1 provides a short description of the IE task. In Section 2.2 we outline the architecture of our approach. Section 2.3 briefly describes the named entity recognition task. Section 2.4 reviews STALKER and in Section 2.5 we discuss how STALKER can be used under the proposed approach to perform IE from pages across different sites. In Section 3 we discuss the issue of post-processing the output of the STALKER system in order to resolve ambiguous fields. Section 4 presents experimental results on four-language datasets, all describing laptop products. Related work is presented in Section 5. Finally we conclude in Section 6, discussing potential improvements of our approach.

2   Information Extraction from Multiple Web Sites

2.1   Definition of the Extraction Task

Let $F = \{f_1...f_W\}$ a set of W extraction *fields* describing a domain of interest, e.g. laptop products, and d, a text page annotated by the domain expert with *instances* of those fields. A field *instance* is a pair $< t(s,e), field >$, where $t(s,e)$ is a text fragment, with s and e the indices of the fragment in page's token table, and *field* $\in F$ the annotated field. Let T, the *template* for page d that contains field instances. A field is typically a *target-slot* in T, while $t(s,e)$ is a *slot-filler*. Table 1 shows a part of a Web page describing laptop products where relevant text is highlighted in bold. Table 2 shows the hand-filled template for this page.

Table 1. Part of a Web page describing laptop products.

> ...**TransPort ZX** \
 \<font size="1"> \<b> **15"**XGA **TFT** Display \</b> \
 Intel \<b> Pentium III 600 MHZ \</b>256k Mobile processor \
 \<b> **256 MB** SDRAM up to 1GB ...

Table 2. Hand-filled populated template for the page of Table 1.

T			Short description for *field*
t(s,e)	*s,e*	*field*	
Transport ZX	47, 49	modelName	Name of laptop's model
15"	56, 58	screenSize	Size of laptop's screen
TFT	59, 60	screenType	Type of laptop's screen
Intel \<b> Pentium III	63, 67	processorName	Name of laptop's processor
600 MHZ	67, 69	processorSpeed	Speed of laptop's processor
256 MB	76, 78	ram	Laptop's ram capacity

The IE task can be defined as follows: *given a new document d and an empty template T, find all possible instances for each extraction field within d and populate T*. An extended approach to IE is to group field instances into higher-level concepts, also referred as *multi-slot* extraction [5]. However, the simpler *single-slot* approach addressed here covers a wide range of IE tasks and motivated the development of a variety of learning algorithms, [4, 6, 7, 8, 9].

2.2 The Proposed Framework

Our methodology for IE from multiple Web sites is graphically depicted in Figure 1. Three component modules process each Web page. First, a *named-entity recognizer* that identifies domain-specific named entities across pages from multiple sites. A trained *wrapper induction* system is then applied to perform information extraction as described in section 2.1. Finally, the extraction results are post-processed to improve the extraction performance. All components will be detailed in the following sections.

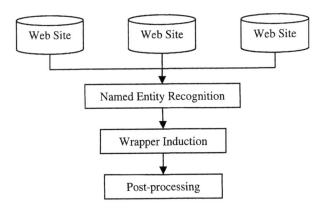

Fig. 1. Generic architecture for information extraction from multiple Web sites

2.3 Named Entity Recognition

Named entity recognition is an important subtask in most language engineering applications and has been included as such in all MUC competitions. Named entity recognition is best known as the first step in a full IE task from free-text sources, as defined in MUC, and involves the identification of a set of basic *entity names*, *numerical expressions*, *temporal expressions*, etc. However, named entity recognition has not received much attention in IE from semi-structured Web sources.

We use named entity recognition in order to identify basic named entities relevant to our task and thus reduce the complexity of IE task. The identified entities are embedded within Web pages as XML tags and serve as a valuable source of information for the wrapper induction system that follows and extracts the relevant information.

The named entity recognizer that we use is a multilingual component of an e-retail product comparison agent [10]. Although it relies on handcrafted rules for identifying domain-specific named entities, it can be rapidly extensible to new languages and domains. Future plans involve the development of a named entity recognizer using machine-learning techniques.

Table 3 shows some of the entity names (*ne*), numerical (*numex*) and temporal (*timex*) expressions, used in the laptop products domain, along with the corresponding examples of XML tags. Table 4 shows the embedded entity names in the page of Table 1.

Table 3. Subset of named entities for the laptop products domain

Entity	Entity Type	Examples of XML tags
Ne	model, process or, term	*<ne type=model>*Presario*</ne>* *<ne type=processor>*Intel Pentium *</ne>* *<ne type=term>* TFT *</ne>*
Numex	capacit y, speed, length	*<numex type=speed>*300 MHz *</numex>* *<numex type=capacity>*20 GB *</numex>* *<numex type=length>*15" *</numex>*
Timex	Duratio n	*<timex type=duration>*1 year *</timex>*

Table 4. Embedded entity names, highlighted in italic, for the page of Table 1.

... *<ne type="model">* **TransPort ZX** *</ne>*
 <font size="1"> <b> *<numex type="length">* 15"*</numex>*XGA *<ne type="term">*TFT *</ne>* Display </b>
 <ne type="processor"> Intel <b> Pentium III *</ne>* *<numex type="speed">* **600 MHZ** *</speed>* </b> *<numex type="speed">* 256k *</numex>* Mobile processor
 <b> *<numex type="capacity">* **256 MB** *<numex>* SDRAM up to *<numex type="capacity">*1GB *</numex>*...

By examining Table 4, we note that the IE task has been simplified, due to the additional named entity tags. For example, in order to identify instances of the field *modelName*, a wrapper has to be induced that identifies the left delimiter "<ne type=model>" and the right delimiter "</ne> within a page and then extract the content between the two delimiters. Such a wrapper could efficiently extract *modelName* instances within pages from multiple vendor sites by exploiting the delimiters embedded by the named entity recognizer.

The penalty, however, for the simplification of the IE task is a potential loss in the precision. Examining Table 4 we note that not all of the identified named entities correspond to the relevant information that we wish to extract. For example, the text fragment "256k" is a numerical entity of type "speed". However it is not relevant to our IE scenario. The fragment "1GB" is a numeric entity of type capacity. However it is also not relevant to our IE scenario, according to the hand-filled template of Table 2. Therefore a post-processing step is required, as will be described in section 3, aiming to remove a high proportion of the erroneously identified instances.

2.4   The STALKER Wrapper Induction System

STALKER [4] is a sequential covering rule learning system that performs *single-slot* extraction from highly-structured Web pages. *Multi-slot* extraction –i.e. linking of the isolated field instances- is feasible through an *Embedded-Catalog (EC) Tree* formalism, which may describe the common structure of a range of Web pages. The EC tree is constructed manually, usually for each site, and its leaves represent the individual fields. STALKER is capable of extracting information from pages with tabular organization of their content, as well as pages with hierarchically organized content.

Each extraction rule in STALKER consists of two ordered lists of *linear landmark automata* (LA's – also called *disjuncts*), which are a subclass of nondeterministic finite state automata. The first list constitutes the *start* rule, while the second list constitutes the *end* rule. Each rule consists of *landmarks*, i.e. groups of consecutive tokens or *wildcards* that enable the location of a field instance within a text page. A wildcard represents a class of tokens, e.g. *Number* or *HtmlTag*. A rule for extracting a field instance x within page p, consists of a *start* rule that consumes the prefix of p with respect to x, and an *end* rule, which consumes the suffix of p with respect to x. Thus the training data for inducing a start rule consists of sequences of tokens (and wildcards) that represent the *prefixes* (or *suffixes* for end rule) that must be consumed by the induced rule. Table 5 shows some examples of start rules for the laptop-products domain.

Table 5. Examples of start rules induced by STALKER.

R1 = SkipTo(type="model">)
R2 = SkipTo (type="term") OR SkipUntil (TFT)
R3 = SkipTo (type="capacity")

The rules listed in Table 5 identify the start indices of *modelName*, *screenType* and *ram* field instances respectively. Each argument of a "SkipTo" or "SkipUntil" construct is a landmark. A group of "SkipTo" and/or "SkipUntil" functions represents a linear landmark automaton. The meaning of the rule R1 is: ignore everything in the page's token table until the sequence of tokens *type="model"* is found. The rule R2 consists of an ordered list of two LA (disjuncts). The difference between "SkipTo" and "SkipUntil" constructs is that the landmark argument of "SkipUntil" is not consumed. The meaning of R2 is: ignore everything in the page's token table until the sequence of tokens *type="term"* is met. If the matching is successful then terminate. Otherwise a new search starts and everything is ignored until the token *TFT* is met, but without consuming it.

Examining Table 5 we note that STALKER's rules rely heavily on the named entity information, embedded within a page. Using STALKER's EC tree as a guide, the extraction in a given page is performed by applying –for each field- the LA's that constitute the start rule in the order in which they appear in the list. As soon as a LA is found that matches within the page, the matching process terminates. The process is symmetric for the end rule. More details on the algorithm can be found in [4].

2.5 Adapting STALKER to Multi-site Information Extraction

The EC tree formalism used in STALKER is generally not applicable for describing pages with variable markup structure. Different EC trees need to be manually built for different markup structures and thus different extraction rules to be induced. In this paper, we are seeking for a single domain-specific trainable system, without having to deal with each page structure separately. The paper focuses on the widely-used approach of single-slot extraction. Our motivation is that if isolated field instances could be accurately identified, then it is possible to link those instances separately on a second step. We therefore specify our task as follows:

For each field, try to induce a *list iteration* rule as depicted in Figure 2.

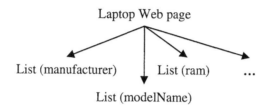

Fig. 2. Simplification of the EC tree. A list iteration rule is learned for each field and applies to the whole content of a page, at run-time

The EC tree depicted in Figure 2 has the following interpretation: a Web page that describes laptop products consists of a list of instances of the field *manufacturer* (e.g. "Compaq"), a list of instances of the field *modelName* (e.g. "Presario"), a list of *ram* instances (e.g. "256MB"), etc. The system, during runtime, exhaustively applies each rule to the content of the whole page. This simplified EC tree is independent of any particular page structure. The proposed approach relies on the page-independent named entities to lead to efficient extraction rules.

Since each extraction rule applies exhaustively within the complete Web page, rather than being constrained by the EC tree, we expect an extraction bias towards recall, i.e., overgeneration of instances for each field. The penalty is a potential loss in precision, since each rule applies to text regions that do not contain relevant information and may return erroneous instances. For example, in the page of Table 4, a rule that identifies the left delimiter *<numex type="capacity">* and the right delimiter *</numex>*, correctly identifies the text fragment "256MB" as *ram*. However the text fragment "1GB" is incorrectly identified as *ram*, since both fragments share the same left and right delimiters. Therefore we seek a post-processing mechanism capable of discarding the erroneous instances and thus improving the overall precision.

3 Post-processing the Extraction Results

In single-slot IE systems, each rule is applied independently of the others. This may naturally cause identical or overlapping matches among different rules resulting in multiple ambiguous fields for those matches. We would like to resolve such ambiguities and choose the correct field. Choosing the correct field and removing all the others shall improve the extraction precision.

3.1 Problem Specification

In this paper we adopt a post-processing approach in order to resolve ambiguities in the extraction results of the IE system. Given that $t_i(s_i, e_i)$ is a text fragment within a page p and s_i and e_i are the start and end token bounds respectively in the token table of p, then the task can be formally described as follows:

1. Let $I = \{i_j \mid i_j = <t_j, field_j>\}$ be the set of instances extracted by all the rules, where $field_j$ is the predicted field associated with the text fragment t_j.
2. Let DT be the list of all *distinct* text fragments t_j, appearing in the extracted instances in I. Note that $t_1(s_1, e_1)$ and $t_2(s_2, e_2)$ are different, if either $s_1 \neq s_2$ or $e_1 \neq e_2$. The elements of DT are sorted in ascending order of s_i.
3. If for a distinct fragment t_i in DT, there exist at least two instances i_k and i_l so that $i_k : <t_i, field_k>$ and $i_l : <t_i, field_l>$, $k \neq l$, then $field_k$ and $field_l$ are ambiguous fields for t_i.
4. The goal is to associate a single field to each element of the list DT.

To illustrate the problem, if for the fragment $t(24,25) = $"16x" in a page describing laptops, there are two extracted instances i_k and i_l, where $field_k = dvdSpeed$ and $field_l = cdromSpeed$, then there are two ambiguous fields for t_i. One of them must be chosen and associated with t_i.

3.2 Formulate the Task as a Hill-Climbing Search

Resolving ambiguous fields can be viewed as a *hill-climbing* search in the space of all possible sequences of fields that can be associated with the sequence DT of distinct text fragments.

This hill-climbing search can be formulated as follows:

1. Start from a hypothetical empty node, and transition at each step j to the next distinct text fragment t_j of the sorted sequence DT.

2. At each step apply a set of operations $Choose(field_k)$. Each operation associates t_j with the $field_k$ predicted by an instance $i_k = <t_j, field_k>$. A *weight* is assigned to each operation, based on some predefined metric. The operation with the highest weight is selected at each step.

3. The goal of the search is to associate a single field to the last distinct fragment of the sorted list DT, and thus return the final unambiguous sequence of fields for DT.

To illustrate the procedure, consider the fictitious token table in Table 6(a), which is part of a page describing laptop products.

Table 6(b) lists the instances extracted by STALKER for the token table part of Table 2(a). The DT list consists of the three distinct fragments t_1, t_2, t_3. Table 6(c) shows the two possible field sequences that can be associated with DT. After the *processorSpeed* field prediction for t_1, two operations apply for predicting a field for t_2: The *choose (ram)* and *choose (HDcapacity)* operations, each associated with a *weight*, according to a predefined metric. We assume that the former operation returns a higher weight value and therefore *ram* is the chosen field for t_2. The bold circles in the tree show the chosen sequence of fields {*processorSpeed, ram, HDcapacity*} that is attached to the sequence t_1, t_2, t_3. Table 5(6) illustrates the final extracted instances, after the disambiguation process. In this paper we explore three metrics for assigning weights to the choice operations:

1. *Confidence scores*, estimated for each field by the wrapper induction algorithm.
2. *Field-transition* probabilities, learned by a bigram model.
3. The *product* of the above probabilities, based on a simple multiplicative model.

Selecting the correct instance, and thus the correct field, at each step and discarding the others, results in improving the overall precision. However, an incorrect choice harms both the recall and the precision of a certain field. The overall goal of the disambiguation process is to improve the overall precision while keeping recall unaffected.

Table 6. (a) Part of a token table of a page dscribing laptops. (b) Instances extracted by STALKER. (c) The tree of all possible field paths (d) The extracted instances after the disambiguation process.

...	33	34	35	36	37	38	39	40	...
...	1,6	GHz	/	1	GB	/	80	GB	...

(a)

$t_i(s_i, e_i)$	$field_k$
$t_1(33,34)$	processorSpeed
$t_2(36,37)$	ram
$t_2(36,37)$	HDcapacity
$t_3(39,40)$	HDcapacity

(b)

(c)

$t_i(s_i, e_i)$	$field_k$
$t_1(33,34)$	processorSpeed
$t_2(36,37)$	ram
$t_3(39,40)$	HDcapacity

(d)

3.3   Estimating Confidence Scores

The original STALKER algorithm does not assign confidence scores to the extracted instances. In this paper we estimate confidence scores by calculating a value for each extraction rule, i.e. for each field. That value is calculated as the average *precision* obtained by a three-fold cross-validation methodology on the training set. According to this methodology, the training data is split into three equally-sized subsets and the learning algorithm is run three times. Each time two of the three pieces are used for training and the third is kept as unseen data for the evaluation of the induced extraction rules. Each of the three pieces acts as the evaluation set in one of the three runs and the final result is the average over the three runs. A three-fold cross-validation methodology for estimating confidence scores has been also used in other studies [7].

At runtime, each instance extracted by a single-slot rule will be assigned the *precision* score of that rule. For example, if the text fragment "300 Mhz" was matched by the *processorSpeed* rule, then this fragment will be assigned the confidence associated with *processorSpeed*. The key insight into using confidence scores is that among ambiguous fields, we can choose the one with the highest estimated confidence.

3.4   Learning Field Transition Probabilities

In many extraction domains, some fields appear in an almost fixed order within each page. For instance, a page describing laptop products may contain instances of the *processorSpeed* field, appearing almost immediately after instances of the *processorName* field. Training a simple bigram model is a natural way of modeling such dependencies and can be easily implemented by calculating ratios of counts (maximum likelihood estimation) in the labeled data as follows:

$$P(i \rightarrow j) = \frac{c(i \rightarrow j)}{\sum_{j \in K} c(i \rightarrow j)} , \tag{1}$$

where the nominator counts the transitions from field i to field j, according to the labeled training instances. The denominator counts the total number of transitions from field i to all fields (including self-transitions). We also calculate a *starting probability* for each field, i.e. the probability that an instance of a particular field is the first one appearing in the labeled training pages.

The motivation for using field transitions is that between ambiguous fields we could choose the one with the highest transition probability given the preceding field prediction. To illustrate that, consider that the text fragment "16 x" has been identified as both *cdromSpeed* and *dvdSpeed* within a page describing laptops. Assume also that the preceding field prediction of the system is *ram*. If the transition from *ram* to *dvdSpeed* has a higher probability, according to the learned bigram, than from *ram* to *cdromSpeed*, then we can choose the *dvdSpeed* field. If ambiguity occurs at the first extracted instance, where there is no preceding field prediction available, then we can choose the field with the highest starting probability.

3.5   Employing a Multiplicative Model

A simple way to combine the two sources of information described above is through a multiplicative model, assigning a score to each extracted instance $i_k = < t_i, field_k >$, based on the *product* of the confidence score estimated for $field_k$ and the transition probability from the preceding instance to $field_k$. Using the example of Table 6 with the two ambiguous fields *ram* and *HDcapacity* for the text fragment t_2, Table 7 depicts the probabilities assigned to each field by the two methods described in sections 3.3 and 3.4 and the multiplicative model.

Table 7. Probabilities assigned to each of the two ambiguous fields of Table 6.

$t(36,31) = $ "1 GB"	Confidence score	Bigram score	Multiplicative score
ram	0,7	0,3	0,21
HDcapacity	0,4	0,5	0,20

Using the confidence scores by the wrapper induction algorithm, the *ram* field is selected. However, using bigram probabilities, the *HDcapacity* is selected.

4   Experiments

4.1   Dataset Description

Experiments were conducted on four language corpora (Greek, French, English, Italian) describing laptop products[1].

Approximately 100 pages from each language were hand-tagged using a Web page annotation tool [11]. The corpus for each language was divided into two equally sized data sets for *training* and *testing*. Part of the test corpus was collected from sites not appearing in the training data. The named entities were embedded as XML tags within the pages of the training and test data, as illustrated in Table 4. A separate named entity recognition module was developed for each of the four languages of the project.

---

[1] http://www.iit.demokritos.gr/skel/crossmarc. Datasets are available on this site.

A total of 19 fields (listed in Table 8) were hand-filled for the laptop product domain. The pages were collected from multiple vendor sites and demonstrate a rich variety of structure, including tables, lists etc.

Table 8. Hand-filled fields for the laptop products domain

Field	Short description
manufacturer	The manufacturer of the laptop, e.g. HP
modelName	The model name, e.g. ARMADA 110
processorName	The processor name, e.g. Intel Pentium III
processorSpeed	Processor's speed , e.g. 600 MhZ
ram	RAM, e.g. 512 MB
HDcapacity	The hard disk capacity, e.g. 40 GB
price	The price of the laptop
warranty	The laptop's warranty, e.g. 2 years
screenSize	The screen size, e.g. 14''
screenType	The type of the screen, e.g. TFT
preinstalledOS	The operating system that is preinstalled, e.g. Windows XP
preinstalledSoftware	Software that is preinstalled, e.g. Norton AntiVirus
modemSpeed	The speed of the modem, e.g. 56K
weight	The weight of the laptop
cdromSpeed	The speed of the cdrom player, e.g. 48x
dvdSpeed	The speed of the dvd player (if any)
screenResolution	The resolution of the screen, e.g. 1024x768
batteryType	The type of the laptop's battery, e.g. Li-Lon
batteryLife	The duration of the battery, e.g. 3,5 h

4.2 Results

Our goal was to evaluate the effect of named entity information to the extraction performance of STALKER and compare the three different methods for resolving ambiguous fields.

We, therefore, conducted two groups of experiments. In the first group we evaluated STALKER on the testing datasets for each language, with the named entities embedded as XML tags within the pages. Table 9 presents the results. The evaluation metrics are *micro-average recall* and *micro-average precision* [12] over all 19 fields. The last row of Table 9 averages the results over all languages.

Table 9. Evaluation results for STALKER in four languages

Language	Micro Precision (%)	Micro Recall (%)
Greek	60,5	86,8
French	64,1	93,7
English	52,2	85,1
Italian	72,8	91,9
Average	**62,4**	**89,4**

The exhaustive application of each extraction rule to the whole content of a page resulted, as expected, in a high recall, accompanied by a lower precision. However, named-entity information led a pure wrapper induction system like STALKER to achieve a bareable level of extraction performance across pages with variable structure. We also trained STALKER on the same data without embedding named entities within the pages. The result was an unacceptably high training time, accompanied by rules with many disjuncts that mostly overfit the training data. Evaluation results on the testing corpora provided recall and precision figures below 30%.

In the second group of experiments, we evaluated the post-processing methodology for resolving ambiguous fields that was described in Section 3. Results are illustrated in Table 10.

Table 10. Evaluation results after resolving ambiguities

Language	Micro Precision (%)			Micro Recall (%)		
	Conf. score	Bigram	Mult.	Conf. score	Bigram	Mult.
Greek	69,3	73,5	73,8	76,9	81,6	81,9
French	77,0	78,9	79,4	82,1	84,1	84,6
English	65,9	67,5	68,9	74,4	76,2	77,5
Italian	84,4	83,8	84,4	87,6	87,0	87,6
Average	**74,2**	**75,9**	**76,6**	**80,3**	**82,2**	**82,9**

Comparing the results of Table 9 to the results of Table 10, we conclude the following:

1. Choosing among ambiguous fields, using any of the three methods, achieves an overall increase in precision, accompanied by a lower decrease in recall. Results are very encouraging, given the difficulty of the task.
2. Using bigram field transitions for choosing among ambiguous fields achieves better results that using confidence values. However, the simple multiplicative model outperforms slightly the two single methods.

To corroborate the effectiveness of the multiplicative model, we counted the number of correct choices made by the three post-processing methods at each step of the hill-climbing process, as described in section 3.2. Results are illustrated in Table 11.

Table 11. Counting the ambiguous predictions and the correct choices

Language	Distinct t(s,e)	Ambiguous t(s,e)	Corrected (Confidence score)	Corrected (Bigram score)	Corrected (Multiplicative score)
Greek	549	490	251	331	336
French	720	574	321	364	374
English	2203	1806	915	996	1062
Italian	727	670	538	458	483
Average	**1050**	**885**	**506**	**537**	**563**

The first column of Table 11 is the number of distinct text fragments t_i, as defined in section 3.1, for all pages in the testing corpus. The second column counts the t_i with more than one –ambiguous- fields (e.g. the t_2 in Table 6). The last three columns count the correct choices made by each of the three methods.

We conclude that by using a simple multiplicative model, based on the product of bigram probabilities and STALKER-assigned confidence scores we make more correct choices than by using either of the two methods individually.

5 Related Work

Extracting information from multiple Web sites is a challenging issue for the wrapper induction community. Cohen and Fun [13] present a method for learning page-independent heuristics for IE from Web pages. However they require as input a set of existing wrappers along with the pages they correctly wrap. Cohen *et al.* [14], also present one component of a larger system that extracts information from multiple sites. A common characteristic of both the aforementioned approaches is that they need to encounter separately each different markup structure during training. In contrast to this approach, we examine the viability of trainable systems that can generalize over unseen sites, without encountering each page's specific structure.

An IE system that exploits shallow linguistic pre-processing information is presented in [6]. However, they generalize extraction rules relying on lexical units (tokens), each one associated with shallow linguistic information, e.g., lemma, part-of-speech tag, etc. We generalize rules relying on named entities, which involve contiguous lexical units, and thus providing higher flexibility to the wrapper induction algorithm.

An ontology-driven IE system from pages across different sites is presented in [15]. However, they rely on hand-crafted (provided by an ontology) regular expressions, along with a set of heuristics, in order to identify single-slot fields within a document. On the other hand, we try to induce such expressions using wrapper induction. Another ontology-driven IE system is presented in [16]. The accuracy of the induced wrappers, however, highly depends on how representative is the manually-constructed ontology for the domain of interest.

All systems mentioned in this section experiment with different corpora, and thus cannot easily be comparatively evaluated.

6 Conclusions and Future Work

This paper presented a methodology for extracting information from Web pages across different sites, which is based on using a pipeline of three component modules: a named-entity recognizer, a standard wrapper induction system, and a post-processing module for disambiguating extracted fields. Experimental results showed the viability of our approach.

The issue of disambiguating fields is important for single-slot IE systems used on the Web. For instance, *Hidden Markov Models* (HMMs) [8] are a well-known learning method for performing single-slot extraction. According to this approach, a single HMM is trained for each field. At run-time, each HMM is applied to a page, using the *Viterbi* [17] procedure, to identify relevant matches. Identified matches across different HMMs may be identical or overlapping resulting in ambiguous fields. Our post-processing methodology can thus be particularly useful to HMM extraction tasks.

Bigram modeling is a simplistic approach to the exploitation of dependencies among fields. We plan to explore higher-level interdependencies among fields, using higher order n-gram models, or probabilistic FSA, e.g. as learned by the *Alergia* algorithm [18]. Our aim is to further increase the number of correct choices made for ambiguous fields, thus further improving both recall and precision. Dependencies among fields shall be also investigated in the context of *multi-slot* extraction.

A bottleneck in existing approaches for IE is the labeling process. Despite the use of a user-friendly annotation tool [11], the labeling process is a tedious, time-consuming and error-prone task, especially when moving to a new domain. We plan to investigate *active learning* techniques [19] for reducing the amount of labeled data required. On the other hand, we anticipate that our labeled datasets will be of use as benchmarks for the comparative evaluation of other current and/or future IE systems.

Acknowledgements. This work has been partially funded by first author's research grant -provided by the NCSR "Demokritos"- and CROSSMARC, a EC-funded research project. The authors are grateful to Georgios Sakis for implementing the STALKER system.

References

1. Defense Advanced Research Projects Agency (DARPA), *Proceedings of the 4th Message Understanding Conferences (MUC-4)*, McLean, Virginia, Morgan Kaufmann (1992).
2. Defense Advanced Research Projects Agency (DARPA), *Proceedings of the 5th Message Understanding Conferences (MUC-5)*, San Mateo, CA, Morgan Kaufmann (1993).
3. Kushmerick N., Wrapper induction for Information Extraction, *PhD Thesis, Department Of computer Scienc, Univ. Of Washington* (1997).
4. Muslea, I., Minton, S., Knoblock, C., Hierarchical Wrapper Induction for Semistructured Information Sources. *Journal Of Autonomous Agents and Multi-Agent Systems*, 4:93-114 (2001).
5. Sonderland, S., Learning Information Extraction Rules for Semi-structured and Free Text, *Machine Learning*, 34-(1/3), 233-272 (1999).
6. Ciravegna, F., Adaptive Information Extraction from Text by Rule Induction and Generalization. *In Proceedings of the 17th IJCAI Conference*. Seattle (2001).
7. Freitag, D., Machine Learning for Information Extraction in Informal Domains, *Machine Learrning*, 39, 169-202 (2000).
8. Freitag, D., McCallum, A.K., Information Extraction using HMMs and Shrinkage. *AAAI-99 Workshop on Machine Learning for Information Extraction*, p.31-36 (1999).

9. Freitag, D., Kushmerick, N., Boosted Wrapper Induction, *In Proceedings of the 17th AAAI*, 59-66 (1999).
10. Grover C., McDonald S., Gearailt D.N., Karkaletsis V., Farmakiotou D., Samaritakis G., Petasis G., Pazienza M.T., Vindigni M., Vichot F., Wolinski F., Multilingual XML-based Named Entity Recognition for E-Retail Domains, *In Proceedings of the LREC –2002*, Las Palmas, May (2002).
11. Sigletos, G., Farmakiotou, D., Stamatakis, K., Paliouras, G., Karkaletsis V., Annotating Web pages for the needs of Web Information Extraction Applications. *Poster at WWW 2003*, Budapest Hungary, May 20-24 (2003).
12. Sebastiani F., Machine Learning in Automated Text Categorization, *ACM Computing Surveys*, 34(1):1-47 (2002).
13. Cohen, W., Fan, W., Learning page-independent heuristics for extracting data from Web pages. *In the Proceedings of the 8th international WWW conference (WWW-99)*. Toronto, Canada (1999).
14. Cohen, W., Hurst, M., Jensen, L., A Flexible Learning System for Wrapping Tables and Lists in HTML Documents. *Proceedings of the 11th International WWW Conference*. Hawaii, USA (2002).
15. Davulcu, H., Mukherjee, S., Ramakrishman, I.V., Extraction Techniques for Mining Services from Web Sources, *IEEE International Conference on Data Mining*, Maebashi City, Japan (2002).
16. Embley, D.W., Campbell, D.M., Jiang, Y.S., Liddle, S.W., Lonsdale, D.W., Ng Y.K., Smith, R.D., Conceptual model-based data extraction from multiple-record web documents, *Data and Knowledge Engineering*, 31(3), 227-251 (1999).
17. Rabiner, L., A tutorial on hidden Markov models and selected applications in speech recognition. *Proceedings of the IEEE* 77-2 (1989).
18. Carrasco, R., Oncina, J., Learning stochastic regular grammars by means of a state-merging method. *Grammatical Inference and Applications, ICGI'94*, p. 139-150, Spain (1994).
19. Muslea, I., Active Learning with multiple views. *PhD Thesis*, University of Southern California (2002).

Web Community Directories:
A New Approach to Web Personalization

Dimitrios Pierrakos[1], Georgios Paliouras[1], Christos Papatheodorou[2],
Vangelis Karkaletsis[1], and Marios Dikaiakos[3]

[1] Institute of Informatics and Telecommunications, NCSR "Demokritos",
15310 Ag. Paraskevi, Greece
{dpie, paliourg, vangelis}@iit.demokritos.gr
[2] Department of Archive & Library Sciences, Ionian University 49100, Corfu, Greece
papatheodor@ionio.gr
[3] Department of Computer Science, University of Cyprus
CY1678, Nicosia, Cyprus
mdd@ucy.ac.cy

Abstract. This paper introduces a new approach to Web Personalization, named Web Community Directories that aims to tackle the problem of information overload on the WWW. This is realized by applying personalization techniques to the well-known concept of Web Directories. The Web directory is viewed as a concept hierarchy which is generated by a content-based document clustering method. Personalization is realized by constructing community models on the basis of usage data collected by the proxy servers of an Internet Service Provider. For the construction of the community models, a new data mining algorithm, called Community Directory Miner, is used. This is a simple cluster mining algorithm which has been extended to ascend a concept hierarchy, and specialize it to the needs of user communities. The data that are mined present a number of peculiarities such as their large volume and semantic diversity. Initial results presented in this paper illustrate the use of the methodology and provide an indication of the behavior of the new mining method.

1 Introduction

The hypergraphical architecture of the Web has been used to support claims that the Web will make Internet-based services really user-friendly. However, at its current state, the Web has not achieved its goal of providing easy access to online information. Being an almost unstructured and heterogeneous environment it creates an information overload and places obstacles in the way users access the required information.

One approach towards the alleviation of this problem is the organization of Web content into thematic hierarchies, also known as *Web directories*. A Web directory, such as Yahoo! [21] or the Open Directory Project [17], allows Web users to locate information that relates to their interests, through a hierarchy navigation process. This approach suffers though from a number of problems.

B. Berendt et al. (Eds.): EWMF 2003, LNAI 3209, pp. 113–129, 2004.
© Springer-Verlag Berlin Heidelberg 2004

The manual creation and maintenance of the Web directories leads to limited coverage of the topics that are contained in those directories, since there are millions of Web pages and the rate of expansion is very high. In addition, the size and complexity of the directories is cancelling out any gains that were expected with respect to the information overload problem, i.e., it is often difficult for a particular user to navigate to interesting information.

An alternative solution is the personalization of the services on the Web. *Web Personalization* [12] focuses on the adaptability of Web-based information systems to the needs and interests of individuals or groups of users and aims to make the Web a friendlier environment. Typically, a personalized Web site recognizes its users, collects information about their preferences and adapts its services, in order to match the users' needs. A major obstacle towards realizing Web personalization is the acquisition of accurate and operational models for the users. Reliance to manual creation of these models, either by the users or by domain experts, is inadequate for various reasons, among which the annoyance of the users and the difficulty of verifying and maintaining the resulting models. An alternative approach is that of *Web Usage Mining* [20], which uses data mining methods to create models, based on the analysis of usage data, i.e., records of how a service on the Web is used. Web usage mining provides a methodology for the collection and preprocessing of usage data, and the construction of models representing the behavior and the interests of users [16].

In this paper, we propose a solution to the problem of information overload, by combining the strengths of Web Directories and Web Personalization, in order to address some of the above-mentioned issues. In particular we focus on the construction of usable Web directories that correspond to the interests of groups of users, known as *user communities*. The construction of user community models with the aid of Web Usage Mining has so far only been studied in the context of specific Web sites [15]. This approach is extended here to a much larger portion of the Web, through the analysis of usage data collected by the proxy servers of an Internet Service Provider (ISP). The final goal is the construction of community-specific Web Directories. Web Community Directories can be employed by various services on the Web, such as Web portals, in order to offer their subscribers a more personalized view of the Web. The members of a community can use the community directory as a starting point for navigating the Web, based on the topics that they are interested in, without the requirement of accessing vast Web directories. In this manner, the information overload is reduced by presenting only a "snapshot" of the initial Web Directory which is directly related with the users' interests. At the same time the service offers added value to its customers since user's navigation time inside the Web Directory is reduced.

The construction of community directories with usage mining raises a number of interesting research issues, which are addressed in this paper. The first challenge is the analysis of large datasets in order to identify community behavior. In addition to the heavy traffic expected at a central node, such as an ISP, a peculiarity of the data is that they do not correspond to hits within the boundaries of a site, but record outgoing traffic to the whole of the Web. This fact leads to the increased dimensionality and the semantic incoherence of the data, i.e., the Web pages that have been accessed. In order to address these issues we create a thematic hierarchy of the Web pages by examining their content, and assign the Web pages to the categories of this hierarchy. An agglomerative clustering approach is used to construct the hierarchy with nodes representing content categories. A community construction method then exploits the constructed hierarchy and specializes it to the interests of particular communities. The basic data mining algorithm that has been developed for that purpose, the *Community Directory Miner* (CDM), is an extension of the *cluster mining* algorithm, which has been used for the construction of site-specific communities in previous work [15]. The new method proposed here is able to ascend an existing directory in order to arrive at a suitable level of semantic characterization of the interests of a particular community.

The rest of this paper is organized as follows. Section 2 presents existing approaches to Web personalization with usage mining methods that are related to the work presented here. Section 3 presents in detail our methodology for the construction of Web community directories. Section 4 provides results of the application of the methodology to the usage data of an ISP. Finally section 5 summarizes the most interesting conclusions of this work and presents promising paths for future research.

2   Related Work

In recent years, the exploitation of usage mining methods for Web personalization has attracted considerable attention and a number of systems use information from Web server log files to construct user models that represent the behavior of the users. Their differences are in the method that they employ for the construction of user models, as well as in the way that this knowledge, i.e., the models, is exploited. Clustering methods, e.g. [8], [11] and [22], classification methods, e.g. [14], and sequential pattern discovery, e.g. [18], have been employed to create user models. These models are subsequently used to customize the Web site and recommend links to follow.

Usage data have also been combined with the content of Web pages in [13]. In this approach content profiles are created using clustering techniques. Content profiles represent the users' interests for accessed pages with similar content and are combined with usage profiles to support the recommendation process. A similar approach is presented in [7]. Content and usage data are aggregated and clustering methods are employed for the creation of richer user profiles. In [5], Web content data are clustered for the categorization of the Web pages that are accessed by users. These categories are subsequently used to classify Web usage data.

Personalized Web directories, on the other hand, are mainly associated with services such as Yahoo! [21] and Excite [6], which support manual personalization by the user. A semi-automated approach for the personalization of a Web Directory like ODP, is presented in [19]. In this work, a high level language, named *Semantic Channel Specification Language (SCSL)*, is defined in order to allow users to specify a personalized view of the directory. This view consists of categories from the Web Directories that are chosen by exploiting the declarations, offered by SCSL.

Full automation of the personalization process, with the aid of usage mining methods is proposed in the Montage system [1]. This system is used to create personalized portals, consisting primarily of links to the Web pages that a particular user has visited, organized into thematic categories according to the ODP directory. For the construction of the user model, a number of heuristic metrics are used, such as the interest in a page or a topic, the probability of revisiting a page, etc. An alternative approach is the construction of a directory of useful links (bookmarks) for an individual user, as adopted by the PowerBookmarks system [9]. The system collects "bookmark" information for a particular user, such as frequently visited pages, query results from a search engine, etc. Text classification techniques are used for the assignment of labels to Web pages. An important issue regarding these methods is the scalability of the classification methods that they use. These methods may be suitable for constructing models of what a single user usually views, but their extendibility to aggregate user models is questionable. Furthermore, the requirement for a small set of predefined classes complicates the construction of rich hierarchical models.

In contrast to existing work, this paper proposes a novel methodology for the construction of Web directories according to the preferences of user communities, by combining document clustering and usage mining techniques. A hierarchical clustering method is employed for document clustering using the content of the Web pages. Subsequently, the hierarchy of document categories is exploited by the Web usage mining process and the complete paths of this hierarchy are used for the construction of Web community directories. This approach differs from the related work mentioned above, where the content of the Web pages is clustered in order to either enhance the user profiles or to assign Web usage data to content categories. The community models are aggregate user models, constructed with the use of a simple cluster mining method, which has been extended to ascend a concept hierarchy, such as a Web directory, and specialize it to the preferences of the community.

The construction of the communities is based on usage data collected by the proxy servers of an Internet Service Provider (ISP), which is also a task that has not been addressed adequately in the literature. This type of data has a number of peculiarities, such as its large volume and its semantic diversity, as it records the navigational behavior of the users throughout the Web, rather than within a particular Web site. The methodology presented here addresses these issues and proposes a new way of exploiting the extracted knowledge. Instead of link recommendation or site customization, it focuses on the construction of Web community directories, as a new way of personalizing services on the Web.

3   Constructing Web Community Directories

The construction of Web community directories is seen here as the end result of a usage mining process on data collected at the proxy servers of a central service on the Web. This process consists of the following steps:

- Data Collection and Preprocessing, comprising the collection and cleaning of the data, their characterization using the content of the Web pages, and the identification of user sessions. Note that this step involves a separate data mining process for the discovery of content categories and the characterization of the pages.
- Pattern Discovery, comprising the extraction of user communities from the data with a suitably extended cluster mining technique, which is able to ascend a thematic hierarchy, in order to discover interesting patterns.
- Knowledge Post-Processing, comprising the translation of community models into Web community directories and their evaluation.

An architectural overview of the discovery process is given in Figure 1, and described in the following sections.

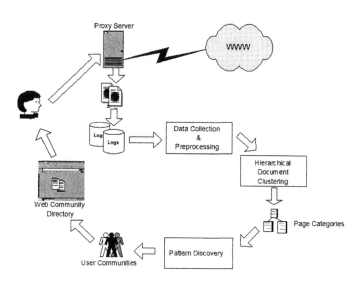

Fig. 1. The process of constructing Web Community Directories.

3.1   Data Collection and Preprocessing

The usage data that form the basis for the construction of the communities are collected in the access log files of proxy servers, e.g. ISP cache proxy servers. These data record the navigation of the subscribers through the Web. No record of the user's identification is being used, in order to avoid privacy violations. However, the data collected in the logs are usually diverse and voluminous. The outgoing traffic is much higher than the usual incoming traffic of a Web site and the visited pages less coherent semantically. The task of data preprocessing is to assemble these data into a consistent, integrated and comprehensive view, in order to be used for pattern discovery. The first stage of data preprocessing involves data cleaning. The aim is to remove as much noise from the data as possible, in order to keep only the Web pages that are directly related to the user behavior. This involves the filtering of the log files to remove data that are downloaded without a user explicitly requesting them, such as multimedia content, advertisements, Web counters, etc. Records with HTTP error codes that correspond to bad requests, or unauthorized accesses are also removed.

The second stage of data preprocessing involves the thematic categorization of Web pages, thus reducing the dimensionality and the semantic diversity of data. Typically, Web page categorization approaches, e.g. [4] and [10], use text classification methods to construct models for a small number of known thematic categories of a Web directory, such as that of Yahoo!. These models are then used to assign each visited page to a category. The limitation of this approach with respect to the methodology proposed here, is that it is based on a dataset for training the classifiers, which is usually limited in scope, i.e., covers only part of the directory. Furthermore, a manually-constructed Web directory is required, suffering from low coverage of the Web.

In contrast to this approach, we build a taxonomy of Web pages included in the log files. This is realized by a document clustering approach, which is based on terms that are frequently encountered in the Web pages. Each Web page is represented by a binary feature vector, where each feature encodes the presence of a particular term in the document. A hierarchical agglomerative approach [23] is employed for document clustering. The nodes of the resulting hierarchy represent clusters of Web pages that form thematic categories. By exploiting this taxonomy, a mapping can be obtained between the Web pages and the categories that each page is assigned to. Moreover, the most important terms for each category can be extracted, and be used for descriptive labeling of the category. For the sake of brevity we choose to label each category using a numeric coding scheme, representing the path from the root to the category node, e.g. "1.4.8.19" where "1" corresponds to the root of the tree.

This document clustering approach has the following advantages: first a hierarchical classification of Web documents is constructed without any human expert intervention or other external knowledge; second the dimensionality of the space is significantly reduced since we are now examining the page categories instead of the pages themselves; and third the thematic categorization is directly related to the preferences and interests of the users, i.e. the pages they have chosen to visit.

The third stage of preprocessing involves the extraction of access sessions. An access session is a sequence of log entries, i.e., accesses to Web pages by the same IP address, where the time interval between two subsequent entries does not exceed a certain time interval. In our approach, pages are mapped onto thematic categories that correspond to the leaves of the hierarchy and therefore an access session is translated into a sequence of categories.

Access sessions are the main input to the pattern discovery phase, and are extracted as follows:

1. Grouping the logs by date and IP address.
2. Selecting a time-frame within which two records from the same IP address can be considered to belong in the same access session.
3. Grouping the Web pages (thematic categories) accessed by the same IP address within the selected time-frame to form a session.

Finally, access sessions are translated into binary feature vectors. Each feature in the vector represents the presence of a category in that session.

Note that in the current approach we are simply interested of the presence or absence of category in a given session. There are though cases, where a certain category has multiple occurrences in a session that probably shows that a user is particularly interest in the topic that this category represents. This information is lost where the sessions are translated into binary vectors. This is an important issue for the personalization of the Web directories that we be handled in a future work.

3.2   Extraction of Web Community Directories

Once the data have been translated into feature vectors, they are used to discover patterns of interest, in the form of community models. This is done by the *Community Directory Miner* (CDM), an enhanced version of the cluster mining algorithm. This approach is based on the work presented in [15] for site-specific communities.

Cluster mining discovers patterns of common behavior by looking for all maximal fully-connected subgraphs (cliques) of a graph that represents the users' characteristic features, i.e., thematic categories in our case. The method starts by constructing a weighted graph $G(A, E, WA, WE)$. The set of vertices A corresponds to the descriptive features used in the input data. The set of edges E corresponds to feature co-occurrence as observed in the data. For instance, if the user visits pages belonging to categories "1.3.5" and "1.7.8" an edge is created between the relevant vertices. The weights on the vertices W_A and the edges W_E are computed as the feature occurrence and co-occurrence frequencies respectively.

Cluster mining does not attempt to form independent user groups, but the generated clusters group together characteristic features of the users directly. If needed, a user can be associated with the clique(s) that best match the user's behaviour. Alternatively each user can be associated probabilistically with each of the cliques. The focus of our work is on the discovery of the behavioural patterns of user communities. For this reason, no attempt is made to match individual users with the cliques generated by the cluster mining algorithm.

Figure 2 shows an example of such a graph. The connectivity of the graph is usually very high. For this reason we make use of a connectivity threshold aiming to reduce the edges of the graph. This threshold is related to the frequency of the thematic categories in the data. In our example in Figure 2, if the threshold is 0.07 the edge ("1.3.5", "1.3.6") is dropped.

Once, the connectivity of the graph has been reduced,the weighted graph is turned to an unweighted one. This is realised by replacing in the adjacency matrix of the original graph the remaining weights with 1's and the removed weights, due to the threshold, with 0's. This is a simplified approach for handling the initial weights of the graph and further work is required in order to be able to include these weights in the process. Finally all maximal cliques of the unweighted graph are generated, each one corresponding to a community model. One important advantage of this approach is that each user may be assigned to many communities, unlike most user clustering methods.

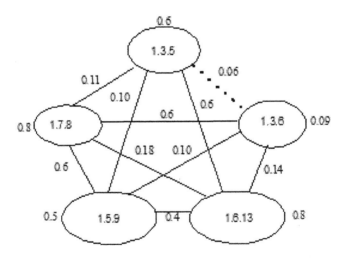

Fig. 2. An example of a graph for cluster mining.

CDM enhances cluster mining so as to be able to ascend a hierarchy of topic categories. This is achieved by updating the weights of the vertices and the nodes in the graph. Initially, each category is mapped onto a set of categories, corresponding to its parent and grandparents in the thematic hierarchy. Thus, the category "1.6.12.122.258" is also mapped onto the following categories: "1", "1.6", "1.6.12", "1.6.12.122". The frequency of each of these categories is increased by the frequency of the initial child category. Thus, the frequency of each category corresponds to its own original frequency, plus the frequency of its children. The underlying assumption for the update of the weights is that if a certain category exists in the data, then its parent categories should also be examined for the construction of the community model. In this manner, even if a category (or a pair of categories) have a low occurrence (co-occurrence) frequency, their parents may have a sufficiently high frequency to be included in a community model. This enhancement allows the algorithm to start from a particular category and ascend the topic hierarchy accordingly. The result is the construction of a topic tree, even if only a few nodes of the tree exist in the usage data.

The CDM algorithm can be summarized in the following steps:

1. **Step 1:** *Compute frequencies of categories that correspond to the weights of the vertices.* More formally, if a_{ij} is the value of a feature i in the binary feature vector j, and there are N vectors, the weight w_i for that vertex is calculated as follows:

$$w_i = \frac{\sum_{j=1}^{N} a_{ij}}{N} \tag{1}$$

2. **Step 2:** *Compute co-occurrence frequencies between categories that correspond to the weights of the edges.* If a_{ik}^j is a binary indicator of whether features i and k co-occur in vector j, then the weight of the edge w_{ik} is calculated as follows:

$$w_{ik} = \frac{\sum_{j=1}^{N} a_{ik}^j}{N} \tag{2}$$

3. **Step 3:** *Update the weights of categories, i.e. vertices, by adding the frequencies of their children.* More formally, if w_p is the weight of a parent vertex p and w_i is the weight of a child vertex i, the final weight w_p' of the parent is computed as follows:

$$w_p' = w_p + \sum_i w_i \tag{3}$$

This calculation is repeated recursively ascending the hierarchy of the Web directory. Similarly, the edge weights are updated, as all the parents and grandparents of the categories that co-occur in a session, are also assumed to co-occur.

4. **Step 4:** *Turn the weighted graph of categories into an unweighted one by removing all the weights from the nodes and the edges and find all the maximal cliques.* [3].

3.3   Post-processing the Web Community Directories

The discovered patterns are topic trees, representing the community models, i.e., behavioral patterns that occur frequently in the data. That means that each clique generated by the CDM algorithm contains the complete path of each of the categories, i.e. the category itself as well as its parent categories. These models are usable as Web community directories, and can be delivered by various means to the users of a community. A pictorial view of such a directory is shown in Figure 3, where the community directory is "superimposed" onto the hierarchy of categories. Grey boxes represent the categories that belong to a particular community, while white boxes represent the rest of the categories in the Web directory. Each category has been labelled using the most frequent terms of the Web pages that belong to this category. The categories "12.2", "18.79" and "18.85" appear in the community model, due to the frequency of their children. Furthermore, some of their children, e.g. "18.79.5" and "18.79.6" (the spotted boxes) may also not be sufficiently frequent to appear in the model. Nevertheless, they force their parent category, i.e., "18.79" into the model.

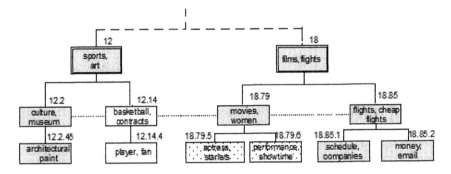

Fig. 3. An example of a Web community directory.

Thus, the initial Web Directory is shrinked, as some of the categories are completely removed. For example the categories labelled "12" and "12.2" do not appear in the final Web Community Directory, since the sibling of node "12.2" has been removed and therefore nodes "12" and "12.2" deterministically lead to the leaf category "12.2.45". However, some of the categories that do not belong in the community directory, according to the CDM algorithm, are maintained and presented to the final user. In particular, we ignore the bottom-up pruning of the directory, achieved by CDM. In our example although the category "18.79" has been identified as a leaf node of the Web Community Directory, in the presentation of the directory to the user we keep the child categories "18.79.5" and "18.79.6". The reason for ignoring the bottom-up pruning of the directory, is that although we end up with a smaller tree, the number of Web pages included in the higher-level nodes is bound to be overwhelming for the user. In other words, we prefer to maintain the original directory structure below the leaf nodes of the community directory, rather than associating a high-level category with a large list of Web pages, i.e., the pages of all its sub-categories. Clearly, this removes one of the gains from the CDM algorithm and further work is required in order to be able to selectively take advantage of the bottom-up pruning.

4   Experimental Results

The methodology introduced in this paper for the construction of Web community directories has been tested in the context of a research project, which focuses on the analysis of usage data from the proxy server logs of an Internet Service Provider. We analyzed log files consisting of 781,069 records. In the stage of pre-processing, data cleaning has been performed and the remaining data has been characterized using the hierarchical agglomerative clustering mentioned in section 3.1. The process resulted in the creation of 998 distinct categories. Based on these characterized data, we constructed 2,253 user sessions, using a time-interval of 60 minutes as a threshold on the "silence" period between two consecutive requests from the same IP. After mapping the Web pages of the sessions to the categories of the hierarchy, we translated the sessions into binary vectors and analyzed them by the CDM algorithm, in order to identify community models, in the form of topic trees.

The evaluation process consisted of two phases. In the first phase we evaluated the methodology that we employed to construct our models, whilst in the second phase we evaluated the usability of our models, i.e. the way that real-world users can benefit from the We Community Directories approach that we have employed.

4.1   Model Evaluation

Having generated the community models, we need to decide on their desired properties, in order to evaluate them. For this purpose, we use ideas from existing work on community modeling and in particular the measure of distinctiveness [15]. When there are only small differences between the models, accounting for variants of the same community, the segmentation of users into communities is not interesting. Thus, we are interested in community models that are as distinct from each other as possible. We measure the distinctiveness of a set of models M by the ratio between the number of distinct categories that appear in M and the total number of categories in M. Thus, if J the number of models in M, A_j the categories used in the j-th model, and A' the different categories appearing at least in one model, distinctiveness is given by equation 4.

$$Distinctiveness(M) = \frac{\|A'\|}{\sum_j A_j} \qquad (4)$$

As an example, if there exits a community model with the following simple (one-level) communities:

Community 1: 12.3.4, 18.3.2, 15.6.4
Community 2: 15.6.4, 2.3.6
Community 3: 12.3.4, 2.3.6

then the number of distinct categories is 4, i.e., 12.3.4, 18.3.2, 15.6.4, and 2.3.6, while the total number of categories is 7. Thus, the distinctiveness of the model is 0.57. The optimization of distinctiveness by a set of community models indicates the presence of useful knowledge in the set. Additionally, the number of distinct categories A' that are used in a set of community models is also of interest as it shows the extent to which there is a focus on a subset of categories by the users.

Figures 4 and 5 present the results that we obtained, using these two model evaluation measures.

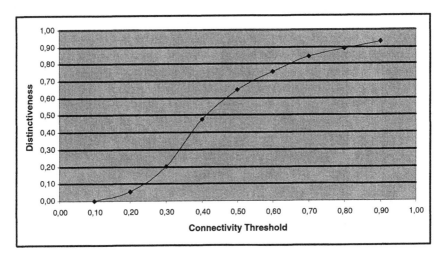

Fig. 4. Distinctiveness as a function of the connectivity threshold.

Figure 4 shows how the distinctiveness of the resulting community models increases as the connectivity threshold increases, i.e., as the requirement on the frequency of occurrence/co-occurrence becomes "stricter". The rate of increase is higher for smaller values of the threshold and starts to dampen down for values above 0.7. This effect is justified by the decrease in the number of distinct categories, as shown in Figure 5. Nevertheless, more than half of the categories have frequency of occurrence greater than 600 (threshold 0.6), while at that threshold value the level of distinctiveness exceeds 0.7, i.e. 70% of the categories that appear in the model are distinct. These figures provide an indication of the behavior and the effectiveness of the community modeling algorithm. At the same time, they assist in selecting an appropriate value for the connectivity threshold and a corresponding set of community models. Not that, in the current approach the selection of the proper value of the connectivity threshold is done manually, although we are examining more sophisticated techniques in order to automate this process.

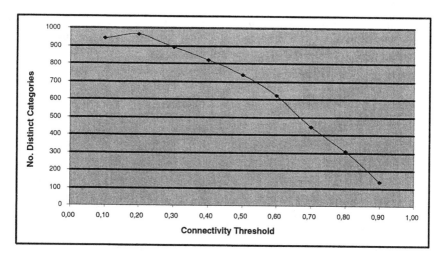

Fig. 5. Number of distinct categories as a function of the connectivity threshold.

4.2 Usability Evaluation

Apart from evaluating the composition of our model we have also considered a methodology that shows how a real-world user can benefit from our approach. This methodology has focused on: (a) how well our model can predict what the user is looking for, and (b) what the user gains by using a Web Community Directory against using the original Web Directory.

In order to realize this, we followed a common approach used for recommendation systems [2], i.e., we have hidden the last hit, i.e. category, of each user session, and tried to see whether and how the user can get to it, using the community directory to which the particular user session is assigned. The hidden category is called the "target" category here. The assignment of a user session to a community directory is based on the remaining categories of the session and is done as follows:

1. For each of the categories in the user session, excluding the "target" category, we identified the community directories that contain it, if any.
2. Since the categories in the access sessions might belong to more than one community directory, we identified the three most prevalent community directories, i.e. the directories that contain most of the categories in a particular access session.
3. From these three prevalent community directories a new and larger directory is constructed by joining the three hierarchies. In this manner, a session-specific community directory is constructed.

The resulting, session-specific directories are used in the evaluation.

The first step of the evaluation process was to estimate the coverage of our model, which corresponds to the predictiveness of our model, i.e. the number of target categories that are covered by the corresponding community directories. This is achieved by counting the number of user sessions, for which the community directory, as explained before, covers the target category. The results for various connectivity thresholds are shown in Figure 6.

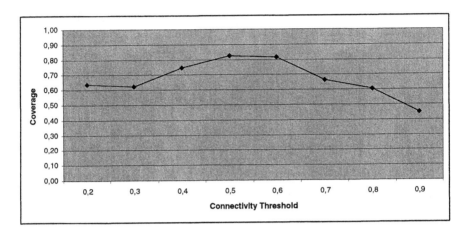

Fig. 6. Model Coverage as a function of the connectivity threshold.

The next step of the usability evaluation was to estimate the actual gain that a user would have by following the community directory structure, instead of the complete Web directory. In order to realize this we followed a simple approach that is based on the calculation of the effort that a user is required to exert in order to arrive at the target category. We estimated this effort based on the user's navigation path inside a directory, in order to arrive at the target category. This is estimated by a new metric, named *ClickPath*, which takes into account the depth of the navigation path as well as the branching factor at each step. More formally:

$$ClickPath = \sum_{j=1}^{d} b_j, \tag{5}$$

where d the depth of the path and b_j the branching factor at the j-th step.

Hence, for each user session whose target category is covered by the corresponding community directory, we calculated the ClickPath for the community directory and for the original Web Directory. The final user gain is estimated as the ratio of these two results, and for various thresholds it is shown in Figure 7.

From the above figures we can conclude that regarding the coverage of our model more than 80% of the target categories can be predicted. At the same time the user gain is around 20%, despite the fact that we completely ignore the bottom-up pruning that can be achieved by the CDM algorithm, as explained in

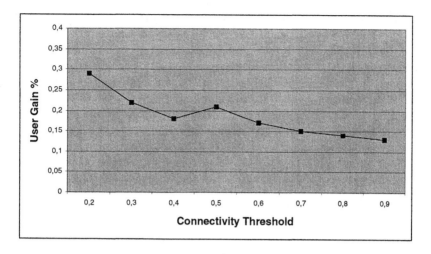

Fig. 7. User Gain as a function of the connectivity threshold.

section 3.3. These numbers give us an initial indication of the benefits that we can obtain by personalizing Web Directories to the needs and interests of user communities. However, we have only estimated the gain of the end user and we have not weighted up any "losses" that could be encountered in the case the user would not find the interesting category that is looking for in the personalised directory. This issue would be examined in a future work.

5   Conclusions and Future Work

This paper has introduced the concept of a Web Community Directory, as a Web Directory that specialises to the needs and interests of particular user communities. Furthermore, it presented a novel methodology for the construction of such directories, with the aid of document clustering and Web usage mining. In this case, user community models take the form of thematic hierarchies and are constructed by a cluster mining algorithm, which has been extended to take advantage of an existing directory, and ascend its hierarchical structure. The initial directory is generated by a document clustering algorithm, based on the content of the pages appearing in an access log.

We have tested this methodology by applying it on access logs collected at the proxy servers of an ISP and have provided initial results, indicative of the behavior of the mining algorithm and the usability of the resulting Web Community Directories. Proxy server logs have introduced a number of interesting challenges, such as their size and their semantic diversity. The proposed methodology handles these problems by reducing the dimensionality of the problem, through the categorization of individual Web pages into the categories of a Web directory, as constructed by document clustering. In this manner, the corresponding community models take the form of thematic hierarchies.

The combination of two different approaches to the problem of information overload on the Web, i.e. thematic hierarchies and personalization, as proposed in this paper, introduces a promising research direction, where many new issues arise. Various components of the methodology could be replaced by a number of alternatives. For instance, other mining methods could be adapted to the task of discovering community directories and compared to the algorithm presented here. Similarly, different methods of constructing the initial thematic hierarchy could be examined. Moreover, additional evaluation is required, in order to test the robustness of the mining algorithm to a changing environment.

Another important issue that will be examined in a further work is the scalability of our approach, to larger datasets,i.e. for larger log files that would result in a larger number of sessions. However, the performance of the the the whole process, together with the CDM algorithm itself, gave us promising indications for the scalability of our method. Finally, more sophisticated metrics could also be employed for examining the usability of the resulting community directories.

Acknowledgements. This research has been partially funded by the Greece-Cyprus Research Cooperation project "Web-C-Mine: Data Mining from Web Cache and Proxy Log Files".

References

1. C. R. Anderson and E. Horvitz. Web montage: A dynamic personalized start page. In *11th WWW Conference*, Honolulu, Hawaii, USA, May 2002.
2. J. S. Breese, D. Heckerman, and C.M Kadie. Empirical analysis of predictive algorithms for collaborative filtering. In *14th International Conference on Uncertainty in Artificial Intelligence, (UAI)*, pages 43–52, University of Wisconsin Business School, Madison, Wisconsin, USA, July 24-26 1998. Morgan Kaufmann.
3. C. Bron and J. Kerbosch. Algorithm 457—finding all cliques of an undirected graph. *Communications of the ACM*, 16(9):575–577, 1973.
4. H. Chen and S. T. Dumais. Bringing order to the web: automatically categorizing search results. In *CHI'00, Human Factors in Computing Systems*, pages 145–152, The Hague, Netherlands, April 1-6 2000.
5. R. Cooley. *Web Usage Mining: Discovery and Application of Interesting Patterns from Web Data*. PhD thesis, University of Minnesota, May 2000.
6. Excite. http://www.excite.com.
7. J. Heer and Ed H. Chi. Identification of web user traffic composition using multimodal clustering and information scent. In *Workshop on Web Mining, SIAM Conference on Data Mining*, pages 51–58, 2001.
8. T. Kamdar and A. Joshi. On creating adaptive web sites using weblog mining. Technical report, Department of Computer Science and Electrical Engineering, University of Maryland, Baltimore County, 2000.
9. W-S. Li, Q. Vu, E. Chang, D. Agrawal, Y. Hara, and H. Takano. Powerbookmarks: A system for personalizable web information organization, sharing, and management. In *8th International World Wide Web Conference, Toronto, Canada*, May 1999.

10. D Mladenic. Turning yahoo into an automatic web-page classifier. In *13th European Conference on Artificial Intelligence, ECAI'98*, pages 473–474, Brighton, UK, 1998. ECCAI Press.

11. B. Mobasher, R. Cooley, and J. Srivastava. Creating adaptive web sites through usage-based clustering of urls. In *IEEE Knowledge and Data Engineering Exchange Workshop, KDEX99*, 1999.

12. B. Mobasher, R. Cooley, and J. Srivastava. Automatic personalization based on web usage mining. *Communications of the ACM*, 43(8):142–151, 2000.

13. B. Mobasher, H. Dai, T. Luo, Y. Sung, and J. Zhu. Integrating web usage and content mining for more effective personalization. In *International Conference on E-Commerce and Web Technologies, ECWeb2000*, pages 165–176, Greenwich, UK, 2000.

14. D. S. W. Ngu and X. Wu. Sitehelper: A localized agent that helps incremental exploration of the world wide web. In *6th International World Wide Web Conference*, volume 29, pages 691–700, Santa Clara, California, USA,, April 7-11 1997.

15. G. Paliouras, C. Papatheodorou, V. Karkaletsis, and C. D Spyropoulos. Discovering user communities on the internet using unsupervised machine learning techniques. *Interacting with Computers Journal*, 14(6):761–791, 2002.

16. D. Pierrakos, G. Paliouras, C. Papatheodorou, and C. D Spyropoulos. Web usage mining as a tool for personalization: a survey. *User Modeling and User-Adapted Interaction*, 13(4):311–372, 2003.

17. Open Directory Project. http://dmoz.org.

18. M. Spiliopoulou and L. C Faulstich. Wum: A web utilization miner. In *EDBT Workshop of Web and databases WebDB98*, 1998.

19. N. Spyratos, Y. Tzitzikas, and V. Christophides. On personalizing the catalogs of web portals. In *FLAIRS Conference*, pages 430–434, 2002.

20. J. Srivastava, R. Cooley, M. Deshpande, and P. T Tan. Web usage mining: Discovery and applications of usage patterns from web data. *SIGKDD Explorations*, 1(2):12–23, 2000.

21. Yahoo. http://www.yahoo.com.

22. T. W. Yan, M. Jacobsen, H. Garcia-Molina, and U. Dayal. From user access patterns to dynamic hypertext linking. In *5th World Wide Web Conference (WWW5)*, pages 1007–1014, Paris, France, May 1996.

23. Y. Zhao and G Karypis. Evaluation of hierarchical clustering algorithms for document datasets. In *CICM*, 2002.

Evaluation and Validation of Two Approaches to User Profiling

F. Esposito, G. Semeraro, S. Ferilli, M. Degemmis,
N. Di Mauro, T.M.A. Basile, and P. Lops

Dipartimento di Informatica
Università di Bari
via E. Orabona, 4 - 70125 Bari - Italia
{esposito,semeraro,ferilli,degemmis,nicodimauro,basile,lops}@di.uniba.it

Abstract. In the Internet era, huge amounts of data are available to everybody, in every place and at any moment. Searching for relevant information can be overwhelming, thus contributing to the user's sense of information overload. Building systems for assisting users in this task is often complicated by the difficulty in articulating user interests in a structured form - a profile - to be used for searching. Machine learning methods offer a promising approach to solve this problem. Our research focuses on supervised methods for learning user profiles which are predictively accurate and comprehensible.

The main goal of this paper is the comparison of two different approaches for inducing user profiles, respectively based on Inductive Logic Programming (ILP) and probabilistic methods. An experimental session has been carried out to compare the effectiveness of these methods in terms of classification accuracy, learning and classification time, when coping with the task of learning profiles from textual book descriptions rated by real users according to their tastes.

1 Introduction

The ever increasing popularity of the Internet has led to a huge increase in the number of Web sites and in the volume of available on-line data. Users are swamped with information and have difficulty in separating relevant from irrelevant information. This leads to a clear demand for automated methods able to support users in searching the extremely large Web repositories in order to retrieve relevant information with respect to users' individual preferences. The problem complexity could be lowered by the automatic construction of machine processable profiles that can be exploited to deliver *personalized* content to the user, fitting his or her personal interests.

Personalization has become a critical aspect in many popular domains such as e-commerce, where a user explicitly wants the site to store information such as preferences about himself or herself and to use this information to make recommendations. Exploiting the underlying one-to-one marketing paradigm is essential to be successful in the increasingly competitive Internet marketplace.

B. Berendt et al. (Eds.): EWMF 2003, LNAI 3209, pp. 130–147, 2004.

Recent research on intelligent information access and recommender systems has focused on the content-based information recommendation paradigm: it requires textual descriptions of the items to be recommended [6].

In general, a content-based system analyzes a set of documents rated by an individual user and exploits the content of these documents to infer a model or profile that can be used to recommend additional items of interest.

The user's profile is built and maintained according to an analysis that is applied to the contents of the documents that the user has previously rated. For example, a user profile can be a text classifier able to distinguish between interesting and uninteresting documents. In recent years, text categorization, which can be defined as the content-based assignment of one or more predefined categories to text, has emerged as an application domain to machine learning techniques. Many approaches that suggest the construction of classifiers using induction over preclassified examples have been proposed [13]. These includes numerical learning, such as Bayesian classification [4] or symbolic learning like in [8]. In [5] are presented empirical results on text categorization performance of two inductive learning algorithms, one based on Bayesian classifiers and the other on decision trees. They attempt to study the effect that characteristics of text have on inductive learning algorithms, and what are the performance of purely learning-based methods. They found that feature selection mechanisms are of crucial importance, due to the fact that the primary influence on inductive learning applied to text categorization is the large number of features that natural language provides. In this paper we present a comparison between two different learning strategies to infer models of users' interests from text: an ILP approach and a naïve bayes method. Motivation behind our research is the realization that user profiling and machine learning techniques can be used to tackle the *relevant information problem* already described.

The application of text categorization methods to the problem of learning user profiles is not new: the LIBRA system [7] makes content-based book recommending by applying a naïve Bayes text categorization method to product descriptions in Amazon.com. A similar approach, adopted by Syskill & Webert [10], tracks the users browsing to formulate user profiles. The system identifies informative words from Web pages to be used as boolean features and learns a naïve Bayesian classifier to discriminate interesting Web pages on a particular topic from uninteresting ones. The authors compare six different algorithms from machine learning and information retrieval on the task and they find that the naïve Bayesian classifier offers several advantages over other learning algorithms. They also show that the Bayesian classifier performs well, in terms of both accuracy and efficiency. Therefore, we have decided to use the naïve Bayesian classifier as the default algorithm in our Item Recommender system because it is very fast for both learning and predicting, which are crucial factors in learning user profiles. The learning time of this classifier is linear in the number of examples and its prediction time is independent of the number of examples. Moreover, our research aims at comparing this technique with a symbolic approach able to induce profiles that are more readable from a human understandability viewpoint.

Experiments reported in this paper evaluated the effects of the ILP and the Bayesian methods in learning intelligible profiles of users' interests. The experiments were conducted in the context of a content-based profiling system for virtual bookshop on the World Wide Web. In this scenario, a client side utility has been developed in order to download documents (book descriptions) for a user from the Web and to capture user's feedback regarding his liking/disliking on the downloaded documents. Then this knowledge can be exploited by the two different machine learning techniques so that when a trained system encounters a new document it can intelligently infer whether this new document will be liked by the user or not. This strategy can be used to make recommendations to the user about new books. The experiments reported here investigate also the effect of using different representations of the profiles.

The structure of the remainder of the paper is as follows: Section 2 describes the ILP system INTHELEX and its main features, while the next section introduces Item Recommender, the system that implements a statistical learning process to induce profiles from text. Then a detailed description of the experiments is given in Section 4, along with an analysis of the results by means of a statistical test. Section 5 presents how user profiles can be exploited for personalization purposes. Finally, Section 6 draws some general conclusions.

2   INTHELEX

INTHELEX (INcremental THEory Learner from EXamples) [3] is a learning system for the induction of hierarchical theories from positive and negative examples which focuses the search for refinements by exploiting the Object Identity [14] bias on the generalization model (according to which terms denoted by different names must be distinct). It is fully and inherently incremental: this means that, in addition to the possibility of taking as input a previously generated version of the theory, learning can also start from an empty theory and from the first available example; moreover, at any moment the theory is guaranteed to be correct with respect to all of the examples encountered thus far. This is a fundamental issue, since in many cases deep knowledge about the world is not available. Incremental learning is necessary when either incomplete information is available at the time of initial theory generation, or the nature of the concepts evolves dynamically, which are unnegligible issues for learning user profiles. Indeed, generally users' accesses to a source of information are distributed in time, and the system is not free to choose when to start the learning process because a theory is needed since the first access of the user. Hence, for each new access the system tries to assess the validity of the theory (if available) with respect to this new observation. INTHELEX can learn simultaneously various concepts, possibly related to each other, and is based on a closed loop architecture — i.e. the learned theory correctness is checked on any new example and, in case of failure, a revision process is activated on it, in order to restore completeness and consistency.

INTHELEX learns theories expressed as sets of Datalog^{OI} clauses (function free clauses to be interpreted according to the Object Identity assumption). It adopts a full memory storage strategy — i.e., it retains all the available examples, thus the learned theories are guaranteed to be valid on the whole set of known examples — and it incorporates two inductive operators, one for generalizing definitions that reject positive examples, and the other for specializing definitions that explain negative examples. Both these operators, when applied, change the set of examples the theory accounts for.

The logical architecture of INTHELEX is organized as in Figure 1. A set of examples of the concepts to be learned, possibly selected by an Expert, is provided by the Environment. Examples are definite ground Horn clauses, whose body describes the observation by means of only basic non-negated predicates of the representation language adopted for the problem at hand, and whose head lists all the classes for which the observed object is a positive example and all those for which it is a negative one (in this case the class is negated). Single classifications are processed separately, in the order they appear in the list, so that the teacher can still decide which concepts should be taken into account first and which should be taken into account later. It is important to note that a positive example for a concept is not considered as a negative example for all the other concepts (unless it is explicitly stated). The set of all examples can be subdivided into three subsets, namely training, tuning, and test examples, according to the way in which examples are exploited during the learning process. Specifically, training examples, previously classified by the Expert, are abstracted and stored in the base of processed examples, then exploited by the Rule Generator to obtain a theory that is able to explain them. Such an initial theory can also be provided by the Expert, or even be empty. Subsequently, the Rule Interpreter checks the validity of the theory against new available examples, also abstracted and stored in the example base, taking the set of inductive hypotheses and a tuning/test example as input and producing a decision. The Critic/Performance Evaluator compares such a decision to the correct one. In the case of incorrectness on a tuning example, it can locate the cause of the wrong decision and choose the proper kind of correction, firing the theory revision process. In this way, tuning examples are exploited incrementally by the Rule Refiner to modify incorrect hypotheses according to a data-driven strategy. The Rule Refiner consists of two distinct modules, a Rule Specializer and a Rule Generalizer, which attempt to correct hypotheses that are too weak or too strong, respectively. Test examples are exploited just to check the predictive capabilities of the theory, intended as the behavior of the theory on new observations, without causing a refinement of the theory in the case of incorrectness on them. Both the Rule Generator and the Rule Interpreter may exploit abduction to hypothesize facts that are not explicitly present in the observations.

The Rule Generalizer is activated when a positive example is not covered, and a revised theory is obtained in one of the following ways (listed by decreasing priority) such that completeness is restored:

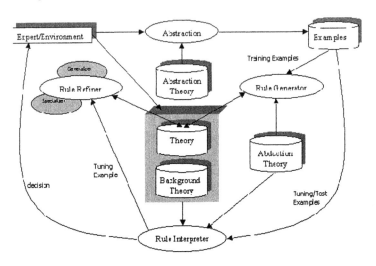

Fig. 1. INTHELEX architecture

– replacing a clause in the theory with one of its generalizations against the problematic example;
– adding a new clause to the theory, obtained by properly turning constants into variables in the problematic example;
– adding the problematic example as a positive exception.

While as regards the Rule Specializer, on the other hand, when a negative example is covered, the system outputs a revised theory that restores consistency by performing one of the following actions (by decreasing priority):

– adding positive literals that are able to characterize all the past positive examples of the concept (and exclude the problematic one) to one of the clauses that concur to the example coverage;
– adding a negative literal that is able to discriminate the problematic example from all the past positive ones to the clause in the theory by which the problematic example is covered;
– adding the problematic example as a negative exception.

An exception contains a specific reference to the observation it represents, as it occurs in the tuning set; new incoming observations are always checked with respect to the exceptions before the rules of the related concept. This does not lead to rules which do not cover any example, since exceptions refer to specific objects, while rules contain variables, so they are still applicable to other objects than those in the exceptions.

It is worth noting that INTHELEX never rejects examples, but always refines the theory. Moreover, it does not need to know *a priori* what is the whole set of concepts to be learned, but it learns a new concept as soon as examples about it are available.

2.1   Learning User Profiles with INTHELEX

We were led by a twofold motivation to exploit INTHELEX on the problem of learning user profiles. First, its representation language (First-Order Logic) is more suitable than numeric/probabilistic approaches to obtain intuitive and human readable rules, which are a highly desirable feature in order to understand the user preferences. Second, incrementality is an undeniable requirement in the given task, since new information on a user is available each time he issues a query, and it would be desirable to be able to refine the previously generated profile instead of completely rejecting it and learning a new one from scratch. Moreover, a user's interests and preferences might change in time, a problem that only incremental systems are able to tackle.

INTHELEX is specifically designed to learn first-order logic theories. In particular, it is suitable when the descriptions of the concepts to be learned are not flat, i.e. they include not only the properties of the objects but also relations between them. However, as we will see later, in the given environment a user profile is described by a list of attributes with an associated value, which corresponds to a propositional representation rather than a first-order one. Hence, in this case the full potentiality of INTHELEX is not entirely exploited, and this should be taken into account when evaluating results.

A further problem that arises in this type of learning task is due to the lack of precise mental schemas in the user for rating a book. Indeed, in many cases, the choice of a book relies on the presence of details appearing in only a few descriptions (e.g., the name of the favourite author). In such a situation, learning a definition for the mental schema of a user becomes more difficult and the resulting profile will be imprecise. This problem is more evident when the system is provided with few users' preferences. On the contrary, when the user's accesses are more frequent, it should (hopefully) be easier to find what is the main trend of the user.

Since INTHELEX is not currently able to handle numeric values, it was not possible to learn preference rates in the continuous interval $[0, 1]$ like in the probabilistic approach. Thus, a discretization was needed. Instead of learning a definition for each of the 10 possible votes, we decided to learn just two possible classes of interest: "likes", describing that the user likes a book, and its opposite "not(likes)". Specifically, the former (positive examples) encompasses all rates ranging from 6 to 10, while the latter (negative examples) included all the others (from 1 to 5). It is worth noting that such a discretization step is not in charge of the human supervisor, since a proper abstraction operator embedded in INTHELEX can be exploited for carrying out this task. Moreover, it has a negligible computational cost, since each numeric value is immediately mapped onto the corresponding discretized symbolic value.

2.2   Representation of Profiles

Each book description is represented in terms of three components by using predicates slot_title(b,t), slot_author(b,au), and slot_annotation(b,an), indicating, respectively, that the book 'b' contains a title, an author and an annotation, where the objects 't', 'au' and 'an' are, respectively, the title, author and annotation of the book 'b'. Any word in the book description is represented by a predicate corresponding to its stem, and linked to both the book itself and the single slots in which it appears. For instance, predicate prolog(slot_title,stp) indicates that object 'stp' has stem 'prolog' and is contained in slot 'slot_title'; in such a case, also a literal prolog(book) is present to say that stem 'prolog' is present in the book description.

Also the number of occurrences of each word in each slot was represented by means of the following predicates: occ_1, occ_2, occ_m, occ_12, occ_2m. A predicate occ_X(Y) indicates that term Y occurs X times, while a predicate occ_XY(Z) indicate that the term Z occurs from X to Y times. Again, such a 'discretization' was needed because numeric values cannot be dealt with in INTHELEX. Note that all the predicates representing intervals to which the value to be represented belongs must be used to represent it; thus, many such predicates can be needed to represent the occurrences of a term. For instance, if a term occurs once, then it occurs also from 1 to 2 (occ_12) times and from 1 to m (occ_1m) times. Figure 2 shows an example for the class likes. Given the specific value in the example, all the intervals to which it belongs are automatically added by the system by putting this information in the background knowledge and exploiting its *saturation* operator. Predicates describing intervals are needed to obtain generalizations based also on the number of word's occurrences in a book. In particular, if a word w occurs once in a description d and twice in a description d', the possible generalizations of the number of occurrences are occ_12, occ_1m.

3   Item Recommender

ITR (ITem Recommender) [2] is a system able to recommend items based on their textual descriptions. It implements a probabilistic learning algorithm to classify texts, the naïve Bayes classifier. Naïve Bayes has been shown to perform competitively with more complex algorithms and has become an increasingly popular algorithm in text classification applications [10,7].

The prototype is able to classify text belonging to a specific category as interesting or uninteresting for a particular user. For example, the system could learn the target concept "*textual descriptions the user finds interesting in the category Computer and Internet*".

Bayesian reasoning provides a probabilistic approach to inference. It is based on the assumption that the quantities of interest are governed by probabilistic distributions and that optimal decision can be made by reasoning about these probabilities together with observed data.

In the learning problem, each instance (item) is represented by a set of *slots*. Each slot is a textual field corresponding to a specific feature of an item.

```
likes(book_501477998) :-
    slot_title(book_501477998, slott),
    practic(slott, slottitlepractic),
    occ_1(slottitlepractic),
    occ_12(slottitlepractic),
    occ_1m(slottitlepractic),
    prolog(slott, slottitleprolog),
    occ_1(slottitleprolog),
    occ_12(slottitleprolog),
    occ_1m(slottitleprolog)
    slot_authors(book_501477998, slotau),
    l_sterling(slotau, slotauthorsl_sterling),
    occ_1(slotauthorsl_sterling),
    occ_12(slotauthorsl_sterling),
    occ_1m(slotauthorsl_sterling),
    slot_annotation(book_501477998, slotan),
    l_sterling(book_501477998),
    practic(book_501477998),
    prolog(book_501477998).
```

Fig. 2. First-Order Representation of a Book

The text in each slot is a collection of words (a bag of word, BOW) processed taking into account their occurrences in the original text. Thus, each instance is represented as a vector of BOWs, one for each slot.

Moreover, each instance is labelled with a discrete rating (from 1 to 10) provided by a user, according to his or her degree of interest in the item.

According to the Bayesian approach to classify natural language text documents, given a set of classes $C = \{c_1, c_2, \ldots, c_{|C|}\}$, the conditional probability of a class c_j given a document d is calculated as follows:

$$P(c_j|d) = \frac{P(c_j)}{P(d)}P(d|c_j)$$

In our problem, we have only 2 classes: c_+ represents the positive class (user-likes, corresponding to ratings from 6 to 10), and c_- the negative one (user-dislikes, ratings from 1 to 5). Since instances are represented as a vector of documents, (one for each BOW), and assumed that the probability of each word is independent of the word's context and position, the conditional probability of a category c_j given an instance d_i is computed using the formula:

$$P(c_j|d_i) = \frac{P(c_j)}{P(d_i)} \prod_{m=1}^{|S|} \prod_{k=1}^{|b_{im}|} P(t_k|c_j, s_m)^{n_{kim}} \tag{1}$$

where $S = \{s_1, s_2, \ldots, s_{|S|}\}$ is the set of slots, b_{im} is the BOW in the slot s_m of the instance d_i, n_{kim} is the number of occurrences of the token t_k in b_{im}.

In (1), since for any given document, the prior $P(d_i)$ is a constant, this factor can be ignored if the only interest concerns a ranking rather than a probability estimate. To calculate (1), we only need to estimate the probability terms $P(c_j)$ and $P(t_k|c_j, s_m)$, from the training set, where each instance is weighted according to the user rating r:

$$w_+^i = \frac{r-1}{9}; \qquad w_-^i = 1 - w_+^i \tag{2}$$

The weights in (2) are used for weighting the occurrence of a word in a document. For example, if a word appears n times in a document d_i, it is counted as occurring $n \cdot w_+^i$ in a positive example and $n \cdot w_-^i$ in a negative example. Weights are used for estimating the two probability terms according to the following equations:

$$\hat{P}(c_j) = \frac{\sum_{i=1}^{|TR|} w_j^i}{|TR|} \tag{3}$$

$$\hat{P}(t_k|c_j, s_m) = \frac{\sum_{i=1}^{|TR|} w_j^i n_{kim}}{\sum_{i=1}^{|TR|} w_j^i |b_{im}|} \tag{4}$$

In (4), n_{kim} is the number of occurrences of the term t_k in the slot s_m of the ith instance, and the denominator denotes the total weighted length of the slot s_m in the class c_j. Therefore, $\hat{P}(t_k|c_j, s_m)$ is calculated as a ratio between the weighted occurrences of the term t_k in slot s_m of class c_j and the total weighted length of the slot.

The final outcome of the learning process is a probabilistic model used to classify a new instance in the class c_+ or c_-. The model can be used to build a personal profile including those words that turn out to be most indicative of the user's preferences, according to the value of the conditional probabilities in (4).

In the specific context of book recommendations, instances in the learning process are the book descriptions. ITR represents each instance as a vector of three BOWs, one BOW for each slot. The slots used are: *title*, *authors* and *textual annotation*. Each book description is analyzed by a simple pattern-matcher that extracts the words, the *tokens* to fill each slot. Tokens are obtained by eliminating stopwords and applying stemming. Instances are used to train the system: occurrences of terms are used to estimates probabilities as described in Equations (3) and (4). An example ITR profile is given in figure 3.

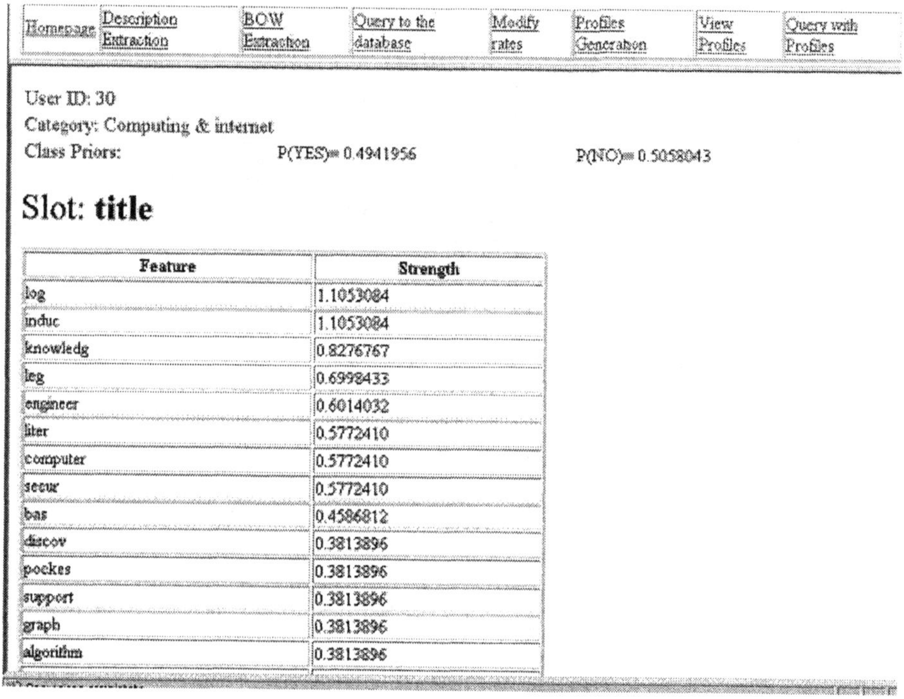

Homepage	Description Extraction	BOW Extraction	Query to the database	Modify rates	Profiles Generation	View Profiles	Query with Profiles

User ID: 30
Category: Computing & internet
Class Priors: P(YES)= 0.4941956   P(NO)= 0.5058043

Slot: **title**

Feature	Strength
log	1.1053084
induc	1.1053084
knowledg	0.8276767
leg	0.6998433
engineer	0.6014032
liter	0.5772410
computer	0.5772410
secur	0.5772410
bas	0.4586812
discov	0.3813896
pockes	0.3813896
support	0.3813896
graph	0.3813896
algorithm	0.3813896

Fig. 3. An example of ITR user profile

4   Experimental Sessions

In this section we describe results from experiments using a collection of textual book descriptions rated by real users according to their tastes. The goal of the experiment has been the comparison of the methods implemented by INTHELEX and ITR in terms of classification accuracy, learning and classification time, when coping with the task of learning user profiles.

The presented experiments are preliminary and should be seen as a baseline study. A new, intensive experimental session will be performed on the Each-Movie data set (http://research.compaq.com/SRC/eachmovie/), that contains 2811983 numeric ratings (entered by 72916 users) for 1628 different movies.

4.1   Design of the Experiments

Eight book categories were selected at the Web site of a virtual bookshop. For each book category, a set of book descriptions was obtained by analyzing Web pages using an automated extractor and stored in a local database. Table 1 describes the extracted information. For each category we considered:

– *Book descriptions* - number of books extracted from the Web site belonging to the specific category;

Table 1. Database information

Category	Book descr.	Books with annotation	Avg. annotation length
Computing & Int.	5378	4178 (77%)	42.35
Fiction & lit.	5857	3347 (57%)	35.71
Travel	3109	1522 (48%)	28.51
Business	5144	3631 (70%)	41.77
SF, horror & fan.	556	433 (77%)	22.49
Art & entert.	1658	1072 (64%)	47.17
Sport & leisure	895	166 (18%)	29.46
History	140	82 (58%)	45.47
Total	**22785**	**14466**	

Table 2. Number of books rated by each user in a given category

UserID	Category	Rated books
37	SF, Horror & Fantasy	40
26	SF, Horror & Fantasy	80
30	Computer & Internet	80
35	Business	80
24c	Computer & Internet	80
36	Fiction & literature	40
24f	Fiction & literature	40
33	Sport & leisure	80
34	Fiction & literature	80
23	Fiction & literature	40

- *Books with annotation* - number of books with a textual annotation (slot annotation not empty);
- *Avg. annotation length* - average length (in words) of the annotations;

Several users have been involved in the experiments: each user were requested to choose one or more categories of interest and to rate 40 or 80 books (in the database) in each selected category, providing 1-10 discrete ratings. In this way, for each user a dataset of 40 or 80 rated books was obtained (see Table 2).

On each dataset a 10-fold cross-validation was run and several metrics were used in the testing phase. In the evaluation phase, the concept of *relevant book* is central. A book in a specific category is considered as relevant by a user if his or her rating is greater than 5. This corresponds in ITR to having $P(c_+|d_i) \geq 0.5$, calculated as in equation (1), where d_i is a book in a specific category. Symmetrically, INTHELEX considers as relevant books covered by the inferred theory. Classification effectiveness is measured in terms of the classical Information Retrieval (IR) notions of *precision (Pr)*, *recall (Re)* and *accuracy (Acc)*, adapted to the case of text categorization [11]. *Precision* is the proportion of items classified as relevant that are really relevant, and *recall* is the proportion of relevant

Table 3. Performance for ITR and INTHELEX on 10 different users

UID	Precision		Recall		Accuracy	
	ITR	INTHELEX	ITR	INTHELEX	ITR	INTHELEX
37	0,767	0,967	0,883	0,5	0,731	0,695
26	0,818	0,955	0,735	0,645	0,737	0,768
30	0,608	0,583	0,600	0,125	0,587	0,488
35	0,651	0,767	0,800	0,234	0,725	0,662
24c	0,586	0,597	0,867	0,383	0,699	0,599
36	0,783	0,9	0,783	0,3	0,700	0,513
24f	0,785	0,9	0,650	0,35	0,651	0,535
33	0,683	0,75	0,808	0,308	0,730	0,659
34	0,608	0,883	0,490	0,255	0,559	0,564
23	0,500	0,975	0,130	0,9	0,153	0,875
Mean	0,679	0,828	0,675	0,4	0,627	0,636
	(0,699)	(0,811)	(0,735)	(0,344)	(0,68)	(0,609)

Table 4. Learning and Classification times (msec) for ITR and INTHELEX on 10 different users

UID	Learning Time		Classification Time	
	ITR	INTHELEX	ITR	INTHELEX
37	3,738	3931,0	0,851	15,0
26	5,378	8839,0	0,969	20,0
30	8,561	51557,0	1,328	53,0
35	9,289	30338,0	1,423	55,0
24c	7,502	29780,0	1,208	44,0
36	5,051	12317,0	0,894	19,0
24f	4,532	18448,0	0,848	19,0
33	5,820	14482,0	0,961	25,0
34	7,592	73708,0	1,209	42,0
23	4,951	1859,0	0,845	20,0
Mean	6,2414	24525,9	1,0536	31,2

items that are classified as relevant; *accuracy* is the proportion of items that are correctly classified as relevant or not.

As regards training and classification times, we tested the algorithms on a 2.4 GHz Pentium IV running Windows 2000.

4.2   Discussion

Table 3 shows the average precision, recall and accuracy of the models learned in the 10 folds for each user. The last row reports the mean values, averaged on all users. Since the average performance for ITR is very low for user 23, we decided to have a deeper insight into the corresponding training file, and noted that all examples were positive, thus indicating possible noise in the data. This led us to recompute the metrics neglecting this user, thus obtaining the results reported in parentheses.

```
likes(A) :-
  learn(A),
  mach(A),
  intellig(A),
  slot_title(A, F),
  slot_authors(A, G),
  slot_annotation(A, B),
  intellig(B, C),
  learn(B, D),
  occ_12(D),
  mach(B, E),
  OCC_12(E).
```

Fig. 4. Rule learned by INTHELEX

In general, INTHELEX provides some performance improvement over ITR. In particular, it can be noticed that INTHELEX produces very high precision even on the category "SF, horror & fantasy", taking into account the shortness of the annotations provided for books belonging to this category. This result is obtained both for user 26, who rated 80 books, and for user 37, who rated only 40 books. Moreover, classification accuracy obtained by INTHELEX is slightly better than the one reached by ITR. On the other hand, ITR yields a better recall than INTHELEX for all users except one (user 23).

For pairwise comparison of the two methods, the nonparametric Wilcoxon signed rank test was used [9], since the number of independent trials (i.e., users) is relatively low and does not justify the application of a parametric test, such as the t-test. In this experiment, the test was adopted in order to evaluate the difference in effectiveness of the profiles induced by the two systems according to the metrics pointed out in Table 3. Requiring a significance level $p < 0.05$, the test revealed that there is a statistically significant difference in performance both for Precision (in favor of INTHELEX) and for Recall (in favor of ITR), but not as regards Accuracy.

Going into more detail, as already stated, ITR performed very poorly only on user 23, whose interests turned out to be very complex to be captured by the probabilistic approach. Actually, all but one rates given by such a user were positive (ranging between 6 and 8), that could be the reason for such a behaviour. With respect to the complete dataset of all users, the accuracy calculated on the subset of all users except user 23 becomes statistically significant in favor of ITR.

Table 4 reports the results about training and classification time of both systems. Training times vary substantially across the two methods. ITR takes an average of 6,2414 msec to train a classifier for a user when averaged over all 10 users. Training INTHELEX takes more time than ITR, but this is not a real problem because profiles can be learnt by batch processes without noise for users. In user profiling application, it is important to quickly classify new instances,

Table 5. Interests of user 39 and user 40 in books belonging to the category "Computing and Internet"

UserID	Interests
39	machine learning, data mining, artificial intelligence
40	web programming, XML, databases, e-commerce

for example to provide users with on-line recommendations. Both methods are very fast in this regard.

In summary, the probabilistic approach seems to have better recall, thus showing a trend to classify unseen instances as positive; on the contrary, the first-order approach tends to adopt a more cautious behavior, and classify new instances as negative. Such a difference is probably due to the approach adopted: learning in INTHELEX is data-driven, thus it works bottom-up and keeps in the induced definitions as much information as possible from the examples. This way, requirements for new observations in order to be classified as positive are more demanding, and few of them pass; on the other hand, this ensures that those that fulfill the condition are actually positive instances.

Another remark worth noting is that theories learned by the symbolic system are very interesting from a human understandability viewpoint, in order to be able to explain and justify the recommendations provided by the system. Figure 4 shows one such rule, to be interpreted as "the user likes a book if its annotation contains stems *intellig*, *learn* (1 or 2 times) and *mach* (1 or 2 times)". Anybody can easily understand that this user is interested in books concerning artificial intelligence and, specifically, machine learning.

The probabilistic approach could be used in developing recommender systems exploiting the *ranked list* approach for presenting items to the users. In this scheme, users specifies their needs in a form and the system presents a usually long list of results, ordered by their predicted relevance (the probability of belonging to the class). On the other hand, the ILP approach could be adopted in situations when the system transparency is a critical factor and it is important to provide an explanation of why a recommendation was made.

From what said above, it seems that the two approaches compared in this paper have complementary *pros and cons*, not only as regards the representation language, but also as concerns the predictive performances. This naturally leads to think that some cooperation could take place between the two in order to reach higher effectiveness of the recommendations. For instance, since the probabilistic theories have a better recall, they could be used for selecting which items are to be presented to the user. Then, some kind of filtering could be applied on them, in order to present to the user first those items that are considered positive by the symbolic theories, that are characterized by a better precision.

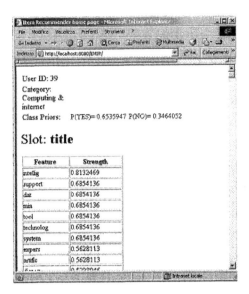

Fig. 5. Profile of user 39.

5   Exploiting Profiles to Personalize Recommendations

In this section, we present an example of how the learned profiles can be exploited to provide Web users with personalized recommendations, delivered using the ranked list approach. In particular, we analyze a usage scenario of the ITR system, in which two users with different interests in books belonging to the category "Computing and Internet" submit the same query to the ITR search engine. Table 5 reports the explicit interests of the two users. Figure 5 and 6 depict the profiles of both users inferred by ITR, and shows some keywords in the slot title, which are indicative of user preferences. When a user submits a query q, the books b_i in the result set R_q are ranked by the classification value $P(c_+|b_i)$, $b_i \in R_q$, computed according to Equation (1). The exact posterior probabilities are determined by normalizing $P(c_+|b_i)$ and $P(c_-|b_i)$, so that their sum is equal to 1. The result set retrieved by ITR in response to the query $q=$ "programming", submitted by user 39, is presented in Figure 7. The first book displayed is "Expert Systems in Finance and Accounting", in accordance with the interests contained in the user profile. In fact, the profile of user 39 contains, in the slot title, stemmed keywords ("intellig", "artific", "system") that reveal the interest of the user in systems exploiting artificial intelligence methods, like expert systems. Conversely, if another user submits the same query, the books in the result set are ranked in a different way, due to the fact that this user has a different profile (user 40 in Figure 6). In this case, the system recommends "Java Professional Library" (the first book in the ranked list) (Figure 8), because the stemmed keywords ("java", "databas", "xml", "program", "jdbc") in the slot title of the profile indicate well known technologies for web developers. Again, the

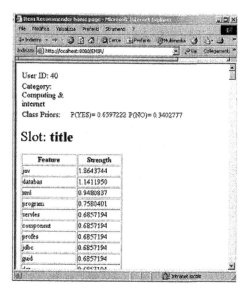

Fig. 6. Profile of user 40.

advice provided by the systems seems to be indicative of the interests supplied by the users.

These scenarios highlight the effect of the personalization on the search process, that is the dependence of the result set on the profile of the user who issued the query. Although the query personalization scenarios presented here suggest a use of the probabilistic profiles for content-based filtering of the search results, thus adopting a passive recommendation strategy, they can be used also for active recommendation. For example, the profile of a user could be used to identify a set of N items that will be of interest to the user in each category of the catalogue (top-N recommendation problem) [12]. Then, the N top-scored items in a category could be recommended when the user is browsing items in that category. As regards the rule-based profiles, since they do not provide a recommendation score, but only a binary judgement (likes/dislikes), they are more suitable for refining the recommendations from among a candidate set, such as a ranked list. To sum up, although this has been designed as a baseline study, it is worth drawing attention to the key finding highlighted by the study: ILP and probabilistic techniques are complementary for the task of learning user profiles from text and could be combined for active or passive recommendation. In our opinion, a cascade hybridization method [1] is the best way to integrate the two approaches. In this technique, the probabilistic profile of a user is exploited first to produce a coarse ranking of candidates, and then the symbolic profile refines the recommendations from among the candidate set, also explaining and justifying the recommendations provided by the system.

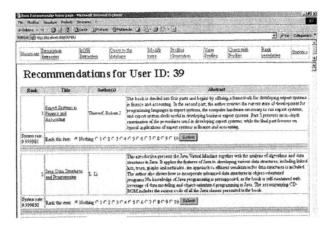

Fig. 7. Books recommended by ITR to user 39, who issued the query "programming".

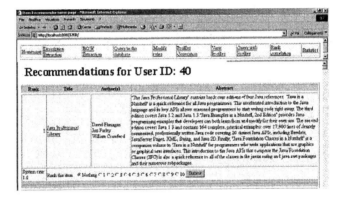

Fig. 8. Books recommended by ITR to user 40, who issued the query "programming".

6   Conclusions

Research presented in this paper has focused on methods for learning user profiles which are predictively accurate and comprehensible. Specifically, an intensive comparison between an ILP and a probabilistic approach to learning models of users' preferences was carried out. Experimental results highlight the usefulness and drawbacks of each one, that can suggest possible ways of combining the two approaches in order to offer better support to users accessing e-commerce virtual shops or other information sources. In particular, we suggest a simple possible way of obtaining a cascade hybrid method. In this technique, the probabilistic approach could be employed first to produce a coarse ranking of candidates and the ILP approach could be used to refine the recommendations from among the candidate set.

Currently we are working on the integration in INTHELEX of techniques able to manage numeric values, in order to treat in a more efficient way numerical features of instances, and hence to obtain theories with a more fine grain size.

References

[1] R. Burke. Hybrid recommender systems: Survey and experiments. *User Modeling and User-Adapted Interaction*, 12(4):331–370, 2002.

[2] M. Degemmis, P. Lops, G. Semeraro, and F. Abbattista. Extraction of user profiles by discovering preferences through machine learning. In M. A. Klopotek, S. T. Wierzhon, and K. Trojanowski, editors, *Information Systems: New Trends in Intelligent Information Processing and Web Mining*, Advances in Soft Computing, pages 69–78. Springer, 2003.

[3] F. Esposito, G. Semeraro, N. Fanizzi, and S. Ferilli. Multistrategy Theory Revision: Induction and abduction in INTHELEX. *Machine Learning*, 38(1/2):133–156, 2000.

[4] D.D. Lewis. Naive (Bayes) at forty: The independence assumption in information retrieval. In Claire Nédellec and Céline Rouveirol, editors, *Proceedings of ECML-98, 10th European Conference on Machine Learning*, number 1398, pages 4–15, Chemnitz, DE, 1998. Springer Verlag, Heidelberg, DE.

[5] D.D. Lewis and M. Ringuette. A comparison of two learning algorithms for text categorization. In *Proceedings of SDAIR-94, 3rd Annual Symposium on Document Analysis and Information Retrieval*, pages 81–93, Las Vegas, US, 1994.

[6] D. Mladenic. Text-learning and related intelligent agents: a survey. *IEEE Intelligent Systems*, 14(4):44–54, 1999.

[7] R.J. Mooney and L. Roy. Content-based book recommending using learning for text categorization. In *Proceedings of the 5th ACM Conference on Digital Libraries*, pages 195–204, San Antonio, US, 2000. ACM Press, New York, US.

[8] I. Moulinier and J.G. Ganascia. Confronting an existing machine learning algorithm to the text categorization task. In *IJCAI, Workshop on New approaches to Learning for Natural Language Processing*, Montréal, 1995.

[9] M. Orkin and R. Drogin. *Vital Statistics*. McGraw-Hill, New York, 1990.

[10] M. Pazzani and D. Billsus. Learning and revising user profiles: The identification of interesting web sites. *Machine Learning*, 27(3):313–331, 1997.

[11] G. Salton and M.J. McGill. *Introduction to Modern Information Retrieval*. McGraw-Hill, New York, 1983.

[12] B. M. Sarwar, G. Karypis, J. Konstan, and J. Riedl. Recommender systems for large-scale e-commerce: Scalable neighborhood formation using clustering. In *Proceedings of the Fifth International Conference on Computer and Information Technology*. East West University, Bangladesh, 2002.

[13] F. Sebastiani. Machine learning in automated text categorization. *ACM Computing Surveys*, 34(1):1–47, 2002.

[14] G. Semeraro, F. Esposito, D. Malerba, N. Fanizzi, and S. Ferilli. A logic framework for the incremental inductive synthesis of datalog theories. In N. E. Fuchs, editor, *Logic Program Synthesis and Transformation*, number 1463 in Lecture Notes in Computer Science, pages 300–321. Springer-Verlag, 1998.

Greedy Recommending Is Not Always Optimal

Maarten van Someren[1], Vera Hollink[1], and Stephan ten Hagen[2]

[1] Dept. of Social Science Informatics, University of Amsterdam,
Roetersstraat 15, 1018 WB Amsterdam, The Netherlands,
{maarten,vhollink}@swi.psy.uva.nl
[2] Faculty of Science, University of Amsterdam,
Kruislaan 403, 1098 SJ Amsterdam, The Netherlands
stephanh@science.uva,nl

Abstract. Recommender systems suggest objects to users. One form recommends documents or other objects to users searching information on a web site. A recommender system can use data about a user to recommend information, for example web pages. Current methods for recommending are aimed at optimising single recommendations. However, usually a series of interactions is needed to find the desired information. Here we argue that in interactive recommending a series of normal, 'greedy', recommendings is not the strategy that minimises the number of steps in the search. Greedy sequential recommending conflicts with the need to explore the entire space of user preferences and may lead to recommending series that require more steps (mouse clicks) from the user than necessary. We illustrate this with an example, analyse when this is so and outline when greedy recommending is not the most efficient.

1 Introduction

Recommender systems typically recommend one or more objects that appear to be the most interesting for a user. A large number of methods have been proposed and a number of systems have been presented in the literature, e.g. [1, 2,8,4,5,6,9,10,16]. These systems collect information about the user, for example documents, screens or actions that were selected by the user, and use this to recommend objects. Some authors view 'return on investment' as the criterion for success of recommendings (e.g. [7]). In this case recommending is a form of advertising and the economic value of objects is of key importance because this will determine the 'return on investment'. A related but different criterion is 'user satisfaction with the recommendation and the recommended object'. A user may be most satisfied with an object that has little 'return on investment' for the site owner but that has a high value for the user. In this case the goal of the recommender can be to maximise either 'return on investment' or user satisfaction. Another dimension of user satisfaction is effort in using the site, for example the number of clicks. A recommender can have as its goal to minimise user effort, for example in a situation where the user will eventually find his target object or information. Of course a recommender can also aim to maximise some

B. Berendt et al. (Eds.): EWMF 2003, LNAI 3209, pp. 148–163, 2004.

- Goal
  - Benefit site owner
  - Benefit user
- Criterion
  - Maximise value of object
  - Minimise effort of finding it
- Preferences distribution (per user)
  - One target and rest flat
  - One target and rest (partially) ordered
  - Multiple targets

Fig. 1. Dimensions of recommender systems

combination of user effort and value of the result. These different recommending tasks require different methods. Advertising can be viewed as a kind of game in which the user and the vendor pursue their own goals and in maximising user satisfaction, user and site owner share the same goal.

If user satisfaction is the goal then another dimension of the recommending task is important: is the users goal a single object or are there many objects that will satisfy the user, as for a user who is just surfing. In the second case, the main goal of recommending is to suggest useful objects, for example something unexpected. If the user has a specific goal then recommending is similar to information retrieval. The purpose of recommending in this case is to help the user to find an object that maximally satisfies the users goal and to minimise his effort in finding it. Information retrieval is normally based on user-defined queries but in some applications users are not able to formulate adequate queries because they are not familiar with the domain, the terminology and the distribution of objects. In this case presenting specific objects can replace or complement a dialogue based on queries. Figure 1 summarises the main dimensions of recommending tasks.

If the criterion is to minimise effort then the choice of an object to recommend depends on two different goals: (1) to offer candidate objects that may satisfy the users interest and (2) to obtain information about the users preferences. A single object may be optimal for both goals but this is not necessarily the case. In this paper we show that different recommendations may be optimal for these goals and that recommending the best candidate ('greedy recommending') does not always minimise the number of user actions before the target is found. We demonstrate this by introducing an alternative method that exploits a particular type of pattern in user preferences, requiring on average fewer user actions than greedy recommending.

By analogy with greedy heuristic search methods, we use the term *greedy* recommending when the recommender presents objects that it predicts to be closest to the target. This can be seen as a myopic decision making process in which the recommender aims at offering the user immediately the object of interest. If recommending takes information about the user (like the interaction history) into account we call it *user-adaptive* recommending. If recommending takes place over a series of interaction steps that ends with finding a target object, we call it *sequential* recommending in contrast to *one-step* recommending. Most recommendation methods use a form of collaborative filtering (recommending objects which were targets of similar users) or content based filtering (recommending objects which are similar to objects which were positively evaluated before) or a combination of these techniques. We consider in this paper recommender methods that use preferences of objects obtained from many user *and* the session history of the current user to decide about which objects to recommend.

In this paper we note two problems of greedy recommending. The first problem is the *inadequate exploration problem*. The recommender needs data about users preferences. A recommender system generates recommendations but at the same time it has to collect data about user preferences. Greedy recommending may have the effect that some objects are not seen by users and therefore are not evaluated adequately. The collected data (weblog) does not reveal the preferences of the users, but instead it shows the response of the user to the recommended items. This may prevent popular objects from being recommended in future. In section 2 we discuss the inadequate exploration problem.

The second problem is that in sequential recommending settings, greedy recommending may not be the most efficient method for reaching the target. In a setting in which the user is looking for a single target object, a criterion for the quality of recommending is the number of links that needs to be traversed to reach the target. We can view recommending as a classification task where the goal is to 'assign' the user to one of the available objects in the minimal number of steps. It is intuitively clear that 'greedy sequential recommending', presenting the most likely target objects, may not be the optimal method. We introduce a strategy based on binary search and show in an example that *under certain circumstances* this strategy can outperform greedy recommending. In other words: greedy recommending is not optimal under certain circumstances in the sense that it does not minimise the users effort. The circumstances are introduced in section 3 where we specify the specific task and the recommenders are introduced and compared in section 4. We illustrate the difference between the recommenders in a simulation experiment in section 5. The last section discusses the results and contains suggestions for further research.

2   The Inadequate Exploration Problem

Recommenders based on 'social filtering' need data about users. Unfortunately, acquiring the data about user preferences interferes with the actual recommending. There is a conflict between 'exploitation' and 'exploration' (e.g. [13]). In [15] we showed that recommenders might get stuck in a local optimum and never acquire the optimal recommendation strategy. The possible paths through the site which the user can take are determined by the provided recommendations. The user is forced to click on one of the recommended objects even when his target object is not among the recommendations. The system observes which object is chosen and infers that this object was indeed a good recommendation. It increases the probability that the same object is recommended again in the next session and the system never discovers that a different object would have been an even better recommendation. Objects that are recommended in the beginning will become popular because they are recommended, but highly appreciated objects with a low initial estimated appreciation might never be recommended and the system stays with a suboptimal recommendation strategy.

To make sure that the estimation of the popularity of all content objects becomes accurate it is necessary to explore the entire preference space. The system always has to keep trying all objects even if the user population is homogeneous. One way to perform this kind of exploration, is to use the ϵ-greedy exploration method [12]. The greedy object (that is best according to the current knowledge) is recommended with probability $1-\epsilon$ and a random other object with probability ϵ. By taking ϵ small, the system can make good recommendations (exploitation), while assuring all objects will eventually be explored. Note that this agrees with the empirical observations in [14], where it is suggested that recommendations should be reliable in the sense that they guide the users to popular objects. But also new and unexpected objects should be recommended to make sure that all objects are exposed to the user population.

The inadequate exploration problem implies that it is not possible to deduce improvements of a recommender system for recommendations that have not been made. If a site has a static recommender that always recommends the same objects in the same page (e.g. always makes greedy recommendations), then statistics from the weblog may lead to incorrect improvements or suggest no improvements when improvements are still possible. The only way to enrich the data collected in the weblog is by adding an exploratory component to the recommender that sometimes recommends objects not to help the user but to measure how much users are interested in this object. Lack of exploration is thus one cause of suboptimal behaviour by a greedy recommender.

3   The Recommending Task

To enable the analysis we define a specific domain in which we can compare the recommenders.

3.1   The Setting

Although recommending is a single term for the task of supporting users by recommending objects from a large repository, there is actually a wide range of recommendation tasks. We focus on one particular recommendation setting to compare the effects of three recommendation strategies, and we keep the setting as simple as possible to emphasise the differences between these recommendation strategies.

The setting we use has the following properties:

- The recommender recommends elements from a fixed set of content objects: $\{c_1, \cdots, c_n\}$.
- Every user is looking for one particular *target* content object, but this is obviously not the same object for each user.
- In each cycle, the system recommends exactly two content objects to the user.
- After receiving a recommendation the user indicates for one of the objects *"My target is X."* or *"X and Y are both not my target, but object X is closer to what I am looking for than Y."*.
- If the user has found his target then the interaction stops. else he receives two new recommendations.

In this setting the main task of the recommender is to select at each step two content objects to recommend.

Our setting focuses on one aspect of recommending, but usually recommending is a component in a larger system. For example, an information system may include a query facility, menus, a site map and other tools. In this analysis we isolate one aspect of the recommending task, which we believe is fundamental and that its analysis has implications for more realistic settings and settings that are more complicated.

3.2   The Pattern of User Preferences

The recommender can exploit patterns in users preferences to infer the preference of a new user. There are different types of patterns that can be used for this. A common type of pattern is clusters. Clustering methods can detect clusters of users with similar preferences. A new user is classified as belonging to one of these clusters. This reduces the set of candidate objects to those that are preferred by the other members of the cluster. This increases the probability that an object is chosen and thereby it reduces the number of steps to reach it.

We look at a different type of pattern: *scaling patterns*. Suppose that we ask people to compare pairs of objects and to indicate which of each pair they prefer. For this an ordering of objects can be constructed. Now suppose that such orderings are constructed for n persons. It may be possible to order the objects such that each person can be assigned to a point in the ordering such that his ordered objects can be split into two orderings that appear on both sides of 'his' point.

Consider the following example in which two persons have ordered holiday destinations by their preference. Person M prefers destinations with a Mediterranean climate and V prefers destinations with a cooler climate but not too cold:

```
M: Spain - France - Morocco - Italy - Greece -
              Croatia - Scotland - Norway - Sweden - Nigeria
V: Scotland - Norway - Croatia - Sweden - Italy -
              Greece - France - Spain - Morocco - Nigeria
```

We can then construct the following one-dimensional scale:

```
Sweden - Norway - Scotland - France - Spain -
            Italy - Greece - Croatia - Morocco - Nigeria
```

We position M at Spain and V at Scotland. The scale for destinations is then consistent with the orderings constructed from the pairwise comparisons.

One-dimensional scaling methods rely on the idea of 'unfolding': the preference order can be unfolded into two orders that are aligned. Coombs [3] gives a general overview of scaling methods. One-dimensional scaling methods take a (large) number of ratings or comparisons of objects by different persons as input and define an ordering such that each person can be assigned a position on the scale that is consistent with his ratings or comparisons. This means that we obtain a scale and the positions of persons over the scale. More people can have the same position and so we obtain a probability distribution of preferences over the scale.

It is in general not possible to construct a perfect scale for a single variable. Many domains have an underlying multidimensional structure and then there is much random variation. There are methods that construct multi-dimensional scales where a random factor can be quantified as the 'stress': the proportion of paired comparisons that are inconsistent with the constructed scale. In realistic scenarios multidimensional scaling may be more appropriate and this is important to consider for a real recommender system.

We restrict the discussion to one-dimensional scaling because our goal is to demonstrate that a recommender that exploits the user pattern can outperform a greedy recommender. Multi-dimensional scaling (and also clustering) have more 'degrees of freedom' in specifying the preference relations between objects. So choosing a setting that allows for a fair and clear comparison of the performance of different recommenders is hard to find for these methods. For one-dimensional scaling objects only have to be placed in a sequence. In the case of recommending systems we can interpret the user's reaction to recommended objects as a comparison in preference. Combining comparisons of many users then results in a 'popularity' distribution over the one-dimensional scale. This can be easily visualised and specific and exceptional distributions can be enumerated for analysis.

4   Three Recommenders

We distinguish three approaches to sequential recommending that differ in the use of an ordering and in greediness vs. exploration:

- Non-user-adaptive recommending
- Greedy user-adaptive recommending
- Exploratory user-adaptive recommending

Since these methods rely on data about the preferences of users, an important aspect of the recommendation task is to acquire these data. Here the inadequate exploration problem from section 2 has to be addressed.

Non-user-adaptive recommender systems only need statistical data about the user population as a whole. Each individual user will be recommended the same objects in the same situations. Methods which adapt to individual users also need to keep track of the preferences of the current user of the site. This requires that the user can be identified and followed through the session. Cookies can be used for this. The preferences can be received from the user's answers to questions, but they can also be derived from the user's past responses to recommended objects. The complete past can be used, but we only consider the past in the current session alone. So each time someone visits the site the recommender starts as a non-user-adaptive recommender, and at every step in the session some part of the preferences of this user is revealed.

In the following sections we will discuss the advantages and disadvantages of each of the different recommender strategies. The analysis uses the setting from section 3.1. At each presentation there is a probability that the target was presented, resulting in 0 additional presentations. If the user does not accept the presented objects then these are excluded and recommending is applied to the remaining objects. In the worst case, the recommender must present all N objects. Since objects are presented in pairs, this means that the maximum number of presentation cycles equals half the number of objects.

4.1   Non-user-Adaptive Sequential Recommending

The first recommendation strategy that we will discuss is non-user-adaptive recommending. This is a greedy method that does not use information about individual users. It recommends objects ordered by the (marginal) probability that the object is the target. This strategy is often implicit in manually constructed web sites. The designer estimates which objects are most popular and uses this estimate to order the presentation of objects to the user [11]. A recommender that uses this strategy only estimates for each objects the probability that it is target for any arbitrary user.

For this method the upper bound of the number of presentations is simply half number of objects, $N/2$. This will happen to users interested in one of the two least popular objects. The expected number of presentations depends on the distribution of preferences over objects. If this is uniform the notion of *greedy* no longer applies because all objects are equally good in the sense that no objects is preferred over any other object. An alternative, maybe random, selection strategy has to be applied. The expected number of presentations will depend on the ordering resulting from the alternative strategy. Given an arbitrary ordering the excepted number of presentations is half that of the upper bound. So for an uniform distribution the expected number of presentations is $N/4$ and for any other distributions it is lower.

4.2   Greedy User-Adaptive Sequential Recommending

User-adaptive recommenders collect information about the current user during a session and use this to generate *personalised* recommendations. In our setting the only available data about the preferences of a user is a series of rejected objects and preferences that come out of interaction logs. A *greedy* user-adaptive recommender system always recommends the objects with the highest probability of being the target object *given the observed preferences*. If the user has indicated a preference of c_1 over c_2 and c_3 over c_4 et cetera, a greedy user-adaptive recommender recommends c_i with maximal $P(c_i = \text{target}|(c_1 > c_2) \& (c_3 > c_4) \& \ldots)$. If the preference of one object changes the probability that the other object is the target, then this strategy can reduce the expected path length compared to non-user-adaptive recommending.

The greedy user-adaptive recommender always recommends the object with the highest estimated conditional probability of being the target. For this it needs the data to estimate the conditional probabilities of all objects in order to predict the best object. Obviously, estimating the conditional probabilities needs far more data than the marginal probabilities. The one-dimensional scaling pattern from section 3.2 can be seen as an alternative to the estimation of all possible conditional dependencies in user preferences. It serves the same purpose in that user's choices made in the past *change* the probabilities of objects being the target. For the non-user-adaptive recommending these probabilities never change so that it does not need the scaling. For example, in terms of the holiday travel example in section 3.2, a person who prefers Morocco over Spain and Morocco over France, will probably not have his target at Norway or Nigeria. In spite of this the non-user-adaptive recommender may still present Norway or Nigeria at the next step if these are popular holiday destinations. By not presenting these two the user-adaptive recommender increases the probability that the user's target is found faster. It reduces the expected number of presentations compared to the non-user-adaptive recommender.

The upper bound on the number of presentations for this approach is again $N/2$. Again this will happen to users interested in one of the two least popular objects, but now it is possible that these objects are recommended earlier when probabilities of other object being the target become lower during the session. To understand the upper bound of $N/2$, consider a one-dimensional scale where the probability of objects being a target along the scale is monotone decreasing (or increasing). A user interested in the least popular object will get the choice between the two most popular objects. The least popular of the two recommendations is on the scale closest to the object of interest and will be chosen by the user. All other objects are also closest to the recommendation chosen by the user. There are no objects whose probability of being the target is reduced based on the choice of the user, and in the next step the recommender presents the next two object on the scale. This continues until finally the least popular object is presented to the user. This is a specific case in which the greedy user-adaptive recommender behaves exactly like the non-user-adaptive recommender.

For the uniform distribution the difference with the non-user-adaptive recommending is that now at each step the set of objects is expected to be split in half. Also at each step the probability of selecting the target doubles. There is a probability of $\frac{2}{N}$ of no extra presentations, a probability of $2 \cdot \frac{2}{N}(1 - \frac{2}{N})$ of one extra presentation and so on. This results in a polynomial in $\frac{2}{N}$ of order $\frac{N}{2} + 1$ for the expectancy.

4.3 Exploratory User-Adaptive Sequential Recommending

The decision of the greedy user-adaptive sequential recommender about which objects to recommend *only* depends on the (conditional) probabilities of objects being the target. The user pattern is completely ignored. The decrease in expected path length due to the user-adaptivity is more an 'accidental side effect' of the myopic decision making that aims at finishing the path in one step.

Exploratory sequential recommending aims at *minimising* the expected path length in the sense that it tries to increase the probabilities of short paths and increase that of long paths. The method is based on the idea that sequential recommending can be viewed as a kind of classification in which users have to be assigned to the objects that match their interest. Suppose all objects fit perfectly on a one dimensional scale ('stress' is 0) and all users are capable of telling which of the two presented objects is closest to their target. In that case a recommender can be based on a binary search. The set of objects is split in the middle of the scale and two objects, one from each side of the middle, are presented to the user. The user selects the objects closest to the target and all objects on the other side of the middle are discarded in future.

Instead of using only the scale it is possible to weight the objects with their marginal probabilities. Then the set of objects are split with equal probabilities on both sides. This results in exploratory sequential recommending, which consists of repeating the following steps until the target has been found:

1. Find the 'center of probability mass' (CPM), a point CPM such that the sum of probabilities objects on both sides is equal.
2. Find two objects with equal distances to CPM.
3. Present these to the user as recommendations.
4. The user now indicates which of the presented objects he prefers and whether he wants to continue (if neither of the presented objects is the target).
5. If neither of the presented objects is accepted then eliminate *all* objects on the side of the CPM where the least-preferred object is located.

Note that the procedure does not specify which objects should be presented. It is still possible to choose the object with the highest probability, but then the other object should be chosen at the same distance from the CPM. Alternatively one can also decide to always choose two objects far way from the CPM to make sure that the user can clearly discriminate between them.

The upper bound on the number of presentations is again $N/2$. This happens when the probabilities are exponentially decreasing along the scale. Suppose the first object has probability $\frac{1}{2}$, the second $\frac{1}{4}$, the third $\frac{1}{8}$ and so on. The CPM will be between the first and second object and these two objects have to be presented. A user interested in the least popular object will indicate that the second object is closest to the target. Object one and two are removed and the CPM shift between the third and forth object. In this situation the exploratory recommender behaves the same as the other two recommenders.

For a uniform distribution the upper bound or maximum path length can be computed by counting the number of nodes in a full binary three of depth D. Without the root node it has $2^{D+1} - 2$ nodes and so the maximum path length

Table 1. Number of presentations for a site with N objects.

Method	Upper bound	Expected (uniform distribution)
Non-user-adaptive	$N/2$	$N/4$
Greedy user-adaptive	$N/2$	see text
Exploratory user-adaptive	$N/2$	$\frac{4}{N} + \frac{N+2}{N}(\log_2(N+2) - 3)$

$L = D - 1 = \log_2(N + 2) - 2$. This should be rounded up for values of N for which the tree is not completely full. We assume that the tree is full in order to compute the expected path length for this distribution. The number of nodes for each depth is multiplied by the path length and the total sum over all depths is divided by the number of object N. After some manipulations this results in $(4 + (L - 1) * (N + 2))/N$ expected number of presentations.

4.4 Comparison of the Methods

The difference between the three recommenders can be illustrated with a simple example. Suppose a recommender system recommends pieces from a music database consisting of operas and pop songs and in the first cycle the system has recommended the opera 'La Traviata' and the song 'Yellow Submarine'. If the user indicates that he prefers 'La Traviata' over 'Yellow Submarine', it becomes more probable that the user is looking for an opera than a pop song, even if more people ask the database for pop songs. A non-user-adaptive recommender system would not use this information in the next step. Because more people ask for pop songs it will probably presents two pop songs in the next step. The user-adaptive recommenders would use the information and recommend two operas. The greedy user-adaptive recommender will present the two most popular operas, even when they are from the same composer. The exploratory recommender makes sure that it presents two distinguishable operas, like for instance a classic and a modern opera.

Table 1 summarises the number of presentations of the three methods. The upper bound indicates the maximum number of presentations that may be required to find the least popular object in a site for which *any* popularity distribution is possible. This upper bound is the same for all recommenders and it corresponds to presenting all objects. The difference between the recommenders lies in the set of probability distributions of the site for which this situation can occur. The corresponding distribution of the exploratory recommender is a specific subset of the distribution of the greedy user-adaptive recommender, that happens to be a subset of the distribution of the non-user-adaptive recommender. So for an arbitrary site, the need to present all objects is the least likely for the exploratory recommender.

Table 1 also shows the expected path length for a uniform distribution. In this case the non-user-adaptive cannot use the differences in popularity to select the recommendations. The alternative random strategy is responsible for the expected path length that depends linearly on N. This strategy also makes that the set is *not* always split exactly in two for the greedy recommender. This does happen for the exploratory recommender making the expectancy depend logarithmically on N, specially when N becomes very large. So for a uniform distribution, users will find their target faster when the exploratory recommender is used. One may argue that this is not a fair comparison, but for large sites the probability of objects being the target become low for all objects. Differences in probability will not be very significant and the effect of using a greedy recommender will start to resemble that of the random strategy.

It is possible to use exploratory recommendations as alternative strategy when the greedy recommender has to choose between object with the same probabilities. For the comparison in table 1 this could not be used. In practice such hybrid recommender is useful because it shares the benefits of both approaches. The other way around is also possible by taking an exploratory recommender that chooses those two objects around the CPM for which the combined probabilities are maximal. This exploratory recommender maximises the probability of finishing in one step.

5   Simulation Experiment

The purpose of the simulation experiment is to show the differences in the number of presentations for the different recommending strategies. A more realistic experiment would require two identical sites that only differ in the recommender used. In that case we also would not be able to compare results for different distributions of popularity.

We created an artificial site with only 32 objects for which the popularity is given according to the probability of the item being the target. We considered four different popularity distributions:

A **Skewed:** Here the objects are ranked according to their popularity, which can be unrelated to the objects.
B **Triangle:** This corresponds to a site with a specific topic. Most visitors are assume to come for this topic so that these objects are most popular (center). Objects that are less that are less related to this topic are less popular.
C **Uniform:** The popularity of the objects is unknown so assume that everything is equally popular.
D **Peaked:** Here a few known objects are very popular. This corresponds with sites that present a 'most popular' list.

The distributions are shown in Figure 5. These distributions will not appear in reality but they show the effect of properties of the distribution on the effect of the method on the presentation complexity.

We assumed that the user was capable of selecting the object that was closest to the object of interest, when the object of interest was not shown. From the recommender's perspective this is the same as saying that the recommender is capable to predict the choice the user will make given the object of interest. The recommender rejects all object that are closest to the object *not* selected by the user and they will not be considered in future recommendation in the same session. So the recommender has a set of potential target object that is reduced after each click of the user.

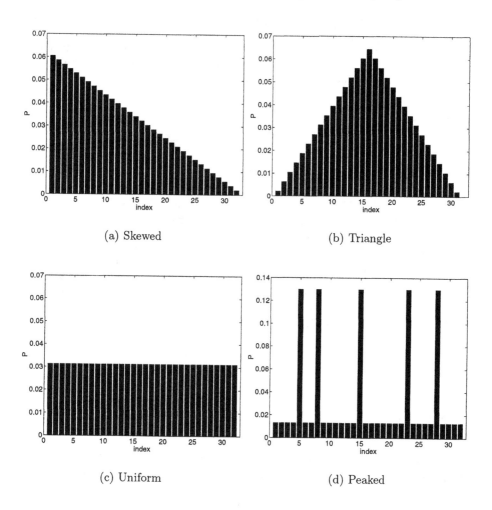

(a) Skewed

(b) Triangle

(c) Uniform

(d) Peaked

Fig. 2. The four different popularity distributions.

We used two recommenders:

- **Greedy:** (Greedy user-adaptive sequential recommending)
  This method attempts to give the user directly the content it wants, by recommending the most popular objects not yet recommended. The recommender selects the two objects with the highest probability according to the assumed distribution. If objects had the same probability the object was picked randomly from the set of highest probabilities.
- **Exploratory:** (Exploratory user-adaptive sequential recommender)
  This methods attempts to increase the set of objects that the user is not interested in so that they do not have to be recommended. First the CPM of the distribution is computed to divide the objects into two sets. The object

Table 2. The results. Here "User" indicates the distribution of the 5000 users, "Site" is the distributions used by the recommender. The "Average" and "Expected" show the number of *extra* clicks of the 5000 users after the presentation of the first two recommendings. The "Worst Case" shows the maximum number of clicks that were needed by at least one user. The bold numbers indicate the lowest result of the two methods.

Distribution		Greedy			Exploratory		
User	Site	Average	Expected	Worst Case	Average	Expected	Worst Case
A	A	8.50	3.07	16	**3.91**	**1.73**	**7**
A	B	5.00	2.58	9	**3.97**	**1.94**	**7**
A	C	3.83	1.97	16	**3.44**	**1.77**	**5**
A	D	3.69	1.89	16	**3.59**	**1.77**	**5**
B	A	8.00	4.00	16	**3.69**	**1.73**	**7**
B	B	4.72	1.74	9	**3.75**	**1.65**	**7**
B	C	3.66	1.90	16	**3.31**	**1.68**	**5**
B	D	3.56	1.84	16	**3.44**	**1.77**	**5**
C	A	8.50	8.50	16	**3.91**	**3.91**	**7**
C	B	5.00	5.00	9	**3.97**	**3.97**	**7**
C	C	3.79	3.79	16	**3.44**	**3.44**	**5**
C	D	3.69	3.69	16	**3.59**	**3.59**	**5**
D	A	8.50	2.00	16	**3.91**	0.87	**7**
D	B	5.00	1.20	9	**3.97**	0.79	**7**
D	C	3.75	0.91	16	**3.44**	0.88	**5**
D	D	3.68	**0.60**	16	**3.59**	0.78	**5**

in the middle of the set with the fewest objects is recommended, together with the object at the same distance form the CPM in the other set.

We did not look at the non-user adaptive recommending because it only removes the previously shown objects and will therefore never outperform the other two approaches.

We simulated the behavior of 5000 users that were interested in only one object. The object of interest was picked randomly from one of the distribution of Figure 5. So we did the experiments with two popularity distributions, one corresponding to the real popularity (user) and the other the 'assumed' popularity used by the recommender (site). The results are presented in Table 2. We looked at:

- **Average:** The average number of presentations for each content object.
- **Expected:** The number of presentations multiplied by the probability of the object according to the user distribution. This indicates the expected number of presentations when an arbitrary user visits the site.
- **Worst Case:** The maximum number of clicks at least one user needed to to find the content object of interest.

The results in table 2 shows that the values for the exploratory recommender is lower than that for the greedy recommender. This implies that the users are able to find the object of interest much faster. Note that this also holds when the recommender uses a distribution that does not correspond to the true popularity distribution of the users. This indicates that the results of the exploratory recommender are more robust for incorrect estimates of user preferences, making this better suited for an adaptive recommender that (probably) starts with a uniform distribution. The only exception is when the user and the site have the same peaked distribution. Here we see that the expected number of presentations is lower for the greedy recommender. So if a site has a few objects that are significantly more popular than the rest, then most users will benefit form the use of a greedy recommending policy.

6   Discussion

A recommender system that aims at helping users of a site needs a strategy for presenting suggestions to these users. A greedy policy recommender is one that only recommends those objects that are considered best according to some criterion, like the popularity of the objects. If the ranking of the objects is available then these can be used to implement the recommender.

A recommender that is adaptive first has to accumulate data from which the recommending strategy can be derived. In section 2 we presented results from earlier work that indicates how recommenders should behave when creating the data set. If recommendations are always greedy then a new recommender derived from the data may not be an improvement. Recommended objects will be chosen more often by the users because they are recommended, and will therefore be recommended by the new recommender as well. To overcome this when creating a data set, a strategy should be used that explores alternatives to the current greedy policy. One way to achieve this is by sometimes randomly replacing the greedy recommendations by objects that are currently not considered the best.

Once a correctly created data set is available the question is how it should be used to obtain a better recommender. In our case the aim of the recommender is to assist users in finding certain content objects, so a natural way to express the performance is the number of click the user needs to find the object of interest. Improving the recommender means reducing the number of clicks. We analysed two sequential recommending policies, where the user's previously made selections are used to reduce the steps to the target object. The *greedy* recommender recommends the popular objects that have a high probability of being the target for any user. The *exploratory* recommender aims at discarding as many objects as possible that are not likely to be target objects according to the choices the user made earlier on in the session.

Our analysis of the two sequential recommenders shows the following:

– Greedy recommending is not always the method that finds the target in the minimal number of interactions (or mouse clicks). Exploratory recommending can be shown to be better under most conditions. The main reason for this is that the greedy recommender aims at finishing the session in one step, ignoring the possible future. Only when a few objects are known to be significantly more popular than the rest, the greedy recommender will perform better. In this case, users interested in less popular objects will not benefit from this and have a harder time finding the their object of interest. Maybe a hybrid solution is needed where the greedy policy is used to help most users immediately and an exploratory policy to help those interested in less popular objects.

– The exploratory recommender perform very well, even when the popularity distribution used by the recommender is different from the real popularity distribution. This is very important for adaptive web sites. After the initialization of the recommender it may take a while before enough data is available to get a reliable estimate of the true popularity distribution. This may also be relevant for static web sites because the interests of a user population can drift.

– We made the assumption that the user is capable of selecting that object that is closest to the target. We can turn this around. If we know what users select given their target objects, we can organise the content of the site accordingly. So instead of having a scaling or clustering that is given, it should be derived from the data by correlating the users behaviors with the objects eventually found. In this way the responsibility of good recommendations is not placed in the hands of the users. Instead the recommender has to make sure that it can estimate the likelihood of object being the target given the selections of the users. Also it should be realised that users exist that do not behave as predicted, so that an additional mechanism is required to make sure that previously discarded objects still can be found.

There are a number of issues that need further work. One is the assumption we made that the content is scalable. In practice there may be cases in which this is not completely possible and then single selections of the users are not enough to discard a set of objects. One solution for this is to make user that the objects outside the scale are never recommended. This would not help the users that are interested in these objects. An other solution is to combine multiple actions until it is clear which objects are not the target of the user. An other issue is the combination with content-based methods. These can be used to model the space in which sequential recommending works and it can be used alone or together with the scaling approach by the exploratory recommender.

Other issues are different forms of recommending. Here we restricted the discussion to a specific recommender setting. We believe that the principle used above is also relevant for other recommending settings, although details may be different. For example, if more than two objects are presented, application of the binary search principle is more complicated and if ratings are used, a different method is needed but the approach remains the same and it is not difficult to adapt the method. If scaling results in a solution with much stress (data that do not fit the scale) a multidimensional method can be tried but if there remains too much randomness, scaling will not work and alteratives such as clustering need to be considered.

References

1. R. Armstrong, D. Freitag, T. Joachims, and T. Mitchell. Webwatcher: A learning apprentice for the world wide web. In *AAAI Spring Symposium on Information Gathering*, pages 6–12, 1995.
2. D. Billsus, C. Brunk, C. Evans, B. Gladish, and M. Pazzani. Adaptive interfaces for ubiquitous web. *Communications of The ACM*, 45(5):34–38, 2002.
3. C. Coombs. *A Theory of Data*. John Wiley, New York, 1964.
4. A. Kiss and J. Quinqueton. Multiagent cooperative learning of user preferences. In *Proceedings of the ECML/PKDD Workshop on Semantic Web Mining 2001*, pages 45–56, 2001.
5. P. Melville, R. Mooney, and R. Nagarajan. Content boosted collaborative filtering. In *Proceedings of the SIGIR-2001 Workshop on Recommender Systems*, 2001.
6. A. Moukas. User modeling in a multiagent evolving system. In *Proceedings of the ACAI'99 Workshop on Machine learning in user modeling*, pages 37–45, 1999.
7. A. Osterwalder and Y. Pigneur. Modelling customer relationships in e-business. In *Proceedings of the 16th Bled eCommerce Conference*, Maribor, Slovenia, 2003. Faculty of Organizational Sciences, University of Maribor.
8. M. Pazzani and D. Billsus. Learning and revising user profiles: The identification of interesting web sites. *Machine Learning*, 27:313–331, 1997.
9. M. Perkowitz and O. O. Etzioni. Adaptive web sites: Automatically syntesizing web pages. In *Proceedings of the 15th National Conference on Artificial Intelligence AAAI98*, pages 727–732, 1998.
10. I. Schwab and W. Pohl. Learning user profiles from positive examples. In *Proceedings of the ACAI'99 Workshop on Machine learning in user modeling*, pages 21–29, 1999.
11. T. Sullivan. Reading reader reaction: A proposal for inferential analysis of web server log files. In *Proceedings of the 3rd Conference on Human Factors and the Web Conference*, 1997.
12. R. Sutton. Generalizing in reinforcement learning: Succesful examples using sparse coarse coding. In *Advances in Neural Information Processing Systems (8)*, 1996.
13. R. Sutton and A. Barto. *Reinforcement Learning: An Introduction*. MIT Press, 1998.
14. K. Swearingen and R. Sinha. Beyond algorithms: An hci perspective on recommender systems. In *Proceedings of the ACM SIGIR 2001 Workshop on Recommender Systems*, New Orleans, Lousiana, 2001.
15. S. ten Hagen, M. van Someren, and V. Hollink. Exploration/exploitation in adaptive recommender systems. In *Proceedings of the European Symposium on Intelligent Technologies, Hybrid Systems and their implementation on Smart Adaptive Systems*, Oulu, Finland, 2003.
16. T. Zhang and V. Iyengar. Recommender systems using lineair classifiers. *Joural of Machine Learning Research*, 2:313–334, 2002.

An Approach to Estimate the Value of User Sessions Using Multiple Viewpoints and Goals

E. Menasalvas[1]*, S. Millán[2], M.S. Pérez[1], E. Hochsztain[3], and A. Tasistro[4]

[1] Facultad de Informática UPM. Madrid Spain
[2] Universidad del Valle. Cali. Colombia
[3] Facultad de Ingeniería - Universidad ORT Uruguay
[4] Universidad de la República. Uruguay

Abstract. Web-based commerce systems fail to achieve many of the features that enable small businesses to develop a friendly human relationship with customers. Although many enterprises have worried about user identification to solve the problem, the solution goes far beyond trying to find out what navigator's behavior looks like. Many approaches have recently been proposed to enrich the data in web logs with semantics related to the business so that web mining algorithms can later be applied to discover patterns and trends. In this paper we present an innovative method of log enrichment as several goals and viewpoints of the organization owning the site are taken into account. By later applying discriminant analysis to the information enriched this way, it is possible to identify the relevant factors that contribute most to the success of a session for each viewpoint under consideration. The method also helps to estimate ongoing session value in terms of how the company's objectives and expectations are being achieved.

1 Introduction

The Internet has become a new communication channel, cheaper and with greater location independency. This, together with the possibility of reaching a potential market of millions of clients and reducing the cost of doing business, accounts for the amazing number of organizations that during the last decade have started operations on the Internet, designing and implementing web sites to interact with their customers. Though the Internet seems to be very attractive for both users and owners of web sites, web-based activities interrupt direct contact with clients and, therefore, fail to achieve many of the features that enable small businesses to develop a warm human relationship with customers. The loss of this one-to-one relationship tends to make businesses less competitive because it is difficult to manage customers when no information about them is available. Although many enterprises have been very worried about getting hold of the identity of the navigator, what is important is not the identity of the user but information about his likes and dislikes, his preferences, or the way he behaves. All this, integrated with information related to the business, will result in successful e-CRM.

The relationship with the users is paramount when trying to develop activities competitively in any web environment. Thus, adapting the web site according to user preferences

---

* Research is partially supported by Universidad Politécnica de Madrid (project Web-RT)

B. Berendt et al. (Eds.): EWMF 2003, LNAI 3209, pp. 164–180, 2004.

is the unavoidable commitment that web-site sponsors must face and, when doing so, preferences and goals of the organization cannot be neglected.

Obtaining and examining the implicit but available knowledge about customers and site owners is the route to be followed to obtain advantages over other competitive Web sites and other communication channels. To analyze the available user navigation data so that knowledge can be obtained, web mining techniques have to be used. This is a challenging activity because the data have not been collected for knowledge discovery processes.

On the other hand, goal achievement has to be measured by the return on investment (ROI)[21]. Measuring the effectiveness of the site from this perspective is also challenging as it should comprise the different company's viewpoints [9]. Each viewpoint will correspond to a particular department or division of the company that will have, at each moment, defined the set of goals to achieve. Each goal will have a particular weight according to the global objetive of the company at a particular moment.

Some approaches (see section 2) have been proposed to measure the effectiveness of web sites but they only consider one viewpoint at a time. The challenge is to have a measure of the success of the site from each viewpoint considered, while also having a combined measure of the global success of the site at a particular moment.

The activity is challenging because the discrepancies among the different criteria used to evaluate business on the Internet often interfere with decision making and with the establishment of proactive actions. A project that has been successfully evaluated by one department is often classified as a failure by another. The first difficulty arises when trying to translate discovered knowledge into concrete actions [22] and trying later to estimate the effect of each action as ROI [12]. More difficulties arise on the Web since actions have to be taken repeatedly on-line as competitors are only a click away.

In this paper, we present an approach for measuring on-line navigation so that proactive actions can be undertaken. The approach is based on the evaluation of user behavior from different viewpoints and further action derivation. A method based on discriminant analysis is proposed so that in addition to obtaining an estimation of the value of the session, those factors that contribute most to the success of a session are identified. Since the exploitation approach is made in a dynamic environment and requires several coordinated and dependent actions, we propose to deploy the whole approach by means of a three-tier agent-based architecture in which agents for preprocessing, classification and proactive actions are identified. Agent technology allows applications to adapt successfully to complex, dynamic and heterogeneous environments, making the gradual addition of functionalities also possible [30].

The remainder of the paper is organized as follows. Section 2 presents the related work. Section 3 introduces the factors that have to be taken into account to estimate the value of a session when dealing with multiple viewpoints. The proposed methodology and a complete description of all the steps of the process presented in section 4. One of the key questions of the approach is the predictive method to estimate the value of the session. In this case, the method is based on discriminant analysis and is further explained in section 5. The architecture we proposed to deploy in our approach is shown in section 6. Section 7 presents experimental results and section 8 presents the main conclusions and further developments.

2 Related Work

Most enterprises are investing great amounts of money in order to establish mechanisms to discover Internet's user behavior. Many tools, algorithms and systems have been developed to provide Web site administrators with information and knowledge useful to understand user behavior and improve Web site results. Our work is related to three main topics: Web usage mining, Web agents and measures to evaluate site success.

2.1 Web Usage Mining

A way to evaluate the quality of a particular site is to determine how well a Web site's structure adjusts to the intuition of Web site users, represented in their navigation behaviour [3].

First, approaches to do this concentrated on analyzing clickstream data in order to obtain user's navigation patterns using data mining techniques [4] [16] [24] [26] [29]. However, Web mining results can be improved when they are enhanced with Web semantic information [2]. In this sense, several approaches, most of them based on ontologies, have been proposed in order to take site semantics into account. Berendt et al. [3] propose enriching Web log data with semantic information that could be obtained from textual content included in the site or using conceptual hierarchies based on services. On the other hand, Chi et al. [5] introduce an approach that, taking into account information associated to goals inferred from particular patterns and information associated to linked pages, makes it possible to understand the relationship between user needs and user actions. Oberle et al. [18] represent user actions based on an ontology's taxonomy. URL's are mapped to applications events depending on whether they represent actions (i.e. buy) or content.

However, most of these approaches and methods have concentrated on understanding user behaviour without taking Web business goals into account, whether these goals are diverse and dependent for different organizational departments. In [15] we propose an algorithm that takes into account both the information of the server logs and the business goals, improving traditional Web analysis. In this algorithm, however, the value of the links is statically assigned.

In this paper, we consider multiple business viewpoints and factors in order to understand Web user behaviour and act accordingly in a proactive way.

2.2 Web Agents

In this paper we introduce an architecture based on software agents. Taking into account that software agents exhibit a degree of autonomous behavior and attempt to act intelligently on behalf of the user for whom they are working [14][19], Web agents included in the architecture deal with all tasks of the proposed method.

In Web domain, software agents have been used for several purposes: filtering, retrieval, recommending, categorizing and collaborating.

A market architecture that supports multi-agent contracting implemented, with the use of the system MAGNET (Multi AGent NEgotiation Testbed), is presented in [6]. According to the authors, the system provides support for different kinds of transactions, from simple buying and selling of goods and services to complex multi-agent negotiation of contracts with temporal and precedence constraints. MARI (Multi-Attribute Resource Intermediary) [28] consists of an intermediary architecture that allows both buyer and seller to exercise control over a commercial transaction. MARI makes it possible to specify different preferences for the transaction partner. Furthermore, MARI proposes an integrative negotiation protocol between buying agents and selling agents.

Based on knowledge represented by multiple ontologies, in [20], agents and services are defined in order to support navigation in a conference-schedule domain. ARCH (Adaptive Retrieval based on Concept Hierarchies) [23] helps the user in expressing an effective search query, using domain concept hierarchies.

Most of these systems have been designed as user-side agents to assist users in carrying out different kinds of tasks. The agent-based architecture proposed in this paper has been designed taking the business point of view into account. Agents, in our approach, could be considered as business-side agents.

2.3   Measuring the Effectiveness of the Site

In spite of the huge volume of data stored on the Web, the relationship between user navigation data and site effectiveness, in terms of site goals when trying to design "good pages" or users, is still difficult to understand. Several approaches, models and measures have been proposed in order to evaluate and improve Web sites. Decision-making criteria related to the design and content of Web sites are needed so that user behavior is mapped onto the objectives and expectations of Web site owners.

Spiliopoulou et al. introduce in [25] a methodology useful for improving the success of a site and several success measures are proposed. The success of a site is evaluated based on the business goals. According to the authors it is necessary to identify one goal of the site at a time, in order to determine how different pages (action and target) on the site contribute to reach this goal. Besides, service-based concept hierarchies are introduced in order to transform Web site pages into action and target pages. User sessions are considered active sessions if they contain activities towards reaching the goal.
A set of metrics useful to evaluate the effectiveness of a Web market is proposed in Lee et al.[13]. The metrics definition, called micro-conversion rates, takes into account several shopping steps in online stores. Metrics have been integrated into an interactive visualization system and they provide information about store effectiveness.
Based on micro-conversion rates [13] and life-cycle metrics, Teltzrow and Berendt [27] propose and formalize several Web usage metrics to evaluate multi-channel businesses. Metrics are implemented into an interactive system that offers the user a visualization approach to analyze Web merchandizing.

3   Web Site Success Factors

Most of the approaches to evaluate the success of a Web site are stated in terms of efficiency and quality. In these approaches efficiency is generally measured by means of the number of pages accessed and served, duration of a session, and the action performed by the users (e.g. buy, download, query). Quality is measured by the response time, accessability of pages, and number of visitors of the site. The success of a company is measured by means of indicators such as profitability, costs, cost-effectiveness, ROI, gross sales, volume of business and turnover.

Thus, executive directors are often both amazed and disappointed by the differences between the criteria used to determine if the investment on a Web site is successful and the criteria used to evaluate the success of a project outside the Web. Department managers recognized that little consideration is given to the financial and commercial aspects of e-business projects [7] [8].

Due to the fact that the traditional criteria based on the ROI cannot be avoided when evaluating investments in Internet projects [21], some approaches that consider success both from the technological perspective (content, design of the Web pages) and the commercial perspective (achievement of company's goals) [9] have arisen.

Nevertheless, considering the commercial aspects of the site is not the only require-ment for measuring the success of the site. The global success of a company is the result of the contribution of each department to the fulfilment of the company goals. It is not reasonable to think that a company has only one success criterion (independently of the fact that the Web is being used as channel). On the contrary, and particularly in the Web sphere, by its presence on the Web always tries to achieve more than one goal, depending on particular environment conditions. Thus, both the goals and their weight for different viewpoints have to be taken into account when measuring the success of the site.

3.1   Different Viewpoints, Different Goals

As it has been already mentioned (see section 2), previous approaches assume that the analysis concerns one objective at a time characterizing this objective as the goal of the site. However, the Web site is not the aim but the means to achieve a company's goals. The significance of goal achievement differs for each company and each department of a company. In retailing domains, it is often the case that the only viewpoint under consideration is merchandizing, so that success is measured as the number of purchases. But for the marketing department the number of times a product is accessed is the goal rather than the number of final purchases. Thus, success or failure is not a one viewpoint function but it depends on different viewpoints each of which defines its own success criteria and goals. The goals of a company then depend on the viewpoint of the different departments, sections or divisions of the same company, defining in each case its own weights for the set of goals. It is often the case that different departments will assign weights to different goals in a contradictory way. In any case, the importance of each goal will depend on the environment conditions.

All that has been stated above, can be equally applied to businesses that use the Web only as a communication channel. In this sense, for example, the greatest significance for the marketing department will be assigned to the attractiveness and ease of use of the Web site by the user, while the department in charge of the design of the pages will give more importance to the site's design. In contrast, the sales department's most significant goal will be increasing the number of purchases.

Under any circumstances, the global success criteria will depend on the particular conditions. Hence, the goal established as: fulfill the user's needs at the same time as the company's goals are fulfilled can be measured as a function that depends, at least, on the following factors:

- Goals to be achieved
- Viewpoints that are considered
- Environment conditions
- User information on navigation and satisfaction
- Pages content

We formally express these factors in the following definitions.

Definition 1 *The set $Goals = \{g_1, g_2, \ldots, g_s\}$ represents the goals of a company at a particular moment.*

Definition 2 *The set $Viewpoints = \{v_1, v_2, \ldots, v_n\}$ represents different points of view (e.g., marketing, sales).*

Definition 3 *We define w_{ij} as the function that assigns weights to each goal, where i represents the ith viewpoint and j the jth goal. We assume that weights are going to be assigned to different goals depending on the viewpoint and depending on the environment conditions. As we are dealing with a weight function, it has the following properties:*

- $0 <= w_{ij} = w(g_i, v_j) <= l$ *where* $g_i \in Goals$ *and* $v_j \in Viewpoints$
- $\sum_{i \in Goals} w_{ij} = 1$

The set of goals G is made of the goals that the company (every department or just one particular department or division), aims to achieve. The importance of the different goals for the different viewpoints is reflected in the weight the goal has been assigned for each viewpoint. Thus in a way it is possible to say that the weight assigned to a goal is conditioned by the viewpoint under consideration. For each viewpoint the sum of the weights assigned to all the goals is always 1 (it may happen that a particular goal has zero as the weight assigned by a viewpoint meaning that this is not a goal of this viewpoint at this moment), $\sum_{i \in Goals} w_{ij}/v_j = 1$.

The example in table 1 illustrates this particular fact.

In the example of Table 1, goal g_2 is only taken into account by viewpoint number 3. Thus, for the rest of the viewpoints its weight will always be zero.

These assignments will be made at each particular moment by the experts of each department corresponding to different viewpoints. Notice that these assignments may change, for example, because of inside decisions (the company promoting a particular product or section), by actions taken by the competition (a competitor launching a new product), or simply by an environmental event (political events, ...). In order to be proactive the assignments need to always be kept update. Notice that these assignments could also be made on the basis of different user profiles.

Table 1. Example of relationship between goals and viewpoints

Goal	$v_1 = Marketing$	$v_2 =$ Commercial	$v_3 =$ Web Design
$g_1 =$ Long sessions	0.3	0.1	0.3
$g_2 =$ Awards in site design	0	0	0.6
$g_3 =$ Increasing purchases	0.1	0.4	0
$g_4 =$ Purchase different products	0.2	0.2	0
$g_5 =$ Access different products	0.3	0	0.1
$g_6 =$ Session Profit > 0	0.1	0.3	0

3.2   Mapping Pages into Business Goals

Business experts are responsible for the establishment of viewpoints, goals and weights. Once these have been established, the challenge is to add this information to the information about users and their navigation patterns. The only information about user behavior that is available is stored in the Web log (clikstream). The gap to be filled is then the mapping of the business information to the clickstream. In order to capture the business information and to integrate it with the user navigation, we propose pages to be enriched with semantic information related both to the content (as already proposed in [2]) and to the business goals and viewpoints.

In our case, for each site and for each particular viewpoint we define the set of semantics (actions and/or contents) that are relevant to be studied by the site. Notice that this set of semantics can be modified through the site's life time depending on the factors that are relevant to be analyzed at each moment. The relevant information is modelled with the use of ontologies, taxonomies and databases. The way in which this is implemented depends on the technology underlying the site. For example, a site could enrich XML pages themselves with this information. In the case of pages being dynamically generated the enrichment could be done when accessing the database to build the page. The construction of the ontologies and databases containing semantics is outside the scope of this paper as we are concerned with the way we use this information to obtain a predictive model that can compute the value of a session. Thus the important point is that information about the business is obtained and later mapped against the pages.

Possible information to enrich sessions is the length of the session, whether the user has accessed pages in which awards were given, whether he has clicked on a link in the right or left handside part of the page, and whether he has downloaded certain information.

4   Estimating the Result of a Session

We propose to estimate the result of a session while the user is navigating. Our proposal is to map information about navigation onto business information to have a measure of how the goals are being achieved and consequently act. To estimate the result of ongoing sessions we propose a method based on discriminant analysis. The method is twofold: on the one hand, relevant factors to establish the success of a session are obtained and on the other, a measure of the success or failure of the session is obtained. This approach will help classify users on-line taking into account different viewpoints and, consequently, act according to their behavior and the weights each goal has been assigned. The process we propose to undertake includes the following steps:

- Classify historical user sessions as success or failure for the different viewpoints.
- Enrich the information of these sessions with information about the business.
- Apply discriminant analysis to obtain both relevant factors for the success of a session and a method to estimate the result of ongoing sessions.
- Apply the on-line method obtained to estimate the result of the session.
- Act consequently to the estimated result.

4.1 Classify Historical Sessions

The first requirement for obtaining a predictive model is to have historical examples already classified. In our case, the innovative aspect is that sessions have to be classified according to the different viewpoints under consideration.

In classifying sessions we propose two approaches that have been used in the case-study:

- Expert-driven classification: In this approach the expert establishes some criteria for the success of a session, e.g. having asked for information about a certain product. Later, all historical sessions are classified according to the established criteria. In our approach, criteria for the different departments have to be established.
- Improved-expert driven classification. In the second approach the expert is given a set of sessions and instead of giving the criteria to classify them, he classifies them. Then using a classification method (decision tree in our case) the rest of the historical sessions are classified. The main problem of this approach is that the expert is rarely available to manually classify past sessions and if available he will luckily classify a very small set of sessions. Thus, the reliability of the classification method will be under question.

For the future, we propose to use an agent that records, once the session is over, its value (real one) from all the viewpoints considered. These sessions are the input for future improvement of the estimation procedure. This task is performed in the refining stage, as shown in section 6.

4.2 Enrich the Information on the Sessions

The set of sessions already classified enriched with information about the business. Consequently, we obtain a table called **enriched session table**, in which each tuple contains the session identifier and the business information that is taken into account,i.e., information related to action, contents, design of the pages, etc. For each piece of information taken into account, the session can only take values 0 or 1 to specify whether that action occurred during the session. As the approach is multi-goal, in this table we keep, for each department (viewpoint), if the session fulfilled each goal. Nevertheless, we need a global value of the session for each department. In order to obtain this global value, weights of the goals are used. And the resulting values are stored in a new table, named

Results table. Consequently, *Results table* contains information related to the success or failure of each session from each point of view considered.

The innovative aspect of the approach is that several viewpoints and goals are considered at a time. This way, for each session and for each goal we will have a measure of how successful the session occurred to be. Once this information is available, we propose to apply discriminant analysis to obtain the factors that contribute most to the results for each viewpoint and for each goal.

5   Discriminant Analysis Application

We applied a stepwise multivariate predictive model to the set of sessions already classified and enriched. The basic strategy in discriminant analysis is to define a linear combination of the dependent attributes. In our case, the dependent attributes are semantic actions or concepts $s_1, s_2, \ldots, s_t$ that have been used when enriching the sessions. Notice that the aim of our approach is to determine which user actions (s_i) contribute to achieve the department goals. Thus the equation will have the form:

$$L = v_1 s_1 + v_2 s_2 + \ldots + v_t s_t.$$

Once this equation is obtained, the success or failure of a session will be established on the basis of the value of L obtained for that session:

- if $L >= 0$ session success is predicted
- if $L < 0$ session failure is predicted

For simplicity reasons we use here a dichotomic classification. Nevertheless, the extension to deal with more classes is straightforward and can be found in the references. Discriminant analysis is useful in finding the most relevant semantic concepts. In each step of the stepwise discriminant technique the importance of each attribute included can be studied. This is important not only because we will have the equation to estimate the value of a session in the future but also because the method provides the analyst with criteria to understand which actions are most relevant for the success of a session from each viewpoint. The computation of the discriminant function has been done according to [11], [1], [17]. The model estimates the coefficients (values) of each attribute considered (semantic) for each pair of goals and viewpoint considered.

>From this result, it is possible to establish the relationship between semantics and the result of the session. Those coefficients with higher positive value, are associated with sessions successfully ending while those taking negative values are associated with failure sessions.

Hence the proposed approach, provides both the predictive model and the procedure used to establish actions to make a session successful from a certain site viewpoint. Notice that the number of relevant concepts ($N1$) will be much less than the number of pages N ($N1 << N$) in a Web site, so that the problem of analyzing user session decreases in complexity, improving the performance of the methods used to analyze them.

5.1   Applying the Algorithm Online

Once the functions to estimate session value have been obtained, they can be applied on-line to decide the action to be undertaken depending on the estimated result of the session. This activity is again challenging as the result depends on the moment that we apply the model. Due to the fact that it is difficult to predict when a session is to be terminated, let alone finding out how many pages the user will visit, the timing for applying estimation procedures can bias the results.

In our case, we propose to use the algorithm proposed in [10]. According to this algorithm, "breaking" pages in which the user will make a decision can be recognized in the navigation pattern of a user. In the architecture proposed here there will also be agents in charge of this task and according to the breaking pages, the agents will decide the moment of application of the estimation procedure for each on-going session. As a result of the application of the estimation procedure, we will obtain a value of goal achievement for the session and for each viewpoint considered. Furthermore, making use of the weight assignment policies at each moment, another agent will decide on the global value of the session and the action to be taken, if any (i.e., action agents). The action to be taken has to be decided by the business experts and we assume that the information on these actions is stored somewhere in the system and accessed by action agents. Notice that these actions could depend on the user profile if this information were available in the system.

6   Architecture Overview

Web Mining tasks have often been implemented by agents. The agent paradigm offers desirable features such as autonomy, that is, the ability of acting itself and on behalf of others and proactivity, that is, the ability of acting in anticipation of future problems, needs or changes. These characteristics are very suitable in the scenario described in the previous sections because of its dynamic idiosyncrasy. Furthermore, the agent paradigm makes dynamic changes of functionalities feasible. Since Web Mining tasks evolves quickly, we consider that this paradigm is the most suitable one.

Thus, a multiagent architecture is proposed, which is composed of three different layers:

1. Semantic Layer. This layer contains agents related to the logic of the algorithm or method used in the ongoing session result estimation.
2. Optimization/Decision Layer. Corresponds with the agents responsible for optimizing or making decisions depending on the estimated value.
3. Service Provider Layer. This layer contains agents that provide several services other of the agents. These services are generic and independent of the other layers. It also offers an interface, which will be used by any agent asking for a service.

6.1   Semantic Layer

This level is fed directly by the session value estimation methods. The agents of this layer deal with the concepts value estimation and its usage in subsequent sessions. This layer is a multiagent subsystem composed of different specialized agents. They are:

- Preprocessing agents: These agents are responsible for enriching the sessions.
- Classification agents. Classification of a session is made according to an expert, but the criteria used can be automated through the usage of previous classifications and expert knowledge.
- Estimation agents. These agents apply the stepwise multivariate predictive model. In a first phase, this operation is made offline. Nevertheless, the algorithm must be applied online in current Web usage data to estimate the result of a session. Another task that has to be performed by these agents is obtaining the breaking points to decide when the estimation procedure needs to be applied.
- Refining agents. Classification is a continuous task. It is necessary to refine the algorithm with new information (new sessions, new business criteria). This kind of agents must communicate with the estimation agents in order to inform them about changes.

As we can see, using agents in the semantic layer provides adaptivity to the algorithm.

6.2 Optimization/Decision-Making Layer

This layer includes agents that make decisions depending on the information supplied by the semantic layer. We define a generic action agent as an agent template for building agents which allow actions to be taken according to session values. Although it is possible to build other kinds of agents using this template and the needs of the Web site, we have defined the following agents with the aim of optimizing the accesses and personalization usage of the Web site:

- Prefetching agents. These agents prefetch most probably next visited Web pages, depending on the session value. Sessions with a higher estimated value are given higher priority. This way, the Web session load is more efficient and the user feels more comfortable in the Web site.
- Adaptive agents. These agents are responsible for building offers adapted to the preferences of the users. These offers may be shown as popups or Web pages. Any other kind of personalization can be added to the logic of these agents.

6.3 Service Provider Layer

This level includes generic services used for assisting other layer agents. These agents are:

- Data retrieval agents. The goal of these agents is to retrieve data from different information sources. These sources are heterogeneous (e.g., databases, files) and they have different types of information and access requirements. Therefore, these agents can delegate on specialized agents for different sources.
- Locator agents. They are in charge of connecting agents. In order to locate a given agent, the locator agents use its category, that is, the type of agent. If there is no available agent of this type, the system launches a new agent for serving this request.

It is possible to add more services to the architecture. The procedure to do so is to implement the corresponding kind of agent and define the corresponding interface with the rest of the architecture.

Figure 1 represents the three layers of the proposed architecture and the relationship between layers. Notice, that there are both internal and external relationships among different kinds of agents. The different information sources are also shown in the graphic.

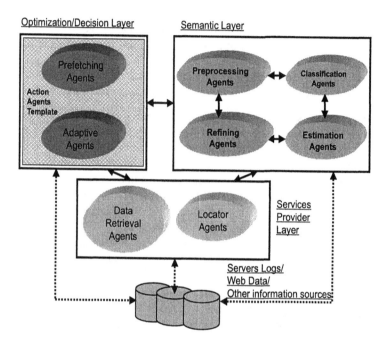

Fig. 1. Web-behavior agent-based architecture layers

7   Case Study – Experimental Results

A company developing its activity both through the Internet and in the traditional way, was taken as the example for the case study. The company under consideration was having difficulties to define success criteria. The departments involved in the study were:

- Marketing
- Commercial
- Web Design
- Technological
- Manufacturing

The e-commerce site contained 2500 pages. We present here the results after analyzing sessions on the server for a month. After filtering out irrelevant entries, the data were segmented into 38058 sessions. The discriminant model has been obtained through a two-step process of test and training (80%)

Table 1 shows the weights of the goals for each viewpoint under consideration. For clarity reason, we only present in this section the results for the commercial department. The main goal of the analysis was applying the proposed method so that the following actions could be undertaken:

– Establishment of concepts or actions behind the visited pages (semantics) that arc more relevant for the success of a session (i.e., those that contribute most to the achievement of goals).
– To provide on-line information to automatically make decisions on what motivates the user (e.g., automatic prefetching, online offers and discounts).

The results of the study found discrepancies between departments and highlighted that the cause of problem was the fact that they were trying to measure the efficiency of the site from a single viewpoint. Viewpoints were identified and success criteria were defined to be integrated in the procedure that estimates the result of a navigation session. The method used to evaluate the sessions combines qualitative and quantitative elements. Qualitative methods included meetings with the managers of the five divisions involved. The aim of interviews was to find the main goals of each department and the importance that each department assigns to each goal.

Some the goals identified include increasing the number of purchases (both in number of purchases and in variety of products in the baskets), awards for the design of site pages, use of contact points at the site by the users.

The quantitative elements were used to measure the achievement of the proposed goals. The first step was to eliminate from the set of goals those that were not directly reflected in the sessions. For example, the goal: "obtaining awards for the design of Web pages" was eliminated.

In a second step, semantic elements were identified to enrich sessions. As most of the pages in the site were dynamically generated, the semantic enrichment in this case was done as the page was generated.

A total of 94 elements were identified to enrich the pages. During the preprocessing and data transformation phases, only 9 out of these 94 elements, were considered relevant. These 9 elements are shown in table 2.

The value of each concept has been established. Results are shown in table 3. The model predicts 93.3 percent of the successful sessions and 82,2 percent of the failure sessions.

The biggest advantage of the proposed method is that helps to determine the importance of each concept for a viewpoint with a high predictive power. A concept is consider to have high predictive value when the model properly classifies more than 70 percent of the sessions.

For the commercial department, the predictive accuracy of the model can be seen in table 3. In this table, we can see that 93.3% of the successful sessions and the 82.2% of the failure sessions were correctly predicted.

Table 2. Examples of semantic elements used to enrich pages

semantic-id	semantic-description
s1	advertising
s2	news
s3	food purchase
s4	cleaning products
s5	cosmetics
s6	download travel information
s7	travel booking
s8	download music information
s9	asking information about promotions

Table 3. Summary discriminant table

	Predicted	
Observed	Success	Failure
Success	93.3	6.7
Failure	17.8	82.2

The discriminant function obtained was:

$$L = 0,431s_1 +, 0,99s_2 + 0,126s_3 + 0,751s_4 - 0,444s_5 - 0,107s_6 + 0,119s_7 + 0,742s_8 + 0,306s_9$$

The proposed analysis helped to establish the relevant factors to take into account when analyzing sessions.

The results of the discriminant function have been depicted in an histogram, where X-axis represents the value of the discriminant function (L) and the Y-axis represents the function of the empiric density. Thus, the area of each rectangle represents the relative frequency of values of the discriminant function for each interval. (Figure 2(a) represents the results for successful sessions and figure 2(b) represents the histogram for failure sessions). The in-depth analysis of the wrong classified sessions helped the site sponsor recognize market niches. Notice that it is more difficult to describe the wrongly classified examples as they resides at the edges.

In 83% of the cases, the number of relevant concepts able to classify a session was 20% or less out of the 94 initial concepts. Finally, when goals were weighted according to each point of view taken into account, an aggregate perception of all goals was obtained for each point of view (i.e., the same session was successful for the Department of Marketing but not for the Sales Department).

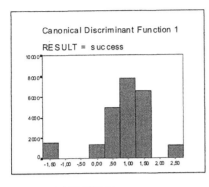
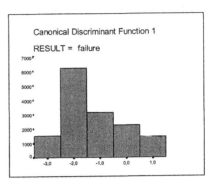

(a) RESULT = success.   (b) RESULT = failure.

Fig. 2. Canonical Discriminant Function 1

8   Conclusions

The global success of a company is the result of the contribution of each department to the fulfilment of the company goal. Based on this fact, in this paper we have presented a method to estimate the value of a navigation session according to different viewpoints. This is the innovative aspect of the approach as it makes it possible to analyze user behavior by a global measurement related to all the relevant goals of the company. Besides, an agent-based architecture has been defined with the aim of providing dynamism to method deployment.

The main drawback of the method proposed in this paper, is that it requires a set of sessions already classified by the experts of each department. To solve this problem we have also proposed a semi-automatic method to classify sessions but the methods still depends heavily on the expert.

The method has shown to have promising results in the e-commerce site that has been used in the case-study. The results highlighted some market niches and helped the organization to find the factors that made sessions end successfully.

One important factor to measure the success of a session that has been tackled by the proposed approach, is that of dealing with the different goals and viewpoints of the company. However, goals to be achieved by a company also depend on the customer typology, this is to say, for example, that goals to be achieved for very loyal customers may differ from those for the customer who visit the site for the first time.

On the other hand, the proposed method estimates the value of a session based on the presence of some relevant factors the order in which the events occur.

Some open issues that can be developed and addressed by multiple alternatives have been the motivation of current research for improving the proposed method and forecoming work.

Acknowledgments. The research has been partially supported by Universidad Politécnica de Madrid under Project WEB-RT and Programa de Desarrollo Tecnológico (Uruguay).

References

1. R. E. Anderson, R. L. Tatham, and W. C. Black. *Multivariate Data Analysis (5th Edition).* Prentice Hall College Div, Mar 1998.
2. B. Berendt, A. Hotho, and G. Stumme. Towards semantic web mining. *ISWC 2002, LNCS 2342,* pages 264–278, 2002.
3. B. Berendt and M. Spiliopoulou. Analysis of navigation behavior in web sites integrating multiple information systems. *The VLDB Journal,* 9:56–75, 2000.
4. J. Borges and M. Levene. A heuristic to capture longer user web navigation patterns. In *Proc. of the First International Conference on Electronic Commerce and Web Technologies, Greenwich, U.K.,* pages 27–34, September 2000.
5. E. H. Chi, P. Pirolli, and J. Pitkow. The scent of a site: A system for analyzing and predicting information scent, usage, and usability of a web site. In *Proc. of CHI '2000 The Hague, Amsterdam CHI Letters,* 2000.
6. J. Collins, W. Ketter, M. Gini, and B. Mobasher. A multi-agent negotiation testbed for contracting tasks with temporal and precedence constraints. *Int. Journal of Electronic Commerce,* 7(1):35–57, 2002.
7. Jaap Gordijn and Hans Akkermans. Does e-business modeling really help? *Proceedings of the 36th Hawaii International Conference On System Sciences,(HICSS-36 2003),* January 2003.
8. Jaap Gordijn and J.M. Akkermans. Value-based requirements engineering: exploring innovative e-commerce ideas. *Requirements Engineering,* 8(2):114 – 134, July 2003.
9. Jaap Gordijn. Why visualization of e-business models matters. *16th eCommerce Conference eTransformation panel Business models & the mobile industry: Concepts, Metrics, Visualization and Cases,* June 2003.
10. M. Hadjimichael, O. Marbán, E. Menasalvas, S. Millan, and J.M. Peña. Subsessions: a granular approach to click path analysis. In *Proceedings of IEEE Int. Conf. On Fuzzy Systems 2002 (WCCI2002), Honolulu, U.S.A.,* pages 878–883, May 2002.
11. D. G. Keibaun, L. L. Kupper, and K. E. Muller. *Applied Regression Analysis and Other Multivariable Methods.* PWS-KENT Publishing Company, USA, 1988.
12. Ron Kohavi, Neal J. Rothleder, and Evangelos Simoudis. Emerging trends in business analytics. *Communications of the ACM,* 45(8):45–48, August 2002.
13. J. Lee, M. Podlaseck, E. Schonberg, and R. Hoch. Visualization and analysis of clickstream data of online stores for understanding web merchandizing. *Data Mining and Knowledge discovery,* 5(1/2), 2001.
14. P. Maes. Agents that reduce work and information overload. *Communications of the ACM,* 37(7), 1994.
15. E. Menasalvas, S. Millán, and E. Hochsztain. A granular approach for analyzing the degree of afability of a web site. In *Proc. of International Conference on Rough Sets and Current Trends in Computing RSCTC2002,* October 2002.
16. B. Mobasher, H. Dai, T. Luo, M. Nakagawa, and J. Witshire. Discovery of aggregate usage profiles for web personalization. In *Proceedings of the WebKDD Workshop,* 2000.
17. D. Morrison. *Multivariate Statistical Methods.* Duxbury Press; 4th edition, 2002.
18. D. Oberle, B. Berendt, A. Hotho, and J. Gonzalez. Conceptual user tracking. *Advance in Web Intelligence. LNAI 2663. AWIC 2003,* pages 155–164, May 2003.

19. M. Papazoglou. Agent-oriented technology in support of e-business. *Communications of the ACM*, 44(4), 2001.
20. T. R. Payne, R. Singh, and K. Sycara. Browsing schedules - an agent-based approach to navigating the semantic web. *ISWC 2002, LNCS 2342*, pages 469–473, 2002.
21. Gregory Piatetsky-Shapiro. Interview with Jesus Mena. http://www.kdnuggets.com/news/2001/n13/13i.html, 2001. Last update: July 2003.
22. M Schoop, A Becks, C Quix, T Burwick, C Engels, and M Jarke. Enhancing decision and negotiation support in enterprise networks through semantic web technologies. *R. Tolksdorf, R. Eckstein(eds.): XML Technologien für das Semantic Web - XSW Berlin Lecture Notesin Informatics*, Volume P-14:161–167, 2002.
23. A. Sieg, B. Mobasher, S. Lytinen, and R. Burke. Concept based query enhancement in the arch search agent. In *Proceedings of the 4th International Conference on Internet Computing (IC'03), Las Vegas*, June 2003.
24. M. Spiliopoulou, C. Pohle, and L. Faulstich. Improving the effectiveness of a web site with web usage mining. In *Proceedings of the WEBKDD99*, 1999.
25. M. Spiliopoulou and C. Pohle. Data mining for measuring and improving the success of web sites. *Data mining and Knowledge Discovery*, 5(1-2), 2001.
26. J. Srivastava, R. Cooley, M. Deshpande, and P. Tan. Web usage mining: Discovery and applications of usage patterns from web data. *SIGKDD Explorations*, 1:12–23, 2000.
27. M. Teltzrow and B. Berendt. Web-usage-based success metrics for multichannel businesses. In *Proceedings of WebKDD 2003 Workshop August 27h, 2003, Washington DC, USA*, 2003.
28. G. Tewari and P. Maes. Design and implementation of an agent-based intermediary infrastructure for electronic markets. In *Proceedings of the EC'00, Minneapolis, Minnesota*, October 2000.
29. G. Wolfang and S. Lars. Mining web navigation path fragments. In *Workshop on Web Mining for E-Commerce - Challenges and Opportunities Working Notes (KDD2000), Boston, MA*, pages 105–110, August 2000.
30. Michael Wooldridge and Nicholas R. Jennings. Intelligent agents: Theory and practice. *Knowledge Engineering Review*, 1995.

Monitoring the Evolution of Web Usage Patterns

Steffan Baron[1] and Myra Spiliopoulou[2]

[1] Institute of Information Systems, Humboldt-Universität zu Berlin
Spandauer Str. 1, Berlin 10178, Germany
sbaron@wiwi.hu-berlin.de
[2] Institute of Technical and Business Information Systems,
Otto-von-Guericke-Universität Magdeburg,
PO Box 4120, Magdeburg 39016, Germany
myra@iti.cs.uni-magdeburg.de

Abstract. With the ongoing shift from off-line to on-line business processes, the Web has become an important business platform, and for most companies it is crucial to have an on-line presence which can be used to gather information about their products and/or services. However, in many cases there is a difference between the intended and the effective usage of a web site and, presently, many web site operators analyse the usage of their sites to improve their usability. But particularly in the context of the Internet, content and structure change rather quickly, and the way a web site is used may change often, either due to changing information needs of its visitors, or due to an evolving user group. Therefore, the discovered usage patterns need to be updated continuously to always reflect the actual behaviour of the visitors.

In this article, we introduce PAM, an automated *Pattern Monitor*, which can be used to observe changes to the behaviour of a web site's visitors. It is based on a temporal representation of rules in which both the content of the rule and its statistical properties are modelled. It observes pattern change as evolution of the statistical measurements captured for a rule throughout its entire lifetime and notifies the user about interesting changes within the rule base. We present PAM in a case study on the evolution of web usage patterns. In particular, we discovered association rules from a web-server log that show which pages tend to be visited within the same user session. These patterns have been imported into the monitor, and their evolution throughout a period of 8 months has been analysed. Our results show that PAM is particularly suitable to gain insights into the changes of a rule base over time.

1 Introduction and Related Work

Knowledge discovery is an iterative process that reflects the need of extracting knowledge from data that accumulate constantly [6]. The application expert periodically invokes a data mining tool to extract patterns from the data. Each invocation contributes new insights on the application domain, enriching the expert's domain knowledge and, occasionally, motivating her to revise her beliefs. As the expert becomes gradually familiar with the patterns being extracted, she is increasingly interested in *changes* rather than in already known patterns. Particularly in the context of the Internet, content and structure

B. Berendt et al. (Eds.): EWMF 2003, LNAI 3209, pp. 181–200, 2004.

change rather quickly, and the way a web site is used may change often or even permanently, either due to the changing information needs of its visitors, or due to an evolving user group. Therefore, the discovered usage patterns need to be updated continuously to always reflect the actual behaviour of the visitors. In the case of a heavily used web site with thousands of users per day, the question arises how this can be achieved with a reasonable amount of effort.

One major problem is the large number of discovered rules, and the identification of *interesting* patterns has become a widely discussed topic [9,7]. Even for small datasets this a problem and makes the inspection of all rules impractical. In some cases, it may be possible to assess the interestingness of rules manually or with respect to the application context, e.g. if the occurrence of a particular pattern suggests an application error. However, this is usually quite time consuming, and there are approaches that offer application independent solutions to this problem based on the statistical properties of patterns [21, 12,13]. The problem of interestingness arises also when evaluating the changes that have affected a rule. A commonly used approach to protect the domain expert from inspecting too many rule changes is the definition of limits for e.g. the steepness of change for the observed statistical measurements. When these limits are exceeded, the corresponding rule change is considered to be interesting. Furthermore, a pattern classified as interesting may only change slightly over time, whereas a pattern that is actually not interesting may exhibit strong changes which are of particular importance to the domain expert. Therefore, the selection of rules should not be limited to *conventional* methods which assess rules statically, they should rather be evaluated embracing their *temporal* dimension.

When data, as in the case of web-server logs, is continuously collected over a potentially long period, the concepts reflected in the data will change over time. Due to internal and/or external factors, the distribution and/or the composition of the dataset may change. This requires the user to monitor the discovered patterns continuously, which is of particular importance for applications that timestamp data. One possible way to deal with the temporal dimension is to use an appropriate partitioning scheme. However, if the partitions are too big or too small the user may miss important rules and/or changes. Generally, partitioning is highly application depended. However, there is research into formal methods for application independent partitioning of data. Chen and Petrounias focus on the identification of valid time intervals for previously discovered association rules [9]. They propose a mechanism that finds (a) all contiguous time intervals during which a specific association holds, and (b) all interesting periodicities that a specific association has. Chakrabarti et al. propose the discovery of surprising, i.e. unexpected and therefore interesting, patterns in market basket analysis by observing the variation of the correlation of the purchases of items over time [8]. The underpinnings of that work come from time series analysis, so that the emphasis is on partitioning the time axis into such intervals that the rule statistics change dramatically between two consecutive intervals.

In the last years, a number of methods and techniques for maintaining and updating previously discovered knowledge have emerged which are able to deal with dynamic datasets. A widely used approach is that of *incremental mining* in which the knowledge about already extracted patterns is re-used in subsequent periods. Originally, the emphasis of incremental mining was on optimising the miners performance from one invocation of the miner to the next. Most of this research focuses on the update of association rules

[10,2,20,22], frequent sequences [23], and clusters [11]. They aim at efficiently updating the content of discovered rules, thus avoiding a complete re-run of the mining algorithm on the entire, updated dataset.

The DELI Change Detector of Lee et al. uses a sampling technique to detect changes that may affect previously discovered association rules [17,16]. It invokes an incremental miner to modify the patterns if this turns out to be necessary.

Ganti et al. propose the DEMON framework for data evolution and monitoring across the temporal dimension [15]. DEMON focuses on detecting systematic vs. non-systematic changes in the data and on identifying the data blocks (along the time dimension) which have to be processed by the miner in order to extract new patterns. The emphasis is on updating the knowledge base by detecting changes in the data, rather than detecting changes in the patterns.

Another avenue of research concentrates on the *similarity* of rules and on the statistical properties of rules by considering the *lifetime* of patterns, i.e., the time in which they are sufficiently supported by the data [14,8,9,15]. Ganti et al. propose the framework FOCUS for the comparison of two datasets and the computation of an interpretable, qualifiable deviation measure between them, whereby the difference is expressed in terms of the model the datasets induce [14].

However, all of these proposals consider only part of a pattern, either its content, i.e., the relationship in the data that the pattern reflects, or the statistical properties of the pattern. In [3], we took a first step towards an integrated treatment of these two aspects of a rule. We proposed the *Generic Rule Model* (GRM) which models both the content and the statistics of a rule as a temporal object. Based on these two components of a rule, different types of pattern evolution were defined. Additionally, a simple monitor was implemented which used a user supplied deviation threshold to identify interesting changes to pattern statistics.

Pattern change is usually caused by concept drift. As Kelly et al. point out in [19], adaptive classification algorithms, such as adaptive Bayesian networks are designed to overcome concept drift by considering the impact of each individual new record on the existing classifier and adapting it accordingly. However, the rapid accumulation of records, as in web-server logs, makes the consideration of the impact of each record ineffective. Moreover, individual records that come in large numbers are noisy and reflect trends only partially, especially for trends that manifest themselves slowly, such as a change in preferences or demographics of a user group.

The temporal aspects of patterns are taken into account in the rule monitors of [1,7] and [3,4,5]. In [7], Liu et al. count the significant rule changes across the temporal axis. They pay particular attention on rules that are "stable" over the whole time period, i.e. do not exhibit significant changes, and juxtapose them with rules that show trends of significant increase or decrease. Significance tests form the basis of the experiments. In [1], upward and downward trends in the statistics of rules are identified using an SQL-like query mechanism. Closer to our work is the research of Liu et al. on the discovery of "fundamental rule changes" [18]: they consider rules of the form $r_1, \ldots, r_{m-1} \rightarrow r_m$, and detect changes on support or confidence between two consecutive timepoints by applying a χ^2-test. In our previous work, we model rules as temporal objects, which may exhibit changes of statistics or *content* during the observation period, and we focus on surprising changes, such as the disappearance of a rule and the correlated changes of pairs of rules [3,4]. In [5], we make the distinction between "permanent" rules that are always present (though they may undergo significant changes) and those that appear only temporarily and indicate periodic trends, and discuss methods for identifying them in a *progressive study*.

In this study, we present PAM, an automated pattern monitor, and its theoretical underpinnings. In a case study on the evolution of web usage patterns, we show how the mechanisms implemented by PAM can be used to identify interesting changes in the usage behaviour. In particular, we discovered association rules from a web-server's log that show which pages tend to be visited within the same user session. These patterns have been imported into the monitor, and their evolution throughout a period of 8 months has been analysed.

In the following section, we will introduce the theoretical framework PAM is based upon and its architecture. In Section 3 our experimental results are summarised, and Section 4 concludes our study.

2   A Framework for Pattern Monitoring

We consider data mining as an iterative process which consists of consecutive "mining sessions" initiated at specific points in time t_i, $i = 0, 1, \ldots, n$, where t_0 is the moment of the first analysis. In the mining session at time point t_i the dataset D_i collected in the period $t_i - t_{i-1}$, $i \geq 1$ is analysed.[1] Each session reveals a set of patterns, some of them may be known from previous sessions, and others may be new. Still other patterns may have disappeared from the rule base. As opposed to the incremental mining techniques introduced in Section 1, the statistical properties of known patterns are not *updated*. Instead, the statistics of known patterns are recorded over time, and new patterns are inserted into the rule base. In the general case this has an important impact on the *evolution* of the statistics observed for a pattern.

Example 1. Consider a web site which has 5,000 visitors per week. Analysing the usage of the server over a period of three weeks the site operator has determined that page a.html was accessed in 1,000 sessions per week and page b.html in 1,500 sessions per week. Both pages a.html and b.html were accessed together in 900 sessions in periods t_1 and t_2 and in 600 sessions in period t_3. Table 1 summarises the usage over the three periods. From these session information association rules have been discovered using a support threshold of $\tau_{supp} = 0.1$ and a confidence threshold of $\tau_{conf} = 0.8$.

The last two columns of Table 1 show the results of the incremental approach. While there are no changes for the single item frequencies, both the support and the confidence of the rule "a.html $\Rightarrow$ b.html" decrease in the last period.[2] However, the rule still satisfies the threshold values. When using the monitoring approach the results change perspicuously. Since the data of each period is analysed separately, the influence of the support change between the second and the third period is much stronger and causes the disappearance of the pattern in the last period.

---

[1] In the remainder of the paper we use the terms "time point" and "period" interchangeably where period t_i corresponds to the time interval in which dataset D_i was collected, i.e., between time points t_{i-1} and t_i, $i \geq 1$.

[2] The rule "b.html $\Rightarrow$ a.html" is not considered as it fails to satisfy the confidence threshold in all three periods.

Table 1. Evolution of the site usage

	t_1	t_2	t_3	t_{1-2}	t_{1-3}
# sessions	5,000	5,000	5,000	10,000	15,000
# a.html	1,000	1,000	1,000	2,000	3,000
$supp(\texttt{a.html})$	0.20	0.20	0.20	0.20	0.20
# b.html	1,500	1,500	1,500	3,000	4,500
$supp(\texttt{b.html})$	0.30	0.30	0.30	0.30	0.30
# (a.html $\cup$ b.html)	900	900	600	1,800	2,400
$supp(\texttt{a.html} \cup \texttt{b.html})$	0.18	0.18	0.12	0.18	0.16
$conf(\texttt{a.html} \Rightarrow \texttt{b.html})$	0.90	0.90	0.60	0.90	0.80

This observation reflects a general drawback of the incremental approach: with respect to short-term changes it is far less sensitive than the monitoring approach. The incremental method assumes implicitly that the distribution of the underlying dataset does not change over time. However, in the long run this problem may be alleviated by either using a sliding time window or assigning smaller weights to historical data.

2.1 Temporal Rule Model

As the basis for the temporal representation of patterns we use the *Generic Rule Model* (GRM) [3]. According to this model, a rule R is a temporal object with the following signature:

$$R = ((ID, query, body, head), \{(timestamp, statistics)\})$$

In this signature, ID is a system generated identifier, which ensures that all rules with the same *body* (antecedent) and *head* (consequent) have the same ID. It is used to identify a rule non-ambiguously throughout its entire lifetime. The *query* is the data mining query or similar specification of values for the mining parameters. Note that *query* and ID are invariant across the time axis. Contrary to it, the statistics may vary between two timestamps. The statistics depend on the rule type: We currently consider the support, confidence and certainty factor of association rules. A detailed discussion of the components of the rule signature can be found in [3].

Example 2. Using the GRM, in period t_3 the rule "a.html $\Rightarrow$ b.html" from Example 1 would be represented as

$$R = (\ (\text{``ab''}, \langle \tau_{supp} = 0.1, \tau_{conf} = 0.8 \rangle, \text{``a.html''}, \text{``b.html''}),$$
$$\{\ (t_1, \langle supp = 0.18, conf = 0.9 \rangle),$$
$$(t_2, \langle supp = 0.18, conf = 0.9 \rangle),$$
$$(t_3, \langle supp = 0.12, conf = 0.6 \rangle)\ \}\ ).$$

2.2 Detecting Significant Pattern Changes

We denote a mechanism that identifies significant changes to a rule's statistic as *change detector*. We use the notion of statistical significance to assess the strength of pattern changes. In particular, we use a two-tailed binomial test to verify whether an observed change is statistically significant or not.

For a pattern ξ and a statistical measure s at a time point t_i it is tested whether $\xi.s(t_{i-1}) = \xi.s(t_i)$ at a confidence level α. The test is applied upon the subset of data D_i accumulated between t_{i-1} and t_i, so that the null hypothesis means that D_{i-1} is drawn from the same population as D_i, where D_{i-1} and D_i have an empty intersection by definition. Then, for a pattern ξ an alert is raised for each time point t_i at which the null hypothesis is rejected.

Example 3. Let $supp(t_{i-1}) = 0.1825$ be the support of pattern ξ at time point t_{i-1}, i.e. over dataset D_{i-1}. Let the number of sessions in D_i that support the pattern be 608 (*successes*) upon a total of 2914 sessions in D_i. We test the null hypothesis H_0 that the support of ξ has not changed significantly:

$$H_0 : \quad \xi.supp(t_{i-1}) = \xi.supp(t_i)$$
$$H_1 : \quad \xi.supp(t_{i-1}) \neq \xi.supp(t_i)$$

At $\alpha = 0.01$, the confidence interval ranges from 0.1896 to 0.2287. Since the true support value at time point t_{i-1} is smaller than the lower boundary of the confidence interval we reject H_0 and state that the support has changed significantly from time point t_{i-1} to time point t_i.

These tests are applied to the set of all patterns that appear in a given period. All significant pattern changes are additionally checked for their temporal dimension, i.e., whether they are only of temporary nature. We differentiate between two cases, (a) the value of the statistic returns immediately to its previous level, and (b) the value remains stable at the new level for at least m periods, where m is a user supplied parameter. For this purpose, we again use the binomial test and check if there is a significant change within the interval $[t_{i+1}, t_{i+m}]$ cancelling out the change in period t_i. If so, the second change is not reported to the user because it only represents the return of the measure to its actual level. Instead, the significant pattern change is marked as a *core alert* which may be used as an indicator for a beginning concept drift. Using this approach the temporal dimension of an observed pattern change can be estimated already after $m + 1$ periods.

2.3 Heuristics for Detecting Interesting Pattern Changes

As opposed to the change detector, the heuristics are used to track changes to the statistics of patterns starting at the time point at which the patterns have emerged for the first time, even if they are not continuously in the rule base. Therefore, they can reveal potentially interesting changes also for those patterns that do not satisfy the mining query in all periods. Since the change detector is only aware of patterns that are present in the rule base, this property may be of particular interest to the analyst.

Occurrence-based Grouping. Patterns observed in a given period reflect the properties of the underlying dataset at this specific moment. On the other hand, patterns that are present in each period reflect (part of) the invariant properties of the population. If such patterns change this may be of particular interest to the user.

We, therefore, group rules with respect to their *stability* over time and use the term *occurrence* to denote the proportion of periods in which the rule is present, i.e., the percentage of time points in which its statistics exceeded the threshold values specified in the mining query. In particular, let f be the frequency of appearance of a pattern defined as the ratio of time points at which the observed statistic measure exceeds the thresholds specified by the domain expert. The range of f is $[0, 1]$, which we partition into the intervals $I_L := [0, 0.5)$, $I_M := [0.5, 0.75)$, $I_H := [0.75, 0.9)$, $I_{H+} := [0.9, 1)$ and $I_{permanent} := [1, 1]$. Alternatively, $I_{permanent}$ can be set to $[0.9, 1]$ for large values of n, i.e. for a large number of discrete time points. Then, we label a pattern ξ as L, M, H, $H+$ or *permanent* according to the interval at which $f(\xi)$ belongs. Patterns labelled as H or $H+$ are characterised as *frequent* patterns, whereas L and M form the set of *temporary* patterns.[3]

Then, for a pattern ξ an alert is raised for each time point t_i at which the pattern changes the group it belongs to. Certainly, in order to assess the reliability of patterns, a sufficiently long training phase is needed before meaningful group changes can be observed; in the short run, this approach will be very sensitive to patterns that vanish or emerge.

As mentioned above, one important peculiarity of this approach is that it can identify many significant rule changes which cannot be observed by significance tests. This is caused by the fact that this method will raise an alert when a rule appears/vanishes in/from the rule base. In such cases, changes to the statistics of a rule will usually be significant. However, if a pattern disappears from the rule base its time series is interrupted and a significance test cannot be applied.[4]

Corridor-based Heuristic. For this heuristic, we define a *corridor* around the time series of a pattern. A corridor is an interval of values, which is dynamically adjusted at each time point to reflect the range of values encountered so far. In particular, for a pattern ξ and a statistic measure s, we compute the mean m_i and standard deviation $stddev_i$ of the values $\{\xi.s(t_j)|j = 0, \ldots, i\}$. The corridor at time point t_i is defined as the interval $I(t_i) := [m_i - stddev_i, m_i + stddev_i]$, having a width of one standard deviation in each direction of the mean. Then, for pattern ξ an alert is raised for each time point t_i at which the value of the time series is outside the corridor $I(t_i)$.

The corridor-based heuristic takes account of the values already encountered for a given pattern. It is insensitive to oscillations of the time series around the threshold value used to discover rules. However, it is sensitive to changes that differ from past values but still remain in the interval. Furthermore, the corridor can only be defined reasonably for late time points: at time point t_1, a pattern change is most likely to be signaled because the mean and the standard deviation are not well-defined. Thus, the corridor-based heuristic is more appropriate for a retrospective study of the data; for a progressive

---

[3] Depending on the application the user may opt to choose different intervals.

[4] One possible way to bypass this problem is to use the pattern monitor proposed in [5] which computes the statistics of a rule directly from the underlying dataset.

study, a sufficient number of mining sessions must be performed first. As in the case of the occurrence-based grouping of patterns, this approach may also identify significant changes which cannot be covered by significance tests because corridor violations are tracked starting in the first period a pattern is visible. Therefore, an alert may also be raised when the pattern has disappeared from the rule base. However, such changes may be important for the user, e.g. if the reason for the disappearance is of interest.

Interval-Based Heuristic. For this heuristic, we partition the range of values of the time series into *intervals* of equal width. In particular, we consider the interval $[\tau, M]$, where M is the maximum permissible value per definition of the statistical measure under observation (e.g. support), while τ can be either a threshold provided by the application expert or the minimum permissible value per definition of the statistical measure. This range is partitioned into k equal subintervals. Then, for pattern ξ an alert is raised for each time point t_i at which the value of the time series is in a different interval than for t_{i-1}. An optional parameter ϵ can be supplied to specify the absolute minimum of a change to be considered interesting, i.e., for each signaled interval change it is additionally checked whether $|\xi.s(t_i) - \xi.s(t_{i-1})| \geq \epsilon$.

Example 4. Consider a time series on rule support and a pattern ξ, whose time series on support we denote as $\xi.supp(t_i), i = 0, \ldots, n$. Further, assume that $k = 4$, i.e. the range should be split into four intervals. Then, the range is $[\tau_{supp}, 1]$, where τ_{supp} is the support threshold specified in association rules' discovery.[5] For $\tau_{supp} = 0.2$, we would have four intervals, namely $I_1 = [0.2, 0.4)$, $I_2 = [0.4, 0.6)$, $I_3 = [0.6, 0.8)$ and $I_4 = [0.8, 1]$. A pattern change is signaled for ξ at each $t_i, i \geq 1$ such that

$$\xi.supp(t_i) \in I_j \wedge \xi.supp(t_{i-1}) \in I_{j'} \wedge I_j \neq I_{j'}.$$

While the change detector is used to identify significant changes from a statistical perspective, the heuristics take several aspects of pattern *stability* into account for the identification of interesting pattern changes. The occurrence-based approach detects changes in the frequency of pattern appearance over time, whereas the corridor-based heuristic identifies changes that differ stronger from past values than expected. Finally, the interval-based heuristic looks for absolute changes of a specified strength.

Table 2 provides a comparison of the different approaches with respect to the interestingness measure used, whether a training phase is needed, and which information is taken into account to identify interesting pattern changes. According to these properties and their implications, the domain expert has to decide which approach is appropriate for the application in question. E.g., in order to deliver immediate results, the user may choose the change detector and/or the interval-based approach, whereas for retrospective studies the corridor-based heuristic and occurrence-based grouping may also suit. Furthermore, if the transaction data are not stored in a DBMS the utility of applying the corridor-based and interval-based heuristic may be restricted as they can only reveal interesting changes for visible patterns in this case.

---

[5] This threshold is part of the *query* in the signature of a rule.

Table 2. Comparison of the heuristics with respect to different dimensions.

	change detector	occurrence-based grouping	corridor-based heuristic	interval-based heuristic
interestingness measure	statistical significance	visibility of patterns over time	unexpected deviation from past values	absolute change with respect to the previous period
training phase	no	yes	yes	no
data analysed	pattern statistics	pattern statistics	pattern statistics, transaction data	pattern statistics, transaction data

2.4   Identifying Atomic Changes

The change detector returns at each time point t_i the set of all patterns, whose observed statistic measure has changed with respect to the previous period. Normally, this set will be large, and some of the patterns may be correlated because they overlap in content. In such cases, it is likely that their changes are due to the same drift in the population. Therefore, we try to identify a minimal set of patterns that caused all change. For this purpose, we consider the components of each pattern, assuming that if a pattern change has occurred, it may be traced back to changes of the statistics of its components. We use the term *atomic change* for a change in a pattern which has no component that has itself experienced a change.

According to a rule's signature given in Section 2.1, a rule has a body and a head. We observe them together as components of a pattern ξ that correspond to the rule's itemsets. If a pattern change on ξ is reported at time point t_i, it may be due to a change of one or more of its components. Therefore, at time point t_i we consider all combinations of the elements $e_1, \ldots, e_{length(\xi)}$ constituting ξ, i.e. $\sum_{j=1}^{length(\xi)-1} \binom{length(\xi)}{j}$ components, excluding ξ itself. The following algorithm is used to attribute support changes of a rule to the support changes of its components:

```
Algorithm findCauses(Ξ):
 1   causes := ∅;
 2   for each ξ ∈ Ξ; do
 3      Ω := computeLongestComponents(ξ);
 4      for each ω ∈ Ω; do
 5         if ω ∉ causes and length(ω) > 0; then
 6            if isInteresting(ω) = true; then
 7               causes := causes ∪ ω;
 8               causes := causes ∪ findCauses(ω);
 9            endif;
10         endif;
11      done;
12   done;
13   return causes;
```

The argument of the algorithm is the set of patterns showing significant changes. In line 3 the algorithm computes the set of the longest components for the pattern being processed. Only if a component shows a significant change it is decomposed further, and the subcomponents are checked (cf. lines 6-8). The idea is that only components showing significant changes may have contributed to an observed pattern change; all other components can be ignored.[6] Additionally, a global cache is used to avoid repeated checks of the same component.

The algorithm assumes the base characteristic of association rules, namely that if a rule is frequent, then all its components are also frequent. Hence, for each pattern in the rule base produced at each time point t_i, all its sub patterns are also in the rule base. Since the change detector considers all time series, any pattern that has experienced a change at t_i is placed in Ξ, independently of its components. Thus, if a component of a pattern ξ is found in Ξ, we attribute the change of ξ to it and ignore ξ thereafter.

2.5   Architecture of PAM

PAM encapsulates one or more data mining algorithms and a database that stores data and mining results. Currently, there are interfaces for using the algorithms *k-means* and *Apriori* from the *Weka* tool set [24]. However, in principle any mining algorithm implemented in the Java programming language can be used within PAM.

The general structure of a PAM instance is depicted in Figure 1. The core of PAM

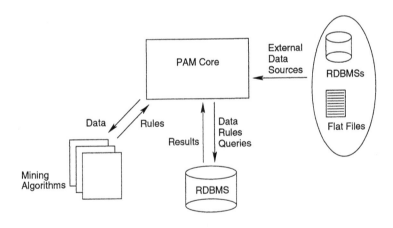

Fig. 1. General structure of a PAM instance.

implements the change detector and heuristics described in the previous paragraphs. When incorporating new data, e.g. the transactions of a new period, these algorithms are used to detect interesting pattern changes. The core offers interfaces to external data sources like databases or flat files. In the database not only the rules discovered by the

---

[6] However, for the user it may also be of interest if a component is stable, i.e. does not show significant changes.

different mining algorithms are stored, but also the (transaction) data. For example, in order to apply the corridor-based heuristic it may be necessary to access the base data, e.g. if the pattern in question could not be found in a particular period. Mining results are stored according to the GRM which has been transformed into a relational schema [5].

3   Experiments

For the experiments, we used the transaction log of a web-server hosting a non-commercial web site, spanning a period of 8 months in total. All pages on the server have been mapped to a concept hierarchy reflecting the purpose of the respective page. The sessionised log file has been split on a monthly basis, and association rules showing the different concepts accessed within the same user session have been discovered. In the mining step, we applied an association rule miner using minimum support of 2.5% and minimum confidence of 80%.

3.1   Overview

Table 3 gives a general overview on the evolution of the number of page accesses, sessions, frequent itemsets and rules found in the respective periods. The last five columns

Table 3. General overview on the dataset.

| period | accesses | sessions | itemsets | number of rules | | | | |
				total	unknown	known	previous	disapp
1	8335	2547	20	22	22	–	–	–
2	9012	2600	20	39	27	–	12	10
3	6008	1799	20	26	4	9	13	26
4	4188	1222	21	24	1	11	12	14
5	9488	2914	20	14	–	1	13	11
6	8927	2736	20	15	1	5	9	5
7	7401	2282	20	13	2	3	8	7
8	9210	3014	20	11	1	2	8	5

are of particular interest as they show the evolution of the entire rule base. The column labelled *total* gives the total number of rules in the respective period, *unknown* gives the number of rules that were found for the first time, and the column *known* shows the number of patterns that are new with respect to the previous period but already known from past periods. The sum of the columns *unknown* and *known* corresponds to the total number of new rules in the respective period. The columns *previous* and *disapp* represent the number of rules that were also present in the previous period, and the number of rules that disappeared from the previous period to the current, respectively.

The first period corresponds to the month October. It can be seen that in periods 3 and 4 (December and January) the site was visited less frequently than in other periods, although the number of discovered rules remains comparably high. The number of frequent itemsets is rather invariant, whereas the total number of rules falls, especially in the second half of the analysis. The number of rules that are found for the first time is quite large up to period 2. Interestingly, it took only two periods to learn almost 85% of all the rules that could be found throughout the entire analysis. It turns out that the fluctuation of the rule base decreases conspicuously in the last three months—both the total number of emerging patterns and the number of disappearing patterns fall. Due to the decrease in the total number of rules, the number of rules that are also present in the previous period declines as well.

In order to assess the stability of the rules found, we grouped them according to their occurrence, i.e., the share of periods in which they were present (cf. Table 4). In

Table 4. Rules grouped by occurrence.

periods present	rules	occurrence	interval
8	3	100.0	$I_{permanent}$
7	4	87.5	I_H
6	4	75.0	
5	2	62.5	I_M
4	2	50.0	
3	6	37.5	I_L
2	15	25.0	
1	22	12.5	

total, there were 58 *distinctive* rules, but only 11 rules were frequent according to the definition in Section 2.3, i.e., they were present in at least 6 periods. Due to the large proportion of rules which appeared only once or twice, there were strong changes to the mining results even for adjacent periods, especially in the first half of the analysis (cf. Table 3). With respect to the number of distinctive rules we can observe a related phenomenon: while there were 54 unique patterns in periods 1 to 4, in periods 5 to 8 only 25 different patterns could be found. Apparently, the usage patterns show a greater extent of diversification in the first half of the analysis.

3.2   Detecting Interesting Pattern Changes

All experiments are solely based on the support of rules, i.e., in order to determine and assess rule changes only the support of a pattern was analysed. However, when analysing changes to the confidence of a rule the same methodology can be used. As described in Section 2.2, we differentiate between short-term and long-term changes to the statistics of rules. For simplicity, we considered only two different scenarios in the experiments, either the support value returned immediately to its previous level, or it remained stable at the new level for at least one more period (core alert), i.e., we used $m = 1$ (cf. Section 2.2).

In total, we observed 164 *cases* over the period of 8 months, whereby the term case refers to the appearance of one rule in one period. However, depending on the heuristic being applied we considered different numbers of cases. For example, the change detector can only be used if the pattern is present in both periods t_i and t_{i-1}. Furthermore, the significance tests cannot be applied in the first period the pattern is present. On the other hand, the heuristics consider pattern changes starting from the first period the pattern was present, whereas two of the heuristics need a training phase.

Table 5 shows the results of applying the change detector and the heuristics. In the second column the number of considered cases is given. Column 3 shows how many of these changes were found to be interesting, and column 4 shows how many interesting changes were also significant.[7] The last column gives the number of significant changes that were core alerts.

Table 5. Results of the different approaches.

approach	number of changes	interesting	significant	core alerts
change detector (comparable)	75	10	10	3
change detector (observed)	142	17	17	11
change detector (all)	344	48	48	32
occurrence-based grouping	178	33	10	6
interval-based heuristic	344	16	12	4
corridor-based heuristic	178	79	22	10

At first we applied the change detector on all cases as they would be available when using conventional mining tools, i.e., we considered only such cases where the pattern was present in period t_i as well as in period t_{i-1}. From a total of 75 cases being considered we found 10 significant changes, 3 of them were core alerts. In the second step we considered all cases discovered by the miner except the 22 cases from the first period, i.e., if a pattern was present in t_i but not in t_{i-1} we computed its statistics in t_{i-1} directly from the data. For this purpose we used the pattern monitor described in [5]. From the resulting 142 cases we found 17 significant changes, 11 of which core alerts. In the third step the change detector was applied to *all* cases that would be considered by the heuristics, i.e., the statistics of a pattern were analysed starting at the first time point at which the pattern was present. In this case 48 out of 344 changes were significant, 32 thereof core alerts.

Despite the fact that all the heuristics operate on the same set of cases, for the occurrence-based and the corridor-based approach the number of cases considered for the *detection* of interesting changes is much smaller. As described in Section 2.3 these two

---

[7] Due to its notion of interestingness, for the change detector the value of column 3 is always equal to the value of column 4.

heuristics need a reasonable training phase before they work reliably. Due to the limited number of periods, we used four periods (starting in the first period in which the pattern was present) as a training phase and observed interesting changes only for the remaining periods. Since equal training phases were used in both cases, the same number of cases were included in the analysis. For the occurrence-based grouping we encountered a total of 33 interesting changes. Using the corridor-based heuristic we identified a total of 79 interesting changes, almost half as much a the number of cases being considered. Although the number of cases considered for the interval-based heuristic was much larger, we found only 16 changes to be interesting. This result was achieved using $k = 25$ intervals, and it turned out that only a drastic increase in k would have led to a larger number of interesting changes. Having a close look at the changes identified by this approach, we encountered a serious problem: depending on whether the value of the time series was close to an interval boundary or not, the same absolute support change led in one case to an interval change, in another case it did not. A possible solution to this problem would be to choose ϵ equal to half of the width of a single interval which, however, is equivalent to checking for an absolute support change of ϵ. The effort required to compute the intervals would only be justifiable if the interval boundaries would have a specific signification, e.g. with respect to the application context.

In order to compare the results of the heuristics and the change detector we also checked the significance of all interesting changes. In total there were 25 significant changes identified by one of the heuristics, which is about half of the total number of significant changes. However, if the same training phases as e.g. in the case of the corridor-based approach would be used for the change detector, only 30 significant support changes would be found. Furthermore, we noticed that the intersection of changes identified by one of the heuristics and the total number of observed cases amounted only to 24. This complies with our assumption from Section 2.3 that the heuristics also reveal interesting changes for patterns that are invisible at the moment. Therefore, the change detector should be used in conjunction with at least one of the heuristics.

Figure 2 shows an example of applying the occurrence-based grouping. The horizontal lines at 0.5, 0.75 and 0.9 represent the borders of the different groups of relative occurrence, the vertical line in period 4 represents the end of the training phase. In the first period the pattern is present (occurrence = 1), in the second period the pattern disappears and the occurrence drops to 0.5. However, since the training phase is not yet finished we do not observe a group change. In the remaining periods the pattern is present and the occurrence grows, except for period 8 in which the pattern again disappears.

In Figure 3, it is shown how the corridor reacts on the changing support of a pattern. The horizontal lines represent the interval borders, the dotted line the corridor borders. Again, the vertical line in period 4 represents the end of the training phase. With respect to the previous period, in periods 5, 6 and 7 the value of the time series is in another interval. All of these changes were also significant. In periods 5, 7 and 8 we observe corridor violations. However, although the support value of the last period is also outside the corridor no alert is raised because there is no significant change back to the previous level. Instead, the alert in period 7 is marked as a core alert which may signal a beginning concept drift.

In summary, there were basically two different results: on the one hand, we had a small number of permanent patterns which changed only slightly throughout the analysis. On the other hand, there were many temporary patterns, especially in the first half of the

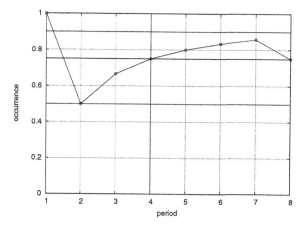

Fig. 2. Evolution of the occurrence of a pattern.

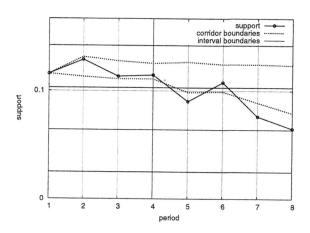

Fig. 3. Evolution of the support of a pattern.

analysis, which changed almost permanently. For example, it turned out that rules which were present in only 2 periods were responsible for 31 corridor violations, whereas the permanent patterns caused only 8 violations.

3.3   Detecting Atomic Changes

All rules returned by the change detector and the heuristics were decomposed into their itemsets, which were checked for significant changes. Table 6 summarises the results of this step. In the second column the number of component changes which were checked for significance is given, the last column contains the number of significant component changes. It turned out that, no matter which approach was used, only about 50% of the

Table 6. Number of significant itemset changes.

approach	component changes	
	checked	significant
change detector (comparable)	28	17
change detector (observed)	59	28
change detector (all)	226	102
occurrence-based grouping	42	18
interval-based heuristic	32	22
corridor-based heuristic	82	51

itemsets of a pattern that changed significantly also showed significant changes. For the user this information is quite interesting as it enables her to track down the causes of the observed pattern changes.

3.4 Discussion

In each period, the change detector and the heuristics output a set of pattern changes which are interesting with respect to the definition of interestingness the actual heuristic is based upon. However, the question whether or not these changes are *really* of interest can only be answered by the domain expert, taking the application context into account. In the following, we will discuss the results of applying our methodology on the example of a specific pattern.

The pattern I11 $\Rightarrow$ I3 suggests that visitors who access the homepage of the concept *information* (I11) also access pages of the concept *overview and navigation* (I3). From the application context the pattern is probably not surprising, but as it is present in all periods the user may pay special attention to it. Table 7 shows the time series of several statistical properties of both the pattern and its components.[8] While lift and confidence show only slight changes (except for period 4), the support of the pattern decreases considerably from period 1 to 8.[9] Since the confidence level is rather stable the support of the concept I11 should show a similar trend. In order to verify this assumption the support of the pattern's components was analysed. It can be seen that I11 shows a comparable trend—after a short increase in period 2 we encounter a conspicuous decrease which is only interrupted in period 6 (cf. Table 7). It is more than likely that the support change of I11 has at least contributed to the support change of the pattern. The other component shows a different development. Its support decreases slightly in period 2, shows an increasing trend from period 4 to 7, and drops in the last period. Interestingly, in period 8 the support of both concepts drops, although the *absolute* number of sessions supporting them increases. Thus, the growth of the total number of sessions in the last period is mainly caused by visitors who do not access those concepts, or access them less frequently. The implications for the domain expert depend on the role of these

---

[8] The results of applying the corridor-based and interval-based heuristic are depicted in Figure 3.

[9] Note that the time series of the total number of sessions shows a different trend (cf. Table 3).

Table 7. Time series of the statistical properties of I11 ⇒ I3 and its components.

period	I11 ⇒ I3				I11		I3	
	support	confidence	lift	number	support	number	support	number
1	0.116	0.843	1.08	295	0.137	350	0.780	1986
2	0.129	0.859	1.12	335	0.150	390	0.766	1992
3	0.113	0.876	1.14	204	0.130	233	0.774	1392
4	0.115	0.870	1.19	140	0.132	161	0.733	896
5	0.090	0.822	1.10	263	0.110	320	0.746	2173
6	0.108	0.853	1.12	295	0.126	346	0.760	2078
7	0.076	0.837	1.05	174	0.091	208	0.796	1817
8	0.065	0.848	1.18	196	0.077	231	0.722	2175

pages. If they are indispensable to achieve the objectives of the site the administrator should investigate the reasons for the observed change and take appropriate actions. In this specific case, the homepage of an entire concept is affected. If the site is strictly hierarchical, without links between the different concepts, the change will have strong effects on the access to all pages belonging to this concept.

3.5   Performance Issues

There are three main aspects influencing the performance of PAM. Firstly, if a pattern disappears its statistics have to be computed. Since the SQL-based computation of the statistics is much more efficient than applying a miner, this is usually not a major issue [5]. While the number of queries depends linearly on the number of rules being monitored $(2n + 1)$, the complexity of the queries depends on the number of items in a rule and on the number of transactions in the respective period. The second aspect refers to the monitoring step which may induce a substantial effort. For the occurrence-based heuristic and interval-based heuristic there are only a few comparisons to be made. However, the significance tests can be quite expensive, especially if a large number of rules is monitored. For the corridor-based heuristic, mean and standard deviation have to be computed. Only if *very* long time series are considered this may be problematic. Lastly, in order to identify atomic changes, additional significance tests have to be done, where the number of tests depends on the number of components in the pattern (cf. Section 2.4).

Table 8 shows the processing time in seconds needed for the different heuristics, including the time to access the database.[10] All the heuristics were applied independently, i.e., we did not use a global cache to remember results produced by another heuristic (cf. Section 2.4). Execution time #1 corresponds to the heuristic itself, #2 refers to the check whether interesting changes were also significant, including the detection of atomic changes. No matter which heuristic is considered, the time needed to check a single pattern change amounts to approximately 0.8 seconds, whereas the time needed for the significance tests decreases with increasing number of tests. This is caused by a

---

[10] All experiments were ran on a P 4/2 GHz/512 MB.

Table 8. Processing time for the different heuristics.

approach	number of changes	execution time #1	interesting changes	execution time #2
change detector (observed)	142	280.0	17	–
occurrence-based grouping	178	147.9	33	98.2
interval-based heuristic	344	281.6	16	60.5
corridor-based heuristic	178	150.4	79	208.7

local cache which ensures that components are not checked twice when detecting atomic changes.

4   Conclusions

In this article, we introduced PAM, an automated pattern monitor, which was used to observe changes in web usage patterns. PAM is based on a temporal rule model which consists of both the content of a pattern and the statistical measures captured for the pattern. We have introduced a set of heuristics which can be used to identify not only significant but also *interesting* rule changes. We argue that the notion of statistical significance is not always appropriate: concept drift as the initiator of pattern change often manifests itself gradually over a long period of time where each of the changes may not be significant at all. Therefore, our heuristics take different aspects of pattern stability into account. E.g., while the occurrence-based grouping identifies changes to the frequency of pattern appearance, the corridor-based heuristic identifies changes that differ stronger from past values than the user would expect. The question which definition is appropriate and, hence, which pattern changes are *really* interesting to the user can only be answered with respect to the application context. In particular, the domain expert will have to inspect the patterns showing interesting changes at least once in order to decide whether or not the used definition was suitable.

We presented PAM in a case study on web usage mining, in which association rules were discovered that show which concepts of the web site analysed tend to be viewed together. Our results show that PAM reveals interesting insights into the evolution of the usage patterns. Particularly the analysis of interesting pattern changes, i.e., the identification of changes which contributed to interesting pattern changes, may be important to the analyst. On the other hand, it turned out that the interval-based heuristic treats changes of equal strength differently, depending on whether or not the respective value is close to an interval border. However, as pointed out in Section 3 the intervals and/or their borders may be of particular importance with respect to the application domain and their computation may be mandatory. Another option is an algorithm which *learns* the intervals, either in order to find as many as possible pattern changes or even to minimise the number of reported changes.

Challenging directions for future work include the application of the proposed methodology to the specific needs of streaming data, and the identification of interdependencies between rules from different periods. In this scenario, each data partition constitutes a transaction in each of which a number of rules (items) appear. These *transactions* can then be analysed to discover periodicities of pattern occurrences and/or temporal relationships between specific rules.

Acknowledgements: Thanks to Gerrit Riessen for his valuable hints.

References

[1] R. Agrawal, G. Psaila, E. L. Wimmers, and M. Zaït. Querying shapes of histories. In *VLDB*, Zürich, Switzerland, 1995.

[2] N. F. Ayan, A. U. Tansel, and E. Arkun. An Efficient Algorithm To Update Large Itemsets With Early Pruning. In *Proceedings of the Fifth ACM SIGKDD International Conference on Knowledge Discovery and Data Mining*, pages 287–291, San Diego, CA, USA, August 1999. ACM.

[3] S. Baron and M. Spiliopoulou. Monitoring change in mining results. In *3rd Int. Conf. on Data Warehousing and Knowledge Discovery - DaWaK 2001*, Munich, Germany, Sept. 2001.

[4] S. Baron and M. Spiliopoulou. Monitoring the Results of the KDD Process: An Overview of Pattern Evolution. In J. M. Meij, editor, *Dealing with the Data Flood: Mining data, text and+multimedia*, chapter 6, pages 845–863. STT Netherlands Study Center for Technology Trends, The Hague, Netherlands, Apr. 2002.

[5] S. Baron, M. Spiliopoulou, and O. Günther. Efficient Monitoring of Patterns in Data Mining Environments. In *Seventh East-European Conference on Advance in Databases and Information Systems (ADBIS'03)*, Dresden, Germany, Sep. 2003. Springer. to appear.

[6] M. J. Berry and G. Linoff. *Data Mining Techniques: For Marketing, Sales and Customer Support*. John Wiley & Sons, Inc., 1997.

[7] Y. M. Bing Liu and R. Lee. Analyzing the interestingness of association rules from the temporal dimension. In *IEEE International Conference on Data Mining (ICDM-2001)*, pages 377–384, Silicon Valley, USA, November 2001.

[8] S. Chakrabarti, S. Sarawagi, and B. Dom. Mining surprising patterns using temporal description length. In A. Gupta, O. Shmueli, and J. Widom, editors, *VLDB'98*, pages 606–617, New York City, NY, Aug. 1998. Morgan Kaufmann.

[9] X. Chen and I. Petrounias. Mining Temporal Features in Association Rules. In *Proceedings of the 3rd European Conference on Principles of Data Mining and Knowledge Discovery*, Lecture Notes in Computer Science, pages 295–300, Prague, Czech Republic, September 1999. Springer.

[10] D. W. Cheung, S. Lee, and B. Kao. A general incremental technique for maintaining discovered association rules. In *DASFAA'97*, Melbourne, Australia, Apr. 1997.

[11] M. Ester, H.-P. Kriegel, J. Sander, M. Wimmer, and X. Xu. Incremental Clustering for Mining in a Data Warehousing Environment. In *Proceedings of the 24th International Conference on Very Large Data Bases*, pages 323–333, New York City, New York, USA, August 1998. Morgan Kaufmann.

[12] A. Freitas. On objective measures of rule surprisingness. In *PKDD'98*, number 1510 in LNAI, pages 1–9, Nantes, France, Sep. 1998. Springer-Verlag.

[13] P. Gago and C. Bento. A Metric for Selection of the Most Promising Rules. In J. M. Zytkow and M. Quafafou, editors, *Principles of Data Mining and Knowledge Discovery, Proceedings of the Second European Symposium, PKDD'98*, Nantes, France, 1998. Springer.

[14] V. Ganti, J. Gehrke, and R. Ramakrishnan. A Framework for Measuring Changes in Data Characteristics. In *Proceedings of the Eighteenth ACM SIGACT-SIGMOD-SIGART Symposium on Principles of Database Systems*, pages 126–137, Philadelphia, Pennsylvania, May 1999. ACM Press.

[15] V. Ganti, J. Gehrke, and R. Ramakrishnan. DEMON: Mining and Monitoring Evolving Data. In *Proceedings of the 15th International Conference on Data Engineering*, pages 439–448, San Diego, California, USA, February 2000. IEEE Computer Society.

[16] S. Lee, D. Cheung, and B. Kao. Is Sampling Useful in Data Mining? A Case in the Maintenance of Discovered Association Rules. *Data Mining and Knowledge Discovery*, 2(3):233–262, September 1998.

[17] S. D. Lee and D. W.-L. Cheung. Maintenance of Discovered Association Rules: When to update? In *ACM-SIGMOD Workshop on Data Mining and Knowledge Discovery (DMKD-97)*, Tucson, Arizona, May 1997.

[18] B. Liu, W. Hsu, and Y. Ma. Discovering the set of fundamental rule changes. In *7th ACM SIGKDD International Conference on Knowledge Discovery and Data Mining (KDD-2001)*, pages 335–340, San Francisco, USA, August 2001.

[19] N. M. A. Mark G. Kelly, David J. Hand. The Impact of Changing Populations on Classifier Performance. In *Proceedings of the 5th ACM SIGKDD International Conference on Knowledge Discovery and Data Mining*, pages 367–371, San Diego, Aug. 1999. ACM.

[20] E. Omiecinski and A. Savasere. Efficient Mining of Association Rules in Large Databases. In *Proceedings of the British National Conference on Databases*, pages 49–63, 1998.

[21] P.-N. Tan, V. Kumar, and J. Srivastava. Selecting the Right Interestingness Measure for Association Patterns. In *Proc. of the Eighth ACM SIGKDD Int'l Conf. on Knowledge Discovery and Data Mining*, 2002.

[22] S. Thomas, S. Bodagala, K. Alsabti, and S. Ranka. An Efficient Algorithm for the Incremental Updation of Association Rules in Large Databases. In *Proceedings of the 3rd International Conference on Knowledge Discovery and Data Mining (KDD-97)*, pages 263–266, Newport Beach, California, USA, Aug. 1997.

[23] K. Wang. Discovering patterns from large and dynamic sequential data. *Intelligent Information Systems*, 9:8–33, 1997.

[24] I. H. Witten and E. Frank. *Data Mining: Practical machine learning tools with Java implementations*. Morgan Kaufmann, San Francisco, 1999.

Author Index

Baron, Steffan   181
Basile, T.M.A.   130
Berendt, Bettina   1

Chevalier, Karine   23

Degemmis, M.   130
Dikaiakos, Marios   113
Di Mauro, N.   130

Esposito, F.   130

Ferilli, S.   130

Ghani, Rayid   43
Grobelnik, Marko   77

Hatzopoulos, Michalis   97
Hochsztain, E.   164
Hollink, Vera   148
Hotho, Andreas   1

Jin, Xin   57

Karkaletsis, Vangelis   113

Lops, P.   130

Menasalvas, E.   164
Millán, S.   164
Mladenić, Dunja   1, 77
Mobasher, Bamshad   57
Mulvenna, Maurice   23

Paliouras, Georgios   97, 113
Papatheodorou, Christos   113
Pérez, M.S.   164
Pierrakos, Dimitrios   113

Semeraro, G.   130
Sigletos, Georgios   97
Singh Anand, Sarabjot   23
Spiliopoulou, Myra   1, 181
Spyropoulos, Constantine D.   97
Stumme, Gerd   1

Tasistro, A.   164
ten Hagen, Stephan   148

van Someren, Maarten   1, 148

Zhou, Yanzan   57

Lecture Notes in Artificial Intelligence (LNAI)

Vol. 3249: B. Buchberger, J.A. Campbell (Eds.), Artificial Intelligence and Symbolic Computation. X, 285 pages. 2004.

Vol. 3245: E. Suzuki, S. Arikawa (Eds.), Discovery Science. XIV, 430 pages. 2004.

Vol. 3244: S. Ben-David, J. Case, A. Maruoka (Eds.), Algorithmic Learning Theory. XIV, 505 pages. 2004.

Vol. 3238: S. Biundo, T. Frühwirth, G. Palm (Eds.), KI 2004: Advances in Artificial Intelligence. XI, 467 pages. 2004.

Vol. 3229: J.J. Alferes, J. Leite (Eds.), Logics in Artificial Intelligence. XIV, 744 pages. 2004.

Vol. 3215: M.G. Negoita, R.J. Howlett, L. Jain (Eds.), Knowledge-Based Intelligent Information and Engineering Systems. LVII, 906 pages. 2004.

Vol. 3214: M.G. Negoita, R.J. Howlett, L. Jain (Eds.), Knowledge-Based Intelligent Information and Engineering Systems. LVIII, 1302 pages. 2004.

Vol. 3213: M.G. Negoita, R.J. Howlett, L. Jain (Eds.), Knowledge-Based Intelligent Information and Engineering Systems. LVIII, 1280 pages. 2004.

Vol. 3209: B. Berendt, A. Hotho, D. Mladenic, M. van Someren, M. Spiliopoulou, G. Stumme (Eds.), Web Mining: From Web to Semantic Web. IX, 201 pages. 2004.

Vol. 3206: P. Sojka, I. Kopecek, K. Pala (Eds.), Text, Speech and Dialogue. XIII, 667 pages. 2004.

Vol. 3202: J.-F. Boulicaut, F. Esposito, F. Giannotti, D. Pedreschi (Eds.), Knowledge Discovery in Databases: PKDD 2004. XIX, 560 pages. 2004.

Vol. 3201: J.-F. Boulicaut, F. Esposito, F. Giannotti, D. Pedreschi (Eds.), Machine Learning: ECML 2004. XVIII, 580 pages. 2004.

Vol. 3194: R. Camacho, R. King, A. Srinivasan (Eds.), Inductive Logic Programming. XI, 361 pages. 2004.

Vol. 3192: C. Bussler, D. Fensel (Eds.), Artificial Intelligence: Methodology, Systems, and Applications. XIII, 522 pages. 2004.

Vol. 3191: M. Klusch, S. Ossowski, V. Kashyap, R. Unland (Eds.), Cooperative Information Agents VIII. XI, 303 pages. 2004.

Vol. 3187: G. Lindemann, J. Denzinger, I.J. Timm, R. Unland (Eds.), Multiagent System Technologies. XIII, 341 pages. 2004.

Vol. 3176: O. Bousquet, U. von Luxburg, G. Rätsch (Eds.), Advanced Lectures on Machine Learning. IX, 241 pages. 2004.

Vol. 3171: A.L.C. Bazzan, S. Labidi (Eds.), Advances in Artificial Intelligence – SBIA 2004. XVII, 548 pages. 2004.

Vol. 3159: U. Visser, Intelligent Information Integration for the Semantic Web. XIV, 150 pages. 2004.

Vol. 3157: C. Zhang, H. W. Guesgen, W.K. Yeap (Eds.), PRICAI 2004: Trends in Artificial Intelligence. XX, 1023 pages. 2004.

Vol. 3155: P. Funk, P.A. González Calero (Eds.), Advances in Case-Based Reasoning. XIII, 822 pages. 2004.

Vol. 3139: F. Iida, R. Pfeifer, L. Steels, Y. Kuniyoshi (Eds.), Embodied Artificial Intelligence. IX, 331 pages. 2004.

Vol. 3131: V. Torra, Y. Narukawa (Eds.), Modeling Decisions for Artificial Intelligence. XI, 327 pages. 2004.

Vol. 3127: K.E. Wolff, H.D. Pfeiffer, H.S. Delugach (Eds.), Conceptual Structures at Work. XI, 403 pages. 2004.

Vol. 3123: A. Belz, R. Evans, P. Piwek (Eds.), Natural Language Generation. X, 219 pages. 2004.

Vol. 3120: J. Shawe-Taylor, Y. Singer (Eds.), Learning Theory. X, 648 pages. 2004.

Vol. 3097: D. Basin, M. Rusinowitch (Eds.), Automated Reasoning. XII, 493 pages. 2004.

Vol. 3071: A. Omicini, P. Petta, J. Pitt (Eds.), Engineering Societies in the Agents World. XIII, 409 pages. 2004.

Vol. 3070: L. Rutkowski, J. Siekmann, R. Tadeusiewicz, L.A. Zadeh (Eds.), Artificial Intelligence and Soft Computing - ICAISC 2004. XXV, 1208 pages. 2004.

Vol. 3068: E. André, L. Dybkjær, W. Minker, P. Heisterkamp (Eds.), Affective Dialogue Systems. XII, 324 pages. 2004.

Vol. 3067: M. Dastani, J. Dix, A. El Fallah-Seghrouchni (Eds.), Programming Multi-Agent Systems. X, 221 pages. 2004.

Vol. 3066: S. Tsumoto, R. Słowiński, J. Komorowski, J.W. Grzymała-Busse (Eds.), Rough Sets and Current Trends in Computing. XX, 853 pages. 2004.

Vol. 3065: A. Lomuscio, D. Nute (Eds.), Deontic Logic in Computer Science. X, 275 pages. 2004.

Vol. 3060: A.Y. Tawfik, S.D. Goodwin (Eds.), Advances in Artificial Intelligence. XIII, 582 pages. 2004.

Vol. 3056: H. Dai, R. Srikant, C. Zhang (Eds.), Advances in Knowledge Discovery and Data Mining. XIX, 713 pages. 2004.

Vol. 3055: H. Christiansen, M.-S. Hacid, T. Andreasen, H.L. Larsen (Eds.), Flexible Query Answering Systems. X, 500 pages. 2004.

Vol. 3040: R. Conejo, M. Urretavizcaya, J.-L. Pérez-de-la-Cruz (Eds.), Current Topics in Artificial Intelligence. XIV, 689 pages. 2004.

Vol. 3035: M.A. Wimmer (Ed.), Knowledge Management in Electronic Government. XII, 326 pages. 2004.

Vol. 3034: J. Favela, E. Menasalvas, E. Chávez (Eds.), Advances in Web Intelligence. XIII, 227 pages. 2004.

Vol. 3030: P. Giorgini, B. Henderson-Sellers, M. Winikoff (Eds.), Agent-Oriented Information Systems. XIV, 207 pages. 2004.

Vol. 3029: B. Orchard, C. Yang, M. Ali (Eds.), Innovations in Applied Artificial Intelligence. XXI, 1272 pages. 2004.

Vol. 3025: G.A. Vouros, T. Panayiotopoulos (Eds.), Methods and Applications of Artificial Intelligence. XV, 546 pages. 2004.

Vol. 3020: D. Polani, B. Browning, A. Bonarini, K. Yoshida (Eds.), RoboCup 2003: Robot Soccer World Cup VII. XVI, 767 pages. 2004.

Vol. 3012: K. Kurumatani, S.-H. Chen, A. Ohuchi (Eds.), Multi-Agnets for Mass User Support. X, 217 pages. 2004.

Vol. 3010: K.R. Apt, F. Fages, F. Rossi, P. Szeredi, J. Váncza (Eds.), Recent Advances in Constraints. VIII, 285 pages. 2004.

Vol. 2990: J. Leite, A. Omicini, L. Sterling, P. Torroni (Eds.), Declarative Agent Languages and Technologies. XII, 281 pages. 2004.

Vol. 2980: A. Blackwell, K. Marriott, A. Shimojima (Eds.), Diagrammatic Representation and Inference. XV, 448 pages. 2004.

Vol. 2977: G. Di Marzo Serugendo, A. Karageorgos, O.F. Rana, F. Zambonelli (Eds.), Engineering Self-Organising Systems. X, 299 pages. 2004.

Vol. 2972: R. Monroy, G. Arroyo-Figueroa, L.E. Sucar, H. Sossa (Eds.), MICAI 2004: Advances in Artificial Intelligence. XVII, 923 pages. 2004.

Vol. 2969: M. Nickles, M. Rovatsos, G. Weiss (Eds.), Agents and Computational Autonomy. X, 275 pages. 2004.

Vol. 2961: P. Eklund (Ed.), Concept Lattices. IX, 411 pages. 2004.

Vol. 2953: K. Konrad, Model Generation for Natural Language Interpretation and Analysis. XIII, 166 pages. 2004.

Vol. 2934: G. Lindemann, D. Moldt, M. Paolucci (Eds.), Regulated Agent-Based Social Systems. X, 301 pages. 2004.

Vol. 2930: F. Winkler (Ed.), Automated Deduction in Geometry. VII, 231 pages. 2004.

Vol. 2926: L. van Elst, V. Dignum, A. Abecker (Eds.), Agent-Mediated Knowledge Management. XI, 428 pages. 2004.

Vol. 2923: V. Lifschitz, I. Niemelä (Eds.), Logic Programming and Nonmonotonic Reasoning. IX, 365 pages. 2004.

Vol. 2915: A. Camurri, G. Volpe (Eds.), Gesture-Based Communication in Human-Computer Interaction. XIII, 558 pages. 2004.

Vol. 2913: T.M. Pinkston, V.K. Prasanna (Eds.), High Performance Computing - HiPC 2003. XX, 512 pages. 2003.

Vol. 2903: T.D. Gedeon, L.C.C. Fung (Eds.), AI 2003: Advances in Artificial Intelligence. XVI, 1075 pages. 2003.

Vol. 2902: F.M. Pires, S.P. Abreu (Eds.), Progress in Artificial Intelligence. XV, 504 pages. 2003.

Vol. 2892: F. Dau, The Logic System of Concept Graphs with Negation. XI, 213 pages. 2003.

Vol. 2891: J. Lee, M. Barley (Eds.), Intelligent Agents and Multi-Agent Systems. X, 215 pages. 2003.

Vol. 2882: D. Veit, Matchmaking in Electronic Markets. XV, 180 pages. 2003.

Vol. 2871: N. Zhong, Z.W. Raś, S. Tsumoto, E. Suzuki (Eds.), Foundations of Intelligent Systems. XV, 697 pages. 2003.

Vol. 2854: J. Hoffmann, Utilizing Problem Structure in Planing. XIII, 251 pages. 2003.

Vol. 2843: G. Grieser, Y. Tanaka, A. Yamamoto (Eds.), Discovery Science. XII, 504 pages. 2003.

Vol. 2842: R. Gavaldá, K.P. Jantke, E. Takimoto (Eds.), Algorithmic Learning Theory. XI, 313 pages. 2003.

Vol. 2838: N. Lavrač, D. Gamberger, L. Todorovski, H. Blockeel (Eds.), Knowledge Discovery in Databases: PKDD 2003. XVI, 508 pages. 2003.

Vol. 2837: N. Lavrač, D. Gamberger, L. Todorovski, H. Blockeel (Eds.), Machine Learning: ECML 2003. XVI, 504 pages. 2003.

Vol. 2835: T. Horváth, A. Yamamoto (Eds.), Inductive Logic Programming. X, 401 pages. 2003.

Vol. 2821: A. Günter, R. Kruse, B. Neumann (Eds.), KI 2003: Advances in Artificial Intelligence. XII, 662 pages. 2003.

Vol. 2807: V. Matoušek, P. Mautner (Eds.), Text, Speech and Dialogue. XIII, 426 pages. 2003.

Vol. 2801: W. Banzhaf, J. Ziegler, T. Christaller, P. Dittrich, J.T. Kim (Eds.), Advances in Artificial Life. XVI, 905 pages. 2003.

Vol. 2797: O.R. Zaïane, S.J. Simoff, C. Djeraba (Eds.), Mining Multimedia and Complex Data. XII, 281 pages. 2003.

Vol. 2792: T. Rist, R.S. Aylett, D. Ballin, J. Rickel (Eds.), Intelligent Virtual Agents. XV, 364 pages. 2003.

Vol. 2782: M. Klusch, A. Omicini, S. Ossowski, H. Laamanen (Eds.), Cooperative Information Agents VII. XI, 345 pages. 2003.

Vol. 2780: M. Dojat, E. Keravnou, P. Barahona (Eds.), Artificial Intelligence in Medicine. XIII, 388 pages. 2003.

Vol. 2777: B. Schölkopf, M.K. Warmuth (Eds.), Learning Theory and Kernel Machines. XIV, 746 pages. 2003.

Vol. 2752: G.A. Kaminka, P.U. Lima, R. Rojas (Eds.), RoboCup 2002: Robot Soccer World Cup VI. XVI, 498 pages. 2003.

Vol. 2741: F. Baader (Ed.), Automated Deduction – CADE-19. XII, 503 pages. 2003.

Vol. 2705: S. Renals, G. Grefenstette (Eds.), Text- and Speech-Triggered Information Access. VII, 197 pages. 2003.

Vol. 2703: O.R. Zaïane, J. Srivastava, M. Spiliopoulou, B. Masand (Eds.), WEBKDD 2002 - Mining Web Data for Discovering Usage Patterns and Profiles. IX, 181 pages. 2003.

Vol. 2700: M.T. Pazienza (Ed.), Extraction in the Web Era. XIII, 163 pages. 2003.

Vol. 2699: M.G. Hinchey, J.L. Rash, W.F. Truszkowski, C.A. Rouff, D.F. Gordon-Spears (Eds.), Formal Approaches to Agent-Based Systems. IX, 297 pages. 2002.